Cooperative Teaching

Cooperative Teaching

Rebuilding the Schoolhouse for All Students

Jeanne Bauwens

Jack J. Hourcade

Illustrations by Will Spearman

8700 Shoal Creek Boulevard
Austin, Texas 78757

pro·ed

© 1995 by PRO-ED, Inc.
8700 Shoal Creek Boulevard
Austin, Texas 78757-6897

Production Manager: Alan Grimes
Production Coordinator: Adrienne Booth
Art Director: Lori Kopp
Reprints Buyer: Alicia Woods
Editor: Tracy Sergo
Editorial Assistant: Claudette Landry

Printed in the United States of America

2   3   4   5   6   7   8   9   10   99   98   97   96   95

"The future is not someplace we are going to, but one we are creating. The paths to it are made, not found, and the activity of making
them changes both the maker and the destination."

—Australian Commission for the Future, 1989

Contents

Foreword

The world of remedial and special education is changing. In special education, the long march from isolation to integration that began before the passage of P.L. 94-142 (Education for All Handicapped Children Act) has placed ever-increasing numbers of students with disabilities in general education classes for most or all of their academic day. There is increasing emphasis on full inclusion, which extends mainstreaming to students who in the past would not have been seen in general education classes, including students with the most severe disabilities. On a parallel track, Chapter 1/Title 1 programs increasingly have moved away from pull-out models toward the use of in-class models and other innovative methods to meet students' needs within the heterogeneous class.

Each of these trends creates opportunities for at-risk children to take their rightful place in the inclusive school and community of their peers. At the same time, each presents teachers and administrators with challenges. How can the needs of all students be met in very heterogeneous classes?

One answer to this is cooperative teaching, a teaming approach between general educators and special educators or other support services providers. Cooperative teaching lets educators work flexibly to enable all students to receive the instruction they need to succeed in a high-expectations curriculum. Cooperative teaching solves many problems in the integration of efforts between general education teachers and support services providers, and it allows each educator to contribute unique skills to facilitate the education of all.

Yet cooperative teaching has its own difficulties. How can partners in cooperative teaching coordinate their efforts? How can they build supportive relationships? How can they deal with scheduling? How can they find time for planning? How can teachers and administrators evaluate the success of their cooperative teaching?

These and many other questions are answered in these pages. Jeanne Bauwens and Jack Hourcade have worked for many years helping schools implement cooperative teaching, and they have assisted many educators in developing and refining collaborative skills. They have seen the problems as well as the potential of cooperative teaching and offer educators moving toward cooperative teaching a practical, thoughtful, and down-to-earth guide to planning, implementation, and self-evaluation. This book provides a wealth of information, experience, and wisdom for schools undertaking reform of their programs for at-risk students. The journey toward cooperative teaching is not one educators should take alone. With this book as a companion, they should experience success in building schools in which all students can achieve their full potential.

— *Robert E. Slavin*
John Hopkins University

Preface

Perhaps the most significant social trend of this century has been toward acknowledgment and greater acceptance of diversity throughout all aspects of society. While travel down this path has been halting and uneven, there is little question that this movement will continue. The reality is that demographic projections clearly predict an increasingly more diverse populace in the future.

In the public schools, the increasing diversity of society is mirrored in the rapidly changing nature of student populations. In more and more schools, so-called cultural and linguistic minority students are actually the majority. Similarly, spurred on largely by the Education for All Handicapped Children Act in 1975 and subsequent legislation (such as the Individuals with Disabilities Education Act of 1990), schools are educating students with disabilities to an ever-greater degree alongside their nondisabled peers in general education classrooms.

Accompanying and facilitating this movement toward inclusion in the classroom has been a greater emphasis on teaching students to work together to develop the knowledge and skills necessary to succeed and thrive in a society where most adults work not in isolation but together. The recent, rapidly growing use of such instructional arrangements as cooperative learning is perhaps the most obvious indicator of this trend.

Given the substantial attention paid over the last 2 decades to inclusion of students with greater diversity in general education classrooms, along with the need for students to learn to work together, surprisingly little attention has been given to educator diversity. That is, while students in heterogeneous classrooms are learning the value of working together rather than in isolation, teachers and other school professionals continue to work as detached and solitary individuals. The model of one educator in one classroom for the entirety of the day is increasingly inappropriate for the schools of the 21st century. In schools throughout the world professional collaboration is emerging as a new paradigm for education, with cooperative teaching leading this movement.

In cooperative teaching, two educators who combine complementary sets of professional knowledge and skills are present simultaneously in general education classrooms. This book is designed for educators who are looking for a more effective way to best serve all students while simultaneously reinvigorating and revitalizing themselves personally and professionally. Using the organizational analogy of remodeling a home, this book explains in a step-by-step fashion how all educators can remodel their professional practice through cooperative teaching.

Organization

Chapter 1, "Surveying the Situation," provides a rationale for and an overview of collaboration, explaining the growing necessity for such an approach in the contemporary educational system.

Chapter 2, "Reviewing the Options," offers several approaches to collaboration, making a distinction between indirect and direct collaboration and noting advantages and disadvantages of each.

Chapter 3, "Developing the Blueprints," highlights one especially promising approach to collaboration, cooperative teaching, and provides a variety of specific practical ways in which cooperative teaching can be implemented.

Chapter 4, "Getting Construction Underway," identifies the real-world issues of time and administrative support and offers a number of suggestions on how to respond effectively to both of these.

Chapter 5, "Inspecting the Job," outlines practical procedures for identifying potential areas of impact of cooperative teaching and explains how each might be evaluated to determine program effectiveness.

Chapter 6, "Moving In," identifies the interpersonal skills and issues such as role changes, trust, and flexibility critical to successful implementation of cooperative teaching and offers ways to minimize problems.

Chapter 7, "Rearranging the Furniture," points out the possibilities for conflict as school professionals adjust to the new and more intense professional relationships inherent in cooperative teaching and supplies a variety of practical strategies for conflict resolution.

Chapter 8, "Reflecting on the Changes," provides the opportunity for educators involved in cooperative teaching to consider the nature of change and to understand how that change can be further nurtured by school principals and other change facilitators. This chapter also provides field-identified ways in which support for change can be elicited and demonstrated.

Finally, Chapter 9, "Having the Open House," explains how the benefits of cooperative teaching can be shared throughout the professional community via dissemination efforts and outlines a number of outlets through which this sharing can take place.

In each chapter a variety of practical examples are included to illustrate fundamental concepts. In addition, field-tested activities are included at the end of each chapter. These activities enable the reader to engage in self-analysis in preparation for moving into cooperative teaching.

Acknowledgments

While the presence of both of our names as authors indicates that collaboration is something we practice as well as preach, the collaboration that has resulted in this book extends far beyond the two listed authors. In particular we would like to thank the thousands of educators we have worked with throughout the world who have developed and implemented cooperative teaching in their schools. The courage to take a chance and change in a most fundamental way how one goes about educating students is perhaps the single most important quality we salute in these professionals.

Our two field reviewers, Lori Korinek of the College of William and Mary and Ed Polloway of Lynchburg College, consistently provided us with a sophisticated yet sensitive mixture of encouragement and suggestions for improvement. We are indebted to both.

Our talented illustrator, Will Spearman, enabled us to clarify basic ideas throughout the book in what we hope to be a clever and entertaining way.

We'd also like to acknowledge the encouragement of our colleagues at Boise State University and elsewhere. Their willingness to listen to and provide feedback on new ideas exemplifies the collaborative spirit.

The staff at PRO-ED have maintained an optimal mix of professionalism and friendliness throughout the book's development. The willingness of Jim Patton, Alan Grimes, Rebecca Fletcher, Lori Kopp, Chris Ann Worsham, and all the other staff at PRO-ED to give us free rein in developing the book's content while still helping us maintain a basic organizational framework is greatly appreciated.

The International Council for Exceptional Children has long been an advocate for collaboration, especially through cooperative teaching. Their encouragement and support for cooperative teaching as a means to facilitate inclusion of students with disabilities has served to bring this approach to collaboration to the attention of thousands of educators.

Finally, we'd like to thank our long-suffering spouses, Laurence Bauwens and Carol Hourcade, as well as our abandoned children, Wendy and Carrie Bauwens and Michael Hourcade, for not complaining as our respective homes fell apart as we instead spent our weekends "rebuilding the schoolhouse." It's time for each of us to follow our own advice and go home to begin our long-delayed family reconstruction projects.

1   Surveying the Situation
An Overview of Collaboration

"Where there is no vision, people perish."
—Proverbs, 29:18

When traveling in any thriving metropolitan area, even the most casual observer cannot help but notice the extensive reconstruction efforts in many of the downtown areas as old buildings are remodeled to better meet present and future needs of their tenants. Similarly, when looking at the professional literature in the field of education today, one cannot help but be struck by the frequency and intensity of calls for "reform," "restructuring," "renewal," and other "re–" words. These widespread calls for dramatic and fundamental changes in the way the educational system is structured are attributable in large part to a variety of substantial developments in society that increasingly are being reflected in the schools.

In classrooms everywhere educators are encountering a degree of diversity in both students' ability levels and their racial, economic, cultural, and linguistic backgrounds that is greater than ever previously encountered in general education classes. By some estimates, the turn of the century will see the majority of students enrolled in U.S. public schools coming from minority backgrounds (Hodgkinson, 1988). This dramatic student demographic shift has unmistakable implications for educators. Perhaps the most significant of these is the fact that students from linguistic and cultural minority backgrounds generally are considered to be more at risk for school failure in traditionally structured schools and classrooms (e.g., Morsink, Thomas, & Correa, 1991).

Similarly, the rise throughout the 1980s of children living in one-parent homes, in poverty, or (as is too often the case) in both is presenting challenges to educators at levels not previously experienced in the public schools. Poverty (and associated problems such as malnourishment and substance abuse) is a correlate of mild mental retardation (Hallahan & Kauffman, 1994) and predisposes children to the development of behavior and learning problems (Baumeister, Kupstas, & Klindworth, 1990). Given this, the rise in the schools in the number of children from impoverished backgrounds occurring simultaneously with a rise in the number of students diagnosed as having mild disabilities is far from surprising, though no less challenging. Essentially what is emerging is an increasing mismatch between what the schools historically have provided students and what these new groups of students require from the schools in order to be successful. Traditional support services (e.g., special education and related services, bilingual education, programs for disadvantaged students) are inadequate to respond to this situation.

One way to conceptualize the traditional role of support services in the educational system is to consider education as a house where students and educators live (i.e., the "schoolhouse"). Traditionally, students who didn't "fit" well in the schoolhouse (for example, they were too big or too small, or they behaved in ways that disturbed the furniture or the efficient and quiet functioning of the household) had a variety of makeshift add-on arrangements built for them so as to avoid a massive remodeling of the schoolhouse itself.

To continue with this analogy, the people in charge of the schoolhouse initially refused to allow many of these "different" students entry (e.g., Hallahan & Kauffman, 1994; Patton, Kauffman, Blackbourn, & Brown, 1991). Even when they were admitted, often these students were placed in the equivalent of the garage, or in lean-

tos attached to the main schoolhouse, or in small houses built just for these students separate from the main schoolhouse (actually, this analogy sometimes comes quite close to the literal reality). In each case, these segregated arrangements allowed educators to leave the main schoolhouse untouched. Students who did not fit perfectly into the preexisting schoolhouse simply were taken out of it and placed in one of these separate structures.

As student populations become more diverse (reflecting equivalent changes in overall society), these makeshift detached arrangements are becoming increasingly more inadequate. The practice of simply continuing to develop stopgap separate arrangements for the ever-greater numbers of students who don't fit the present-day schoolhouse is being questioned (Skrtic, 1991).

When home owners find that their home no longer meets their needs, they have two options: to search for a new home that does fit those needs or to remodel their old home so that it becomes responsive to these new needs. The old schoolhouse that many believed served well in the past simply does not meet the present needs of the more diverse educational family that lives there today. It is likely that these inadequacies will become even more obvious as the needs of the educational family of the future become even more varied. This family and its needs have changed dramatically over the last few decades, with the schoolhouse remaining largely unchanged. This growing discrepancy between needs and functions has resulted in fundamental problems. However, unlike home owners, educators do not have the option of finding another educational house into which to move. Their only choice is to remodel the present system's schoolhouse.

> *Schools as they are now structured are not working for most kids. So the restructuring issue is this. If the schools were working, then you'd say, 'Let's fix them up a little bit; let's work a little harder; let's work a little longer; let's get a little better textbook; let's get a teacher who is slightly better trained.' We're so far away there is no set of improvements (as schools are now structured) that will bring us up to where we can reasonably expect to go. So we've got to think of running schools in ways that are totally different from the ways they are run now; think of what they could be like. They would look different and feel different for parents, teachers, and kids. (Shanker, 1989)*

What is required is that educators begin seeing themselves as educational architects and remodelers. Prior to beginning a remodeling project, an architect surveys the construction site and analyzes the present structures, including their current capabilities and the ongoing as well as emerging functions the structure must support in the future. The results of this analysis then shape the actual remodeling efforts.

Similarly, educators must begin the rebuilding of the schoolhouse by first surveying the existing requirements, functions, and structures of the schoolhouse. This includes a comprehensive analysis of the needs of the various members of the educational family, an examination of the structures presently in place, and a review of their present and future utility. Based on these analyses, a determination of how best to remodel the schoolhouse then can be made.

Overview of Collaboration

Historically, individual educators have worked in near-total isolation from each other. The traditional structure of the schoolhouse has prohibited them from participating in the sort of collaboration that increasingly characterizes the productive and efficient contemporary workplace (Scott & Smith, 1988). Thus it is not surprising that much of the effort to remodel the educational house centers around the

establishment of structures that facilitate greater professional collaboration (e.g., DeBevoise, 1986; Friend & Cook, 1990).

During a home remodeling project, a variety of craftsmen arrive on the scene with different sets of skills, tools, and equipment. A frequent impairment to the efficiency of the remodeling process that many home owners have experienced is that the workers present on any given day may not have the specific skills or tools necessary to do a particular job. These workers then must call in another particular worker and stand aside as this specialist does this work.

The various jobs that are required in such a remodeling project clearly are seen by many of the workers as being someone else's responsibility. Similarly, whenever a job in the schools (e.g., educating a particular student) is out of a narrow range of "normalcy," the general educator traditionally stops teaching the student and requests the assistance of the specialist (i.e., the educator refers the student to a support services provider). This approach is based upon several presumptions.

First, educators often assume that two distinct types or groups of students exist, one of which is "normal" and one of which is "abnormal" (e.g., disabled, non–English speaking, or similarly "deviant"). Second, it often is believed that there exists reliable instrumentation and procedures that can distinguish between the two

groups. Finally, once such a distinction is made, educators presume that two qualitatively distinct sets of instructional procedures, curricula, and materials exist, each of which is appropriate for one group and inappropriate for the other (e.g., Lovitt, 1993).

Each of these presumptions increasingly is being called into question (Lovitt, 1993). The inefficiency of such an approach (as well as many other problems inherent in such a system) has caused educators to look for an alternative way for schools to function.

More and more school professionals are concluding that what is required for them to be successful in their work is a commitment to a higher degree of professional sharing. Specifically, what is required is the sharing of educational tools, the sharing of professional skills, and most importantly, the sharing of responsibility for all students. There is a growing consensus among school professionals that collaboration is an effective unifying work relationship enabling them to achieve this sharing.

For present purposes, effective collaboration will be defined as an ongoing style of professional interaction in which people voluntarily engage in shared program planning, implementation, evaluation, and overall program accountability. The key here is that collaboration is a way for people to interact, not a process or an end in and of itself. Collaboration is best conceptualized as an overall way to think about and organize the shared planning and working relationships through which professionals approach their work, not as a single event. There is not a certain system or administrative structure called *collaboration*; instead, there are a number of different ways in which collaborative efforts might be structured. For example, a distinction might be made between *indirect collaboration*, in which the collaboration primarily takes place at the planning and development stage, with the subsequent program being provided by only one of the professionals, and *direct collaboration*, in which two professionals both plan and deliver the educational program. (The different ways in which collaboration might be structured will be covered in Chapter 2.)

In remodeling the schoolhouse, collaboration can be seen as a large set or book of possible blueprints for the project. There is a wide assortment of blueprints in that set. The particular one selected depends on the unique needs and requirements of that particular schoolhouse. However, regardless of the specific collaborative blueprint chosen and implemented, the same basic function should emerge: to better serve the needs of the people living in the schoolhouse.

Educational collaboration is simply an overall guiding principle based on the shared and ongoing commitment of two or more professionals to joint ownership of, and obligation to, a larger part of a school's educational responsibilities than either professional individually has assumed in traditional school settings. An explanation of fundamental features of collaboration will help to clarify the concept further.

Basic Features of Collaboration

Self-Examination
and Commitment to Change

A fundamental feature of collaboration in the schools is the willingness of the involved educators to, in essence, start from scratch. Educational collaborators must:

(a)   be ready to comprehensively evaluate themselves and the present system;

(b)   be prepared to discard many of their old practices and procedures that are nonfunctional or irrelevant for contemporary educational programs; and

(c)   be active in seeking out or developing, implementing, and evaluating new and more effective procedures.

Assume that a home remodeling project has resulted in a completely redone and modernized kitchen. Prior to that remodeling project, the people in the house may have developed well-established and habitual roles in joint tasks such as cooking and cleanup. After the remodeling, they may well find that the changed physical arrangement of the kitchen makes their old routines inefficient and inappropriate. Yet they also may find it difficult to give up these obsolete and increasingly outdated roles and practices. This problem would have been lessened had the home owners discussed the inevitable need to make changes in their routines prior to actually beginning the remodeling project.

Similarly, as school personnel move into collaborative arrangements they must make similar adaptations to the new structures and features of the remodeled schoolhouse. The process of self-examination and commitment to change involves a three-phase sequence of adjustment. First there must be a willingness to change; second, the identification of current practices and needed procedures; and finally, the implementation of necessary changes.

The roles and requirements inherent in collaboration will demand that participants make substantive and fundamental changes in the way they go about their work as educators. People are reluctant to accept changes in the professional status quo, in which they

likely have become comfortable. For most people change is frustrating and uncomfortable (Brant, 1993). Initially, some in the schools may refuse even to recognize that changes in the way schools function might be useful, much less necessary. The willingness to accept the fundamental changes required to improve the ability of schools to meet the needs of all students is the first stage in this process of self-examination and adjustment. Participants unwilling to recognize that substantive changes are necessary are unlikely to be successful collaborators.

After accepting that fundamental changes are in order, the involved personnel then must identify accurately the old practices and procedures they previously employed that are no longer appropriate for the new environment. This involves the frequently difficult task of discarding old and dear methods that have become second nature to many professionals. For example, educators only recently have begun to accept that so-called pull-out programs (in which students with even mild disabilities routinely are taken from the general education classroom to a special education resource room) may not be the most efficacious way to develop academic skills in these students (e.g., Slavin, 1990).

Finally, the changes that to this point have been only theoretical then must be translated into actual practice in the schools. School professionals may be willing to go through abstract intellectual exercises in identifying the possible changes that collaboration will require. However, in the absence of personal and systemic commitments to actually implementing these changes in practical settings, success is unlikely.

Sharing

One of the most salient features of collaboration is sharing, a component pivotal to collaboration. Traditionally educators have worked as self-contained instructional units. That is, within their individual classrooms educators historically have had great autonomy. The quality of the educational programs provided in those classrooms were determined largely by each individual educator. Each educator had near-total responsibility for those students in his or her class, and almost no responsibility for any other students. The collaborative structures that are evolving in schools throughout the world will require that school professionals adopt a very different perspective, one in which all students are seen as the responsibility of all educators.

In collaboration, sharing occurs in a number of ways and at a number of points. To begin with, the involved professionals must share a similar set of attitudes, beliefs, and values about schools, teaching and learning, and students. Cook and Friend (1991) suggested that collaborative partners must begin by first sharing a common goal, vision, and set of anticipated outcomes for themselves and their students. These shared goals must be specific enough to operationalize and evaluate. In the absence of a high degree of fundamental and shared agreement concerning questions such as the role of the schools; what, how, and where students should be taught; and the desired outcomes of the educational process, collaboration will not approach the potential levels of effectiveness it otherwise possesses.

The collaborators also must share responsibility for decisions that must be made and for the outcomes of those decisions. In collaboration, all activities that are carried out are jointly owned. Similarly, accountability for the outcomes of those activities is shared. If a problem occurs, it too is shared. Such sharing is inherent in the concept that all students in the school are the responsibility of all educators.

In truly collaborative efforts, resources also are shared. These resources include time, money, materials, and, especially, the skills and ideas of the involved professionals. The belief that all aspects of the educational system (including students, responsibilities, and resources) are "ours" instead of "mine" or "yours" is necessary in the development of a truly collaborative approach.

It is important to make a clear distinction between *sharing* and *equality*. While sharing is a constant throughout any sort of collaboration, this does not imply that the educational tasks and responsibilities always are equal. Indeed, at any given time there likely will be some sort of imbalance, with one professional assuming a relatively greater proportion of these responsibilities. The differentiation and identification of roles should be guided by specific program and student needs and by the unique competencies and strengths each professional brings to his or her work, not by the need for a superficial appearance of equality.

Volunteering

Given the power that collaboration has to dramatically improve teaching and learning in the schools, there is a danger that any given collaborative structure may be imposed arbitrarily upon a school or system by administrators. While such an administrative temptation is understandable, the very social nature of collaboration requires a deep and voluntary commitment of the involved participants. In the absence of this commitment, any resulting collaboration will be collaborative in name only, with the educational status quo remaining largely unchanged beneath this thin veneer. Such surface change is unlikely to be long-lasting.

Valuing

A limitation of traditional educational programs is that educators historically have worked in isolation, largely ignorant of the knowledge and skills their colleagues bring to the educational process. As collaboration becomes increasingly more frequent in education, school professionals will be working together on a more intimate basis than has ever been the case. In this process educators must come to see the contributions of their colleagues as valuable, though perhaps different from their own. It must be understood that these varying sets of skills and competencies contributed by all school professionals gain even greater educational impact and value through the synergism of their combination.

Trust in, respect for, and valuing of one's partner all grow over time, as each participant gains experience with the other. Each must feel comfortable giving the other constructive feedback and suggestions. This may include disclosing to the other thoughts and feelings that normally one does not share. This requires trusting that the other will appreciate this openness and similarly reciprocate. Each must value feedback and suggestions from the other, actively soliciting and incorporating these contributions. If an educator does not or cannot value suggestions and input from a collaborator, then any collaboration will occur at best on only a surface level.

Barriers to Implementing Collaboration

When building contractors come in to prepare an estimate for a remodeling job, one of their initial tasks is to identify potential obstacles that may impede their work and to plan accordingly. Similarly, as school professionals seek to remodel the educational system, their efforts are more likely to be successful if they can initially identify potential barriers to the proposed changes.

One way to conceptualize potential barriers to the widespread implementation of collaborative working relationships in the schools is to organize them into three groups: attitudinal barriers, structural

Table 1.1. Types of Barriers to Collaboration

Attitudinal	Structural	Competency
• Power	• Administrative	• Knowledge and Skills
• Tradition	• Legal	
• Cynicism	• Paperwork	
	• Time, Scheduling, and Workload	

barriers, and competency barriers (National Board of Employment, Education and Training Schools Council, 1992). Each of these may be subdivided further as shown in Table 1.1.

Attitudinal Barriers

The first significant potential problem is the attitude of the involved parties concerning change in general and this change toward collaboration in particular. Attitudinal barriers may include such issues as power, tradition, and cynicism.

Historically educators have had great autonomy and personal power in their individual instructional programs. However, the introduction of collaboration to the schools will ask educators to give up some degree of this professional autonomy and independence.

For example, some support services providers have reported a fear that, as they move into collaborative roles in the general classroom, they will lose professional status, with their role becoming the equivalent of an instructional aide. It is not unusual to hear educators say that they agree with collaboration in principle but disagree with it in actual practice in their own programs. The underlying reason for this position is often an unwillingness to share educational responsibilities and duties. This is accompanied by an unstated but deeply felt fear of losing power. A reluctance to engage in power sharing presents a formidable barrier to the implementation of collaboration.

Tradition also carries great weight in the schools. To acknowledge that things should be changed is also to acknowledge that things at present are less than perfect and that one could be doing better. Proposed changes require the abandonment of familiar and comfortable routines, and at least initially result in disruption, discomfort, and possibly more work. Because each school essentially develops its own blueprints for collaboration as it goes along, it is not possible to know beforehand exactly what the final structure will look like. A fear of the unknown and the comfort of tradition are powerful inhibitors.

Over the years many experienced school professionals have seen educational proposals discussed with great excitement, implemented with much fanfare in the schools, and then result in less-than-encouraging outcomes before coming to premature and ignominious ends. After a history of such experiences, many educators develop great cynicism regarding subsequent proposed innovations. This may be especially true if the proposal is perceived as originating from a social (as opposed to educational) foundation, or from a theoretical (as opposed to practical) perspective.

Collaboration should not and cannot be perceived as simply the next educational fad. Instead, it is the natural result of a consistent trend in education over the past several decades. That trend is toward greater integration of educationally heterogeneous students in the schools and general classrooms. Collaboration is simply an effective mechanism to facilitate this movement.

Structural Barriers

Structural barriers include obstacles such as administrative systems, legal considerations, paperwork, and time, scheduling, and workload. Most contemporary educational systems are built around the concept of one educator having primary (if not sole) responsibility for some 25 to 30 students, either for an entire school day (as is typically the case at the elementary level) or for one-hour blocks (at the secondary level). This administrative structure simply was not designed to accommodate programs in which two (or more) school professionals maintain a more shared responsibility for students.

In addition, educators traditionally have relied heavily on administrators for assistance in implementing structural changes in school programs. Certainly, for change to be long-lasting, administrative support must be present (Chapter 8 gives further information on administrative support). However, collaboration functionally begins at the level of the individual educator. Many educators report frustration at either receiving no encouragement from immediate supervisors or receiving encouragement but little real assistance. The lack of guidelines for school administrators to support collaboration is a frequent problem.

The educational system, especially that portion providing programs for students with disabilities, over the years has become encumbered with a variety of laws and regulations concerning the delivery and documentation of specialized educational services. These regulations were developed to assure that students with disabilities and other special needs actually received the services to which they were legally and morally entitled. However, they have resulted in the untenable position of some educators being allowed to teach only those students who have been found to be legally eligible for specialized services. Other students with equivalent educational needs who fail to meet narrowly prescribed and artificially derived eligibility criteria guidelines are denied this assistance. The present administrative structure in essence says that only some students are entitled to additional assistance to meet their needs. This position is incompatible with fundamental educational ethics and conflicts with a central philosophy of collaboration, which is that all educators are responsible for all students.

A second structural problem related to administration is that of paperwork, again especially in the area of educational support services. Most educators identify the quantity of paperwork required in these programs under present administrative requirements as a substantial obstacle to the implementation of more flexible service-delivery strategies, including collaboration. The paperwork required in most support services programs typically requires the use of a bewildering number of forms. For example, for a student with a disability to receive special education throughout most of the United States, the following documentation is either encouraged or required:

- Child Find form

- Prereferral form

- Referral form

- Activity Tracking form

- Parental Notice form

- Parental Rights form

- Parental Consent for Initial Evaluation form

- Parental Consent for Obtaining Information from Non-Education Agencies form

- Individual Evaluation Report form

- Multi-Disciplinary Team Report form

- Individualized Education Program form

- Parental Consent for Periodic Re-evaluation form

- Program Exit form

Given that each of these forms usually has several pages, it is not surprising that paperwork is seen by many as an obstacle to the implementation of widespread collaboration between general educators and support services providers. Many general educators anticipate additional paperwork being added to their already heavy loads and busy schedules should they assume additional educational responsibility for students with special needs.

Certainly the idea that students' educational programs should be legally protected is a good one. However, the point here is that all students should have such protections, not just those labeled by the school as disabled.

In addition, general educators see themselves being asked to take on even greater overall educational responsibilities if these students remain in their rooms and are not pulled out, as they currently are. A common concern among many general educators is that they already are overburdened with job responsibilities and have inadequate time to complete their present work. In implementing collaboration, when professionals in the schools are faced with the prospect of still more responsibilities and the likelihood of (at least initially) a still heavier work load, many understandably show some reluctance.

At present, support services programs typically are provided largely through a pull-out segregated system. That is, students with speech and language needs leave the general education classroom to go to the speech therapy room to work with the speech therapist, students with learning disabilities leave the general education classroom to go to the resource room to work with the special educator, and so on. Professionals providing traditional support services through this rigidly structured approach often are unable to see how they might additionally assume collaborative roles and responsibilities over and above their traditional work loads.

Competency Barriers

Such problems as lack of knowledge and lack of skills are cited frequently by educators and their administrators as barriers to the widespread implementation of collaboration. One study found that over two-thirds of general educators reported that attempting to teach students with a wide range of different learning needs is an area of major difficulty for them (Batten, 1991). While collaborative efforts can serve to address this problem, preservice teacher education programs traditionally have not given educators the necessary knowledge or skills to assume collaboratively based instructional roles.

Historically educators have worked essentially in great professional isolation. While beginning school professionals may move into their roles knowledgeable about what those roles have required in the past, they often have not been prepared in either the planning skills or the interpersonal skills required to move into the more collaborative educational system of the future.

In fact, many educators remain fundamentally uncertain about what these roles might look like in collaborative programs. While perhaps skilled in working with students, they may have little preparation or experience in working with other professionals. The absence of a preexisting and well-defined blueprint for collaboration is unsettling for many.

For example, in many preservice personnel preparation programs, general and special educators receive preservice training along two distinct and separate parallel tracks. Such an approach to the preparation of educators makes the implementation of future professional collaboration more difficult and less likely by providing two discrete sets of knowledge and skills that have minimal overlap. One of the reasons most frequently given by general educators for maintaining a segregated pull-out or withdrawal system for students with disabilities (as opposed to collaborating with a special educator in the general classroom) is professional ignorance about "those kinds of kids." Many general educators feel inadequately prepared in the types of instructional procedures that have been found effective for students who are different from some predetermined "average" student (Gersten & Woodward, 1990; Goodlad & Field, 1993).

Similarly, many special services providers profess a lack of knowledge about topics such as general education curricula, large group instructional procedures and behavior management, and the schools as a whole (Goodlad & Field, 1993). These professional knowledge and skill deficits often are offered as a rationale for maintaining the status quo.

The difficulties inherent in these often formidable obstacles to remodeling the schoolhouse should not be underestimated. Restructuring the schools while simultaneously continuing to provide educational programs has been compared to trying to repair the wing of a 747 while it is in full flight (Donaldson, 1993). However, failure to identify, acknowledge, and resolve these obstacles to collaboration at the onset almost inevitably will lead to yet another educational innovation failing to deliver on its promise. (Chapter 4 further explores barriers to collaboration, especially those specific to cooperative teaching, and offers a variety of field-tested solutions to these obstacles.)

Conclusions

As owners and residents of the schoolhouse, educators increasingly are concluding that an extensive remodeling job is in order. As appropriate as the present structure may have been for the functions and demands of schools in the past, changes in the educational family's roles and needs are making it clear that the present schoolhouse cannot accommodate the educational family of the future. There is little disagreement that this remodeling project will involve, in part, moving the schools from a system in which professionals essentially work in isolation to one in which collaboration and program integration is central. As educators plan for the next century, the question now being addressed is no longer whether education will become more integrated but how and to what extent this integration will be accomplished (e.g., Goodlad & Lovitt, 1993).

As anyone who has lived in a home during a remodeling project will attest, the traumatic disruptions during the construction period create great levels of stress and frustration. The experience often is so unsettling that the decision to do this is questioned frequently during the project itself. However, after the project has been completed and the occupants have become accustomed to the new environment, the home owners often wonder how they managed to live in the home before the changes.

With the completion of this chapter's survey of the educational construction site and the identification of potential barriers in the remodeling project, the next step is to begin studying and evaluating the various possible structural features that might be incorporated in the blueprints for the remodeling of the schoolhouse. Chapter 2 reviews the major collaboration options available to educators in this undertaking, noting the advantages and disadvantages of each.

Chapter I Activity
Collaboration Readiness Scale

For most educators, moving into extensive collaboration represents a substantial departure from the old ways. Rather than blindly leaping into the unknown, it is useful to begin by determining how ready one is to move into collaboration.

The following Collaboration Readiness Scale was adapted from a scale prepared by Conner (1989) to determine the readiness of business professionals to move from traditional ways of conducting business to innovative approaches. The Collaboration Readiness Scale allows educators both to assess their overall readiness to move into collaborative ventures in the schools and to identify any specific aspects of concern about such a move that are especially significant.

Some schools have found it useful to have all educators who are beginning collaborative efforts take the Collaboration Readiness Scale prior to starting any inservice training efforts. In this way the training can be specifically fine-tuned to respond to the specific concerns identified in the pretest. In addition, the scale may be readministered as a posttest after the training to ascertain the effectiveness with which pretraining concerns were resolved. Additional, ongoing administrations of the scale over time can help document educators' growing levels of comfort with the change collaboration represents.

Instructions

Please respond to each of the following items with your truthful personal reaction. The results will be most useful to you if your responses are as honest as possible.

_____ I. **Purpose**. The basic purpose of collaboration

    a. is clear to me.

    b. is unclear to me.

_____ 2. **Need**. I believe that within the schools there is

    a. a high need for collaboration.

    b. a low need for collaboration.

_____ 3. **Involvement in Planning**. In terms of my school's or district's planning for collaboration, I personally feel

    a. very involved.

    b. not very involved.

_____ 4. **Communication**. As information about collaboration is disseminated in my school or district, I believe

    a. little or no miscommunication has taken or will take place.

b. a great deal of miscommunication has taken or will take place.

_____ 5. **Rewards**. Overall I believe collaboration offers

a. relatively low cost and high rewards.

b. relatively high cost and low rewards.

_____ 6. **Compatibility**. As I consider how the philosophies and ideas of collaboration mesh with my school's or district's existing values and beliefs, I see that

a. a good fit exists.

b. direct conflicts exist.

_____ 7. **Advocacy**. As I consider key people in my school or district, I believe that there is

a. good support for collaboration.

b. weak or mixed support for collaboration.

_____ 8. **Social Relationships**. As I consider the implementation of collaboration in my school or district, I believe that social relationships will

a. remain positive or be further improved.

b. remain negative or be adversely affected.

_____ 9. **Administrative Support**. As collaboration is implemented in my school or district, I believe that

a. the necessary supports will be provided.

b. the necessary supports will not be provided.

_____ 10. **Financial Impact**. As collaboration is implemented in my school or district, I believe that there will be

a. minimal negative impact on budgets.

b. a significant negative impact on budgets.

_____ 11. **Speed of Introduction**. As collaboration is implemented in my school or district, I believe that

a. an appropriate amount of time has been allowed between awareness and implementation.

b. not enough time has been allowed between awareness and implementation.

_____ 12. **Habit Patterns**. In terms of planning for my participation in collaboration efforts in my school or district, I feel

a. my habit patterns are being respected.

b. my habit patterns are being ignored.

_____ 13. **Job Characteristics**. In terms of the basic characteristics of my job, I think that implementing collaboration will have

a. positive effects (or at least no negative effects).

b. primarily negative effects.

_____ 14. **Significance of Changes**. I think that the move toward increased collaboration is

a. a meaningful event warranting my attention.

b. just another change for the sake of change to be ignored or tolerated.

_____ 15. **Fear of Failure**. In terms of my personal wishes, I

a. feel the freedom to fail while learning to collaborate.

b. would rather avoid failing by staying with things I already know.

_____ 16. **Security**. There is a certain security in doing things the way they have always been done in the past. This security in doing things the way I've always done them is

a. not important to me.

b. important to me.

_____ 17. **Confidence**. In terms of my own capability and competence, in general I have a

a. high level of confidence in myself and my skills.

b. low level of confidence in myself and my skills.

_____ 18. **Respect and Trust**. As I consider those who are promoting collaboration in my school or district, in general I have

a. a high degree of respect for and trust in them.

b. a low degree of respect for and trust in them.

_____ 19. **Pressure**. In terms of participating in the efforts of my school or district to implement collaboration, in general I

a. do not feel great pressure for results.

b. feel great pressure for results.

_____ 20. **Vested Interest**. As I consider the present system of my school or district, I find that I

a. do not have a strong vested interest in the present system.

b. do have a strong vested interest in the present system.

_____ 21. **Compatibility**. As I consider the efforts of my school or district to implement collaboration, I perceive

a. high congruence between collaborative objectives and my own personal and professional goals.

b. low congruence between collaborative objectives and my own personal and professional goals.

_____ 22. **Status Quo**. As I consider the efforts of my school or district to implement collaboration, I believe that
  a. it should be relatively easy to reverse any consequences if collaborative
  efforts are not fully successful.
  b. if collaborative efforts do not work, it will be difficult or impossible to
  reverse the consequences.

Scoring

Score 3 points for each *a* response you recorded and 1 point for each *b* response.
Your total score is the sum of all these points.

Number of *a* responses x 3 = _____
Number of *b* responses x 1 = _____
Total = _____

Place a mark on the Collaboration Readiness Scale to indicate your total score.

Collaboration Readiness Scale

✕	✕	✕	✕	✕
66	55	44	33	22
High	Moderately High	Caution	Moderately Low	Low

Interpretation

There are a number of ways the scale might be analyzed. Rather than using the
scales only on an individual basis, some school personnel have found it useful to
group the respondents by their professional training and discipline (e.g., general educators, support services providers, administrators). It is not unusual for these subgroups to have specific unique patterns in their concerns. This data can then form
the basis for further individualized training. Specific scoring interpretation is as follows.
  High Readiness (scores of 61–66): Scores in this range suggest strong readiness for collaboration, with very little resistance in evidence. An extremely positive
prognosis for success is indicated.
  Moderate Readiness (scores of 50–60): Scores in this range indicate moderate readiness, though some resistance may exist. Overall the prognosis for effective implementation of collaboration is positive if the strategies designed to implement the collaboration can effectively address and resolve the existing concerns.
  Caution (scores of 39–49): Successful implementation of collaboration is
likely to occur only when readiness factors outweigh hesitation factors. When the
forces are equal, as they are in this category, there exists the risk of investing a great
deal of effort to accomplish very little. Each positive move may be countered by an
equally negative reaction. This may result in the appearance of movement when, in
fact, real change (i.e., collaboration) is not occurring.

Moderate Hesitation (scores of 28–38): Scores in this range suggest a low level of readiness for collaboration, with considerable overt resistance. The prognosis for collaborative success is low unless the involved parties design and implement effective strategies to modify the negative climate concerning collaboration.

High Hesitation (scores of 22–27): Scores at this level indicate virtually no readiness for collaboration and extremely high levels of resistance. The implementation strategy must totally reverse the resistant atmosphere or the prognosis for success is most negative.

In addition to the above overall score, the following individual item comments can be of use to you as you engage in this self-analysis concerning your readiness for collaboration. By reading the explanations of those items to which you responded *b*, you may be able to more clearly determine the underlying reasons for hesitation in moving forward with changes toward collaboration. This determination is a first step in the process of adapting to such fundamental change as collaboration in the schools.

1. The **purpose** of collaboration sometimes is not made completely clear. When educators lack a full understanding of why collaboration is being implemented, anxiety and suspicion usually fill the information vacuum.

2. Educators may not see a **need** for collaboration. Even if educators fully understand the rationale for collaboration, they may differ with others' perspectives and not agree that it is needed.

3. Educators may not be **involved** in the planning. It is only human for people to most fully support what they helped create. If educators do not believe they have a sufficient degree of input into the planning of collaboration, hesitation or even active resistance usually is increased.

4. There may be poor **communication** regarding collaboration. Even if collaboration affects only one other person, communication can be easily distorted.

5. For some educators the perceived **cost** of implementing collaboration is too high, or the rewards inadequate. For educators to be motivated toward collaboration, a reward for accomplishment must be provided in the form of something they truly value. It must compensate for any physical, intellectual, or emotional price they perceive they will have to pay.

6. The **compatibility** of collaboration may be perceived to be low. This idea of compatibility refers to the degree to which educators view the basic philosophies underlying collaboration as aligning with the existing values of their school or district, and with their own personal beliefs. Resistance may be at its highest when collaboration appears to conflict with concerns and issues that educators hold as fundamental or consider to be sacred.

7. At times key people in the school or district may not be seen as truly **advocating** for collaboration. If educators perceive that their principal or other important individuals or groups are not genuinely supportive of collaboration, acceptance is difficult to secure.

8. Educators may perceive that collaboration will have a negative **impact** on their social relations. If educators view collaboration as adversely affecting the way

they relate to people who are significant to them, acceptance is reduced.

9. Sometimes educators sense that there will not be adequate school or district administrative **support** for collaboration. If collaboration requires school or district resources that educators think are inaccessible (e.g., money, time commitments, new equipment or facilities, specialized training), they are likely to become disenchanted with the idea and withdraw.

10. Educators may believe that collaboration will have a negative **impact** on their operating budgets. Due to poor planning or unexpected drops in revenues, operating budgets can be overburdened with the initial training costs involved in planning and implementing collaboration.

11. At times educators and others most impacted by collaboration sense that it is being **introduced** either too quickly or too slowly, in either case causing difficulties. When planning how fast collaboration is to be introduced, it is necessary to think in terms of optimal timing. The most appropriate speed may not correspond to the maximum speed possible.

12. Sometimes educators feel that in the effort to implement collaboration their well-established **habit patterns** are ignored. Promoters of collaboration who lack knowledge about change and sensitivity concerning educators' behavior patterns instead find themselves inadvertently promoting distrust and alienation.

13. Some educators perceive that collaboration will negatively impact **key job characteristics**. Educators will be more resistant to collaboration if they perceive that it generates a decrease in (a) their autonomy, (b) the level of challenge the job offers, (c) the type of feedback they receive, or (d) the degree of importance the school or district places on their job.

14. A common problem in implementing collaboration is that educators have been exposed to a long history of meaningless and/or poorly executed **changes**. If educators see collaboration as simply another in a series of ill-planned events designed primarily to keep educators from being bored, their enthusiasm for collaboration will be greatly diminished.

15. A **fear of failure** is not unique to educators. Collaboration involves learning, and learning usually involves initially higher levels of mistakes. When people are not given the freedom to make mistakes while learning, they become afraid and easily discouraged.

16. Educators, like most human beings, tend to seek **security** in the past. If collaboration produces frustration or anxiety, educators may long for an earlier time when their jobs weren't so complicated.

17. Some educators lack **confidence** in their capacity to implement collaboration. Educators must perceive that they already possess the skills and knowledge required for implementing collaboration or that the necessary training will be provided. In the absence of this fundamental support they are unlikely to welcome change.

18. A not uncommon pitfall is a lack of **respect and trust** in those promoting collaboration. When educators view the change agent as someone they dislike or mistrust, a lack of acceptance and enthusiasm for collaboration will quickly become evident. Trust and respect typically emerge over time, as professionals work with each other and come to recognize the contributions each makes.

19. At times educators will sense excessive **pressure** to accept the proposed change. When educators are already busy and under stress, the additional pressure brought on by the changes inherent in collaboration may be too much for them to assimilate.

20. Some educators sense a **threat** to their vested interests. A major source of resistance is the perception of collaboration as a threat to educators' economic interests or to their professional prestige.

21. At times there is a perceived **incompatibility** between school/district objectives for collaboration and personal goals of educators. Resistance is increased if educators believe collaboration will block or significantly restrict the achievement of their own personal ambitions.

22. Educators may worry that the **status quo** cannot be reestablished if collaboration proves unacceptable. The fewer permanent negative consequences that result from having tried collaboration and the easier it is to reverse collaborative relations, the more likely it is that educators will not resist implementation.

References

Batten, M. (1991). *Recently recruited teachers: Their views and experiences of preservice education, professional development, and teaching.* Canberra, Australia: Department of Employment Education and Training.

Baumeister, A. A., Kupstas, F., & Klindworth, L. M. (1990). New morbidity: Implications for the prevention of children's disabilities. *Exceptionality, 1*(1), 1–16.

Brant, R. (1993). How restructuring applies to me. *Educational Leadership, 51*(2), 7.

Conner, D. (1989). *Managing organizational change: Dangers and opportunities.* Atlanta: Resources.

Cook, L., & Friend, M. (1991). Principles for the practice of collaboration in schools. *Preventing School Failure, 35*(4), 6–9.

DeBevoise, W. (1986). Collaboration: Some principles of bridgework. *Educational Leadership, 43*(5), 9–12.

Donaldson, G. (1993). Working smarter together. *Educational Leadership, 51*(2), 12–16.

Friend, M., & Cook, L. (1990). Collaboration as a predictor of success in school reform. *Journal of Educational and Psychological Consultation, 1*(1), 69–86.

Gersten, R., & Woodward, J. (1990). Rethinking the Regular Education Initiative: Focus on the classroom teacher. *Remedial and Special Education, 11*(3), 7–16.

Goodlad, J. I., & Field, S. (1993). Teachers for renewing schools. In J. I. Goodlad & T. C. Lovitt (Eds.), *Integrating general and special education* (pp. 229–252). New York: Macmillan.

Goodlad, J. I., & Lovitt, T. C. (Eds.). (1993). *Integrating general and special education*. New York: Macmillan.

Hallahan, D. P., & Kauffman, J. M. (1994). *Exceptional children: Introduction to special education* (6th ed.). Needham Heights, MA: Allyn and Bacon.

Hodgkinson, H. (1988). The right schools for the right kids. *Educational Leadership, 45*, 10–15.

Lovitt, T. C. (1993). Recurring issues in general and special education. In J. I. Goodlad & T. C. Lovitt (Eds.), *Integrating general and special education* (pp. 49–72). New York: Macmillan.

Morsink, C. V., Thomas, C. C., & Correa, V. I. (1991). *Interactive teaching: Consultation and collaboration in special programs*. New York: Macmillan.

National Board of Employment, Education and Training Schools Council (1992). *Developing flexible strategies in the early years of schooling: Purposes and possibilities* (Project Paper No. 5). Canberra: Australian Government Publishing Service.

Patton, J. R., Kauffman, J. M., Blackbourn, J. M., & Brown, G. B. (1991). *Exceptional children in focus* (5th ed.). New York: Macmillan.

Scott, J. J., & Smith, S. C. (1988). *From isolation to collaboration: Improving the work environment of teaching*. Elmhurst, IL: North Central Regional Educational Laboratory.

Shanker, A. (1989). *Equity and excellence* [Videotape]. Elmhurst, IL: North Central Regional Educational Laboratory.

Skrtic, T. (1991). *Behind special education: A critical analysis of professional culture and school organization*. Denver: Love.

Slavin, R. E. (1990). General education under the Regular Education Initiative: How must it change? *Remedial and Special Education, 11*(3), 40–50.

2 Reviewing the Options
Types of School Collaboration

"Look ere you leap, for as you sow, ye are like to reap."
—Samuel Butler

Once home owners have made the decision to remodel their home, typically their first step is to check with architects and/or home remodelers to determine the possible features and structures they might want to incorporate in the plans. Their decisions on the various possibilities available through remodeling are based on a number of considerations, including cost, practicality, size of the area, needed functions, availability of materials, and size of their family.

Similarly, once the decision has been made to remodel the schoolhouse by making education more collaborative, the next step for educators is to determine the exact structures and specifications their collaboration remodeling project should incorporate. As is the case with home owners, educators first must be aware of the various structural possibilities that are available. Then, by considering and generating their own unique answers to a series of questions, educators can effectively identify the specific blueprints that will best meet the needs of the educational family.

Naturally, as would anyone else, educators would prefer to see answers offered in simple, concise packages. However, one must keep in mind the following: What would happen to a remodeling business that offered only one standard set of "off-the-shelf" remodeling plans to any client who came in the door, regardless of his or her individual needs and situations? That business would quickly fail, since no one-size-fits-all set of remodeling plans can address adequately the diverse needs of all home owners. Similarly, the heterogeneity of schools makes it difficult to identify the one approach to collaboration that will be equally applicable and successful in all educational situations. As Albert Shanker, president of the American Federation of Teachers, noted, "There is no one blueprint for schools" (1989). Instead, a wide variety of alternative collaborative structures are available to professionals in education.

Each of the alternative ways to structure collaboration has unique features that make it more or less applicable in any given set of circumstances. However, in home remodeling certain general architectural and design principles have come to be especially desirable and thus exist in many variations of popular remodeling plans. It is likely that certain features of collaboration similarly will come to be perceived as especially desirable and thus will be more likely to fit the needs of more schools.

One should keep in mind two fundamental considerations in collaboration. First, the particular approach or approaches selected should be chosen on the basis of what educators need relative to what their students need. This requires that both sets of needs be understood clearly before changes are implemented. Any home owner who goes to a remodeler with the request, "I want a remodeled kitchen," will be presented with hundreds of possibilities. For the home owner to narrow those down to those that will be most useful, he or she must analyze what needs are not being met by the present arrangement and what alternative arrangements might meet those needs more completely. In addition to this, the home owner should think about what aspects of the present arrangement *are* working well, so that those might be retained in any future remodeled structure. Similarly, educators must begin with some sense of those educational needs that presently are unmet in their programs, while also remaining aware of those presently existing educational arrangements that are responding effectively to educator and student needs.

Second (and perhaps needless to say), by its very definition collaboration requires knowledge about and skills in the development and maintenance of interpersonal relationships. In the absence of these prerequisites, collaboration will not reach its ultimate level of potential effectiveness.

Options in Collaboration

Educational collaboration is fundamentally an educator-based support structure. Many schools already have teams of educators working together for a variety of purposes. These include grade-level teams in elementary schools, in which educators discuss issues of curriculum and instruction; departmental teams at the secondary level, which plan directions for their individual content areas; and support services teams, which make determinations about support service programs and instructional procedures for individual students with special needs.

One way to organize collaboration in education is to categorize it as indirect or direct. In *indirect collaboration*, the involved education-

al collaborators meet, plan, and prepare only outside the classroom, leaving the general education teacher alone to provide the instruction. That is, the general educator meets with one or more experts before or after school or during some preparation period to explain areas of difficulty and solicit suggestions. Following this discussion, the general educator then returns alone to the classroom with these suggestions and attempts to implement them with his or her students. This indirect approach, with ultimate instructional responsibility remaining solely with the classroom teacher, has been the traditional format for most collaborative efforts (e.g., Laycock, Gable, & Korinek, 1991).

For example, in indirect collaboration a speech therapist might meet away from the classroom with the teacher of a student who is responding to questions with only one-word answers. After discussing the situation with the student's teacher, the therapist might suggest to the teacher ways he or she can phrase questions during classes to elicit more complete responses from the student.

Direct collaboration refers to a collaborative approach in which the support services provider not only plans beforehand with the general educator but also works in the actual environment with both the classroom teacher and the students who are having difficulty. Direct collaboration is rapidly gaining in acceptance, as it offers a number of significant advantages.

As an example of direct collaboration, a speech therapist might regularly work in the general classroom with the teacher. The two professionals together plan and implement language-enrichment exercises for the entire class, or teach language skills to carefully structured subgroups of students within that class.

There are many possible ways school-based professionals might participate in collaborative efforts. Examples of these include peer coaching, mentoring, and peer supervision. However, four different proposed approaches to collaboration have received significant coverage and wide support in the professional literature. These include:

- collaborative consultation,
- peer collaboration,
- teacher assistance teams, and
- cooperative teaching.

All these approaches propose ways to support general education teachers in educating academically and behaviorally heterogeneous groups of students. Three of these approaches (collaborative consultation, peer collaboration, and teacher assistance teams) are examples of indirect collaboration. The fourth, cooperative teaching, is a direct approach to collaboration.

Indirect Collaboration

Collaborative Consultation. Collaborative consultation originally
was developed to assist general educators who worked with students
who had special needs. As these students with disabilities increasingly were retained in or returned to their regular classrooms from
their previous pull-out programs, many of their teachers reported
lacking the knowledge or skills to effectively teach students whose
needs differed from some average level of ability.

To respond to this need, Idol, Paolucci-Whitcomb, and Nevin
(1986) researched the professional literature in business consultation
to identify how that community responded to problems. In the business world, when a problem exists the involved individuals bring in a
consultant from the outside (that is, outside their own areas of expertise). That outside expert reviews the problem and, based on his or
her experience and expertise in that particular area, develops possible solutions that might then be implemented. This model from business was adapted to meet the needs of educational programs, with
the term *collaborative* added to *consultation* to indicate their perception of the necessary interactive nature of the approach. As defined
by Idol et al. (1986), collaborative consultation is "an interactive
process that enables people with diverse expertise to generate creative solutions to mutually defined problems" (p. 1).

The collaborative consultation approach is a triadic model,
emphasizing three primary components. The first is the *target*, or the
person in whom the behavior change is sought. In school programs
the target would be the student who is having difficulty. The second
component is the *consultant*, the person who has unique knowledge
or skills applicable to the situation. In education this would be the
support services provider (for example, a gifted/talented facilitator, a
speech therapist, or a special educator). Finally, the third component
in this triadic model is the *mediator*, the person who is able to impact
directly upon the target individual's behavior. In schools this is the
general education teacher who is responsible for teaching those students presenting instructional challenges (Idol et al., 1986).

Typically the collaborative consultation approach works as follows. When an educational problem or concern exists in the regular
classroom, that general education teacher (the mediator) seeks out
the expert consultant (e.g., the support services provider). The two
meet outside the classroom, with the general educator describing the
problem of the student (the target) to the expert, who then suggests

possible solutions. The general educator then takes those proposed solutions back to the classroom for implementation, usually reporting back to the specialist about the effectiveness (or lack thereof) of those suggestions.

A concern some educators voice with such an approach is that by its very nature consultation tends to yield an asymmetrical and unbalanced relationship. Idol et al. (1986) suggested that the involved educators share mutual responsibility for the education of the referred student and also share accountability for the success or failure of any developed programs. However, in actual practice the general educator may quite accurately sense that he or she lacks the skills to handle the situation. Otherwise, why would there have been a need to seek assistance from the expert? In such situations, the general educator may simply present a problem to the specialist and then wait passively for a solution.

Conversely, all pressure to solve the problem in this situation lies with the specialist. If the proposed solution is not successful, it is perceived to be the expert's fault. The unstated implication in this situation is that the general educator is automatically absolved of ongoing responsibilities for students who are failing to progress after being referred to the expert. This often occurs even when the student physically remains in that teacher's class.

Implicit responsibility for the student and the student's problem is assumed by the specialist at the point of the referral. In the collaborative consultation approach this individual rarely or never actu-

ally teaches the student and often has never even seen the student in the natural context of the classroom. The primary weakness of this approach is the practical absence of the fundamental philosophy that all students belong to all teachers.

Peer collaboration. Peer collaboration is an outgrowth of the collaborative consultation approach. It was designed to both strengthen the balance of the relationship of the involved professionals and provide structure to facilitate the effectiveness of the ensuing dialogue. To avoid the stilted and unbalanced relationship between an expert and someone who is by definition a "nonexpert," in peer collaboration two true peers (general educators) are paired together. In addition, peer collaboration uses a very structured dialogue format designed to result in solutions (Pugach & Johnson, 1988).

Peer collaboration evolved in part from the sense that the expertise of the general educator, who in the past would have quickly referred the struggling student for special education evaluation, was not being fully utilized. Several reports have concluded that most general education teachers refer students for special services in order to obtain placement outside the regular classroom, not to receive help to teach that student (e.g., Pugach, 1985; Ysseldyke et al., 1983). In traditional support services referral systems, the support services providers almost always eventually assume educational responsibility for students who are referred, since most referred students ultimately are found to be eligible for and receive support services (Strickland & Turnbull, 1990), often away from the general education classroom.

In peer collaboration, the two general educators collaborate by working through a four-step process to identify effective classroom interventions. In the first step, *problem description and clarifying questions*, the teacher whose student is struggling assumes the role of initiator. In this role the teacher writes out and reads to the peer a short description of the problem, and then asks for clarifying questions. Clarifying questions are questions asked by the peer that result in additional relevant information that further defines and clarifies the problem situation. (For example, the facilitator might ask the initiator about significant classroom factors relevant to the student's difficulties.)

Once the problem has been clarified to the satisfaction of both, the initiator then *summarizes the problem* by stating (a) the pattern of the problem, (b) his or her response to the problem, and (c) relevant variables in the classroom that he or she controls. This second step helps in the subsequent development of possible solutions.

In the third step, the initiating teacher *generates at least three practical and minimally disruptive intervention options* and speculates on the possible outcomes of each. The facilitator's primary role here is to systematically guide the initiating teacher through the multiple interventions by discussing and exploring the possibilities and practical limitations of each intervention option. This step culminates in the selection of one intervention strategy.

The final step in peer collaboration is to *plan an evaluation procedure* for the selected intervention strategy. Key considerations include the ease of data collection and a minimal level of intrusiveness. At the end of this step the initiating teacher is ready to begin the intervention, with the two peer collaborators agreeing to meet again in 2 weeks to assess progress or begin the peer collaboration process over again. Once the peer collaborators become experienced in the peer collaboration process, the interaction typically requires approximately an hour from start to finish.

Part of the value underlying this approach is that, as teachers help one another in this questioning fashion, they should come to gain additional skills in asking themselves appropriate questions and ultimately solving problems on their own. This is based on theories underlying metacognitive learning strategies, that is, one's increasing knowledge of one's own learning strategies.

A potential drawback of peer collaboration is that educators sometimes find this structured questioning system too time-consuming, binding, and artificial. It has been suggested that, without careful and ongoing analysis of the interactions, the proceedings have the potential to become so mechanical that a computer program might be equally effective. An additional weakness is that neither peer may have the necessary knowledge or skills to interact productively or to effectively address the significant educational problems.

Teacher Assistance Teams (TAT). One of the earliest approaches suggested to facilitate collaboration among educators is the Teacher Assistance Team (TAT), developed by Chalfant and his colleagues (Chalfant, Pysh, & Moultrie, 1979). The TAT was a response to the then newly passed legislation, the Education for All Handicapped Children Act (P.L. 94-142) (1975), and to the anticipated difficulties educators would have as students with disabilities were returned to their general education classrooms under the "Least Restrictive Environment" directives of that legislation.

The TAT was designed as a means of supporting general education teachers so they could more effectively teach students who were evidencing learning or behavior problems in regular classrooms. The intended results of TAT were a reduction in the number of initial referrals to special education and related services and increased maintenance of special-needs students in the general classrooms. (It is important that the TATs be distinguished from more traditional

multidisciplinary teams whose primary responsibility is to determine special services eligibility of referred students.) In some states TAT-like teams are referred to as School-Wide Assistance Teams (SWAT), Pupil Assistance Committees (PAC), and such.

Traditionally, school districts have responded to perceived staff needs by providing one or more staff development workshops. However, Chalfant and his colleagues determined that this piecemeal approach was inadequate to address the full scope of competencies and skills educators require in order to maintain students with increasingly diverse learning abilities and needs in general classrooms. What instead was required was an ongoing, day-to-day support system.

The Teacher Assistance Team approach is based on the development in a school of a team of four members. Each team has three relatively permanent core members. These individuals are experienced master teachers, elected to participate on the TAT by their colleagues at their school. A fourth and changing member is the educator seeking help. Parents, students, and relevant others also may participate, though this is not required.

In the TAT approach to collaboration, a referring educator brings to the TAT a student problem and describes to team members the student's strengths and needs, as well as interventions that have been attempted. If possible, at least one team member may be asked to observe the student in the classroom prior to the meeting. The team then conducts a problem-solving meeting to help the referring educator clearly define the problem. In this meeting all involved parties brainstorm and then refine possible solutions to the problem, with the educator then taking those ideas back to the classroom. Several weeks later a follow-up meeting is held to monitor the effectiveness of the selected strategies.

Several problems may emerge as a TAT approach is implemented (Bauwens, Hourcade, & Friend, 1989). Typically the permanent team members have received little or no training in providing the types of consultation they now are asked to provide. Thus the effectiveness with which various TATs function may vary significantly.

In addition, the original TAT model proposed that one of the permanent TAT members observe the student in the classroom prior to the first meeting. In practical application, this often does not happen. The ensuing discussions then may be grounded not in the factual reality of the situation but in the referring educator's individual and subjective perception of it.

In fact, in the absence of a "collaborative ethic" (Phillips & McCullough, 1990), the very act of having to bring a problem to the TAT is seen by some educators as a tacit admission of professional inadequacy and failure. This is psychologically a different scenario from the traditional special education referral, in which the referring educator anticipates that the multidisciplinary diagnostic team will determine that the student's failure to learn is due to the presence of a disability (and therefore not the educator's fault), as opposed to the educator's lack of instructional knowledge or skills. If the TAT does not have a record of providing significant amounts of successful help, many educators may come to see the TAT as simply another hurdle to be overcome in the overall process of having a student removed from the classroom and placed in special education.

Direct Collaboration: Cooperative Teaching

Cooperative teaching was initially described by Bauwens, Hourcade, and Friend (1989) as "an educational approach in which general and special educators work in a co-active and coordinated fashion to jointly teach heterogeneous groups of students in educationally integrated settings (i.e., general classrooms). . . . In cooperative teaching both general and special educators are simultaneously present in the general classroom, maintaining joint responsibilities for specified education instruction that is to occur within that setting" (p. 18).

Cooperative teaching differs from the preceding approaches to collaboration in that it is a direct approach to collaboration. That is, the support services provider who is providing assistance to and with

the general educator is actually in the classroom during some portion of the instructional day. The most distinctive feature of cooperative teaching, and the one that most differentiates it from other approaches to collaboration, is this joint *direct* provision of assistance.

Cooperative teaching evolved from analyses of weaknesses experienced by educators using the three preceding approaches to collaboration. Cooperative teaching's direct approach to collaboration, with the simultaneous presence of two professionals in the same classroom, is designed to avoid many of the problems inherent in other collaborative approaches.

Those previously described approaches identified as indirect collaboration all essentially entail the general educator seeking advice from others and then returning alone to the problem situation. In cooperative teaching, though, the support services provider (e.g., speech therapist, gifted/talented facilitator, counselor, special educator, teacher of English as a Second Language, Chapter 1 teacher, and so forth) is present in the general classroom and teaching alongside and in tandem with the general educator. While together, these two professionals determine who teaches what, when, how, and whom not by student categorical labels (e.g., communication disordered, emotionally disturbed, non–English speaking, learning disabled) but by a more global analysis of the needs of the students in the class at any given time and the specific sets of skills and knowledge each professional brings to the classroom.

Traditionally general educators are knowledgeable about curricular sequencing in traditional academic areas and are skilled in large group instruction. Many support services providers are especially skilled in areas such as curricular and instructional adaptations and in the development and provision of individualized instruction. The combination of these previously separate sets of skills for individually determined periods of time provides a powerful instructional package.

Since both professionals are simultaneously present in the classroom, cooperative teaching avoids the question of who has the responsibility for the student with difficulties. Both professionals share the responsibility for the education of all students in that classroom. The relative roles of "expert" and "help-seeker" vary constantly throughout the day, as each professional takes on those responsibilities in which he or she has greater competence.

The social interactions and support system of the involved educators evolve naturally during their work together and are not artificially dictated and constrained by a preordained script. The fact that both are present in the classroom simultaneously means that both will see any student difficulties in the actual instructional environment in which they are based. This yields practical educational interventions that are likely to be more effective. In addition, the development of the working relationship over extended periods of time makes it more likely that each will acquire additional professional skills from the other (Case, 1992).

While cooperative teaching responds effectively to problems inherent in other approaches to collaboration, it does present its own set of challenges. An especially significant challenge is that professionals in the schools may be asked to make significant changes in their well-established professional identities. For example, special educators have long administered programs in which students with special needs were removed from their classrooms into special education programs (e.g., resource rooms or self-contained special classes). Now those special educators are being asked to work in the general education classroom with larger groups of students with more diversity in their learning ability. The potential exists for these individuals to sense the loss of some degree of professional identity and autonomy. If the two involved educators fail to establish an effective working relationship based on mutual trust and respect, they are not likely to implement cooperative teaching effectively.

Nevertheless, cooperative teaching is becoming increasingly popular as the approach to collaboration that can respond most effectively to the need for school professionals to work together to effectively teach educationally diverse groups of students (Friend, Reising,

& Cook, 1993). Though requiring an initially significant commitment of time and resources, it offers benefits in both the short term and the long term. In the short term, the students with special needs receive the powerful instruction they require for educational success in the classroom (Harris et al., 1987; White & White, 1992). In the long term, cooperative teaching builds schoolwide collaborative problem-solving skills and a school culture that supports the ongoing learning of both students and teachers. These outcomes help break the cycle of dependence upon segregated pull-out programs for students with diverse learning needs (Adams & Cessna, 1993; Case, 1992).

Conclusions

Earlier it was noted that no one set of off-the-shelf architectural plans meets the needs of all home owners who are contemplating home remodeling projects. Similarly, it is not likely that any single approach to collaboration can meet the needs of all schools everywhere.

However, certainly there exist architectural plans whose generalized features meet the needs of most home owners, especially when further fine-tuned depending upon individual needs. Similarly, the cooperative teaching approach to collaboration offers most educators a set of unique features and possibilities that are responsive to the problems increasingly common to all schools. Cooperative teaching is the only collaborative proposal that:

(a)   brings together simultaneously in the classroom education professionals from widely differing informational backgrounds who possess complementary sets of skills and perspectives and

(b)   facilitates those professionals integrating those varying sets of knowledge and skills into a comprehensive and complementary instructional system.

As home owners seek to remodel a home, an early accomplishment is finding or developing the architectural plans that will better meet their evolving and changing needs. Educators throughout the world are discovering that the set of cooperative teaching blueprints holds great promise for enabling educators to remodel the schoolhouse for maximum effective educational inclusion of all students, including those of varying cultural, ethnic, and linguistic backgrounds; academic abilities; and behavioral characteristics. Chapter 3 describes in detail exactly how the blueprints of cooperative teaching are transformed into the actual brick and mortar of instruction.

. . . .
Chapter 2 Activity
Self-Examination for Collaboration
. . . .

This chapter has provided an overview of the fundamental features of collaboration and some of the ways in which collaboration can be structured. It is now time to begin a more in-depth, personal, and individualized examination of collaboration, including its background and potential impact relative to one's unique situation.

Instructions

As every educator knows, examinations should include material from varying levels of cognitive complexity, from simple recall of basic factual material to such higher-level skills as synthesis, analysis, and evaluation. The most frequent suggestion is to structure questions along the six levels of Bloom's taxonomy of educational objectives (Bloom, Engelhart, Frost, Hill, & Krathwohl, 1956). These six levels, from the simplest and most concrete level to the most complex and abstract, are:

Knowledge;

Comprehension;

Application;

Analysis;

Synthesis; and

Evaluation.

Unfortunately, many educators find that Bloom's taxonomy is too abstract and requires too much effort and time to use in their programs. To respond to this problem, Weiderhold (1991) constructed a Question Matrix, a user-friendly 6 x 6 matrix based in part on Bloom's taxonomy. Weiderhold's structure moves from simple factual questions in the top left portion of the matrix (e.g., "What is . . . ?") to more complex and demanding questions toward the lower right corner (e.g., "How might . . . ?").

This matrix has been adapted here to allow you to think about, at a number of levels and in a number of ways, collaboration and its potential to change the way teaching is structured at your school. As you read and consider your response to each question, keep in mind that there are no universal right answers to these open-ended items. Rather, these 36 questions are provided simply as an organized structure and framework to help you to more comprehensively analyze yourself and think more deeply about the specifics of your own situation regarding the development and implementation of collaboration in your school or district. The complete Question Matrix, or Q matrix, is provided in Table 2.1.

Table 2.1. Question Matrix

	Event	Situation	Choice	Person	Reason	Means
Present	What is happening now at your school to cause people to consider beginning collaboration?	When is collaboration scheduled to begin?	Which collaborative structure is best suited for the unique needs of your situation?	Who is most involved in collaboration now at your school?	Why is collaboration being considered now?	How is collaboration going to change the way your school's programs now function?
Past	What did you think when you first learned of collaboration?	Where (in what situation) and when did the idea of collaboration at your school first emerge?	Which alternative educational approaches have been tried in the past to target problems in your school?	Who in the past has proposed collaboration at your school? What happened?	Why did no one propose collaboration in the past?	How did the initial thinking about collaboration at your school begin?
Possibility	What can be done to introduce the idea of collaboration most effectively at your school?	Where and when would it be best to prepare potential collaborators at your school?	Which of the many reasons for collaboration can be most easily "sold" to educators at your school?	Who can most effectively "sell" collaboration at your school?	Why can collaboration be successful in your school?	How can the administration most effectively support collaboration?
Probability	What would happen if collaboration were universally instituted throughout all schools?	When would involved professionals be able to get together to review and discuss collaboration?	Which collaborative structure would be seen as the most dramatic departure from the present system?	Who in your school would be most resistant to participating in collaboration?	Why would professionals at your school resist becoming involved in collaboration?	How would the school be affected if only a few professionals chose to participate in collaboration?
Prediction	What will happen if the administration provides only partial support for collaboration in your school?	Where in your school is collaboration likely to be most easily established?	Which comments from parents will be most frequently heard when collaboration is implemented at your school?	Who at your school will emerge as the leading advocate for collaboration?	Why will students at your school welcome the implementation of collaboration?	How will the professional responsibilities inherent in the present day "one teacher–one classroom" structure change with collaboration?
Imagination	What might collaboration change in you personally?	Where might collaboration be less appropriate and less effective than the present system?	Which student characteristics at your school might collaboration be especially well-suited for?	Who will be the most pivotal person at your school to convince of the benefits of collaboration?	Why might some students at your school initially resist collaboration?	How might successful collaborators best develop collaborative networks with other professionals?

Note. From *Cooperative Learning and Critical Thinking: The Question Matrix* by C. Wiederhold, 1991, San Juan Capistrano, CA: Resources for Teachers. Adapted with permission.

References

Adams, L., & Cessna, K. (1993). Metaphors of the co–taught classroom. *Preventing School Failure, 37*(4), 28–31.

Bauwens, J., Hourcade, J., & Friend, M. (1989). Cooperative teaching: A model for general and special education integration. *Remedial and Special Education, 35*(4), 19–24.

Bloom, B. S., Engelhart, M. D., Frost, E. J., Hill, W. H., & Krathwohl, D. R. (1956). *Taxonomy of educational objectives. Handbook 1: Cognitive domain.* New York: David McKay.

Case, A. D. (1992). The special education rescue: A case for systems thinking. *Educational Leadership, 50*(2), 32–34.

Chalfant, J. C., Pysh, M. V. D., & Moultrie, R. (1979). Teacher assistance teams: A model for within–building problem solving. *Learning Disability Quarterly, 2*, 85–96.

Education for All Handicapped Children Act, (EHA), P.L. 94-142, 20 U.S.C. § 1401 *et seq.* (now known as Individuals with Disabilities Education Act [IDEA], P.L. 101-476).

Friend, M., Reising, M., & Cook, L. (1993). Co–Teaching: An overview of the past, a glimpse at the present, and considerations for the future. *Preventing School Failure, 37*(4), 6–10.

Harris, K. C., Harvey, P., Garcia, L., Innes, D., Lynn, P., Munoz, D., Sexton, K., & Stoica, R. (1987). Meeting the needs of special high school students in regular education classrooms. *Teacher Education and Special Education, 10*, 143–152.

Idol, L., Paolucci–Whitcomb, P., & Nevin, A. (1986). *Collaborative consultation.* Austin, TX: PRO-ED.

Laycock, V. A., Gable, R. A., & Korinek, L. (1991). Alternative structures for collaboration in the delivery of special services. *Preventing School Failure, 35*(4), 15–18.

Phillips, V., & McCullough, L. (1990). Consultation–based programming: Instituting the collaborative ethic in schools. *Exceptional Children, 56*, 291–304.

Pugach, M. C. (1985). The limitations of federal special education policy: The role of classroom teachers in determining who is handicapped. *Journal of Special Education, 19*, 123–127.

Pugach, M. C., & Johnson, L. J. (1988). Peer collaboration. *TEACHING Exceptional Children, 20*(3), 75–77.

Shanker, A. (1989). *Equity and excellence* [Videotape]. Elmhurst, IL: North Central Regional Educational Laboratory.

Strickland, B. B., & Turnbull, A. P. (1990). *Developing and implementing individualized education programs* (3rd ed.). Columbus, OH: Merrill.

Weiderhold, C. (1991). *Cooperative learning and critical thinking: The question matrix.* San Juan Capistrano, CA: Resources for Teachers.

White, A. E., & White, L. L. (1992). A collaborative model for students with mild disabilities in middle schools. *Focus on Exceptional Children, 24*(9), 1–10.

Ysseldyke, J. E., Thurlow, M., Graden, J., Wesson, C., Algozzine, B., & Deno, S. (1983). Generalizations from five years of research on assessment and decision making: The University of Minnesota Institute. *Exceptional Education Quarterly, 4*, 75–93.

....

3

Developing the Blueprints
Planning for Cooperative Teaching

....

" . . . look shining at new styles of architecture, a change of heart."
—Wystan Hugh Auden

By this point the home owners who have decided to begin a remodeling project have spent a great deal of time reviewing possible architectural plans for their project and discussing which of these plans and options are best suited for their changing needs. They finally have identified the one set of plans that appears most promising but also have concluded that those plans will require some adaptations and fine-tuning. They now must carefully review those plans for the remodeling project, examining the various features and options to determine how each can be modified to best meet their needs.

Chapter 2 reviewed several potential collaborative structures that schools throughout the country are using in the rebuilding of the schoolhouse. Potential sets of blueprints for this project include collaborative consultation, peer collaboration, teacher assistance teams, and cooperative teaching. Increasing numbers of educators are finding that the unique features of cooperative teaching make it especially well-suited for remodeling the schoolhouse to best meet the needs of students and educators in contemporary society.

Definition of Cooperative Teaching

As is the case with any emerging innovation, the definition of cooperative teaching continues to evolve as the actual practices are refined over time. Chapter 2 provided an early (1989) definition of cooperative teaching. Since that time much field-based experience has been gained as cooperative teaching has been implemented in thousands of schools.

One of the primary developments has been an expansion of cooperative teaching. From its beginnings as a somewhat limited program involving only general and special educators, cooperative teaching has evolved into a substantially more expansive and extensive integrated system involving *all* professional school support staff (e.g., speech therapists, school counselors, special educators, teachers of English as a Second Language, Chapter 1 teachers, gifted/talented facilitators, school nurses) working and teaching directly with their general education colleagues. This development has resulted in this present-day conceptualization of cooperative teaching.

> Cooperative teaching refers to a restructuring of teaching procedures in which two or more educators possessing distinct sets of skills work in a coactive and coordinated fashion to jointly teach academically and behaviorally heterogeneous groups of students in educationally integrated settings, that is, in general classrooms.

In cooperative teaching, two (or more) school professionals possessing clusters of educational knowledge and skills that complement each other are present simultaneously in the general classroom for

some part of the instructional day. In traditional educational arrangements, responsibility for students was divided up according to perceived student characteristics and needs. That is, typically students
whose native language was not English were assigned to ESL teachers; students identified by the school as learning disabled were
assigned to special education teachers; students with other academic deficits were assigned to Chapter 1 teachers; and so on. In cooperative teaching, these students remain in their general education
classrooms, where the cooperative teaching partners provide the pro-
gram(s) necessary for the success of all students there. These educators maintain joint responsibility for all educational outcomes for all
students in that class.

Over the past decade professionals in education have become
increasingly familiar with the practice of "cooperative learning" (e.g.,
Johnson & Johnson, 1986; Slavin, 1987). In cooperative learning,
students are arranged in groups of heterogeneous ability levels in
which they work together to accomplish shared and common goals.
In cooperative teaching, it is educators with diverse backgrounds of
training and experiences who are working and actively teaching
together to more effectively meet the needs of all students. Of course,
cooperative learning and cooperative teaching can be in place simultaneously to take advantage of the unique contributions of both.

Professional Roles in Cooperative Teaching

The professionals who are directly involved in the design and ongoing implementation of cooperative teaching are as diverse as the professional backgrounds of the school's entire faculty. Participants in cooperative teaching include elementary school classroom teachers and secondary content teachers working alongside support services providers such as special education teachers, instructional assistants and aides, speech and language therapists, Chapter 1 and remedial reading teachers, gifted/talented facilitators, teachers of English as a Second Language (ESL), occupational and physical therapists, school nurses, librarians, and school psychologists and counselors.

The essential philosophy of cooperative teaching is simple. In short, *all educators are responsible for all students.* To some extent educator specialization in content areas and skills certainly will continue to occur. However, in cooperative teaching such determinations are based on performance-based assessments of individual educators' skills and strengths, not on artificially determined student categories of presumed differences or disabilities. In this way specific and unique educator capabilities can be more optimally used for the benefit of all students, regardless of administrative labels.

Cooperative teaching effectively uses the specialized sets of knowledge and skills each type of school professional brings to the classroom. For example, most general educators are knowledgeable about curriculum and curricular sequencing, especially in the traditional academic areas. These educators are very familiar with educational standards such as basal series and literature-based texts in reading and spelling, and arithmetic scope and sequence matrices. Especially at the secondary level, these educators additionally are specialists in content areas (e.g., English literature, chemistry, social studies).

In addition, general educators traditionally have been skilled and experienced in large group management procedures. That is, to function effectively in their professional roles, these educators must skillfully manage students in groups of 20 to 40, ensuring that all students in these large groups are effectively engaged in the learning process. These large group management competencies include classroom skills such as effective whole class presentations and assessments, large group discipline, and records management.

Conversely, the use of support services providers evolved with an emphasis on individuals, not large groups. As a result, these professionals have cultivated a significantly different set of school skills. For example, support services providers traditionally have developed expertise in highly detailed individual student assessment. That is, for purposes of both eligibility determination and subsequent curriculum development, support services providers have acquired a wide repertoire of effective evaluation procedures that target individual students. A rapidly evolving related evaluation skill of support services providers is in targeting areas of difficulty within a curriculum and analyzing and adapting instructional materials and instructional strategies. That is, these professionals are skilled and experienced in pinpointing likely areas of difficulty contained in the general education curriculum and materials, and in designing adaptations or modifications of those areas of difficulty appropriate to students with academic difficulties. Conversely, students identified as gifted or talented may require accommodations through enrichment of the standard curricula and materials, as well as possible changes in the manner of instruction. Educator skills in this sort of individualization are becoming more in demand in the general classroom as educators face increasingly heterogeneous student populations.

Most support services providers also have experience in the development of individualized education programs and in applied behavior-analysis procedures. While general educators' classroom management strategies have emphasized group management procedures, support services providers have developed expertise in using systematic behavioral procedures to enhance skill levels and subsequent potential of individual students (or at least small groups).

Instructional assistants and teacher aides have great experience in direct program implementation, often more than the educators under whom they work. Support services providers like speech and language therapists and physical and occupational therapists possess unique knowledge and competencies not found elsewhere among a school's staff. Chapter 1 and remedial reading teachers bring specific diagnostic and intervention skills to students with math and reading difficulties. In addition, these professionals also are especially experienced with the diversity of cultural backgrounds found increasingly in the schools today. The intensive language background ESL teachers can bring to a classroom is also appropriate for the linguistically diverse contemporary classroom, and these professionals also are knowledgeable about imbedding language instruction in the context of typical classroom activities for all students. Psychologists and school counselors may be especially skilled at facilitating social and emotional growth, as well as bringing professional perspectives to areas of concern such as learning strategies and family dynamics.

In short, school professionals representing two or more of these backgrounds working together in cooperative teaching can bring an impressive combination of skills to the integrated classroom. As schools continue to expand their implementation of cooperative teaching, all students will be better served.

Traditionally (and often by law), school decisions regarding the assignment of specific educator responsibilities and duties have been made on the basis of artificial considerations such as areas of administratively determined educator certifications or endorsements, labels of students, and similar concerns. For example, in the past special educators have worked under the assumption that their only educational responsibility was toward those students who had been found legally to be disabled and thus entered into the special education bureaucratic regulatory maze. This position is often justified through overly restrictive and conservative interpretations of federal or state regulations. Similarly, general education teachers often have seen themselves as free of further educational responsibility for such students once a diagnosis of a disability has been made.

Certainly the practical realities of educator certification by state boards of education must be acknowledged. For example, by federal and state regulation, special educators are restricted to providing services only to students legally identified as eligible for these services. If a special educator provides instruction in thinking skills to an entire fifth-grade class, it might be interpreted as a violation of this regulation, since students not eligible for special education services would nonetheless be receiving services from a special educator.

Perhaps the most effective response to this concern is to examine the federal law governing special education. Specifically, the law states that students with disabilities may be removed from the regular education environment only when "education in regular classes with the use of supplemental aids and services cannot be achieved satisfactorily" (Federal Register, 1977, p. 42497).

The primary intention of the law is unmistakable. The preference of the law is clearly for students with disabilities to be taught in the general education classroom with the use of supplemental aids and services. Clearly special educators and other support services providers participating in cooperative teaching are providing such a supplemental service in the classroom as they maintain an active role in the development and implementation of instruction in that classroom. Since cooperative teaching facilitates the provision of a satisfactory education for students with disabilities (as well as all others in the class), then such services are clearly appropriate, warranted, and justifiable. State regulations that are interpreted in a manner contrary to this would appear to be in conflict with both the letter and the spirit of this federal law.

In more and more situations across the country, individual school districts or even entire states are requesting waivers or exemptions from overly restrictive interpretations of regulations, with these waiver requests increasingly granted. It is likely that these state regulatory guidelines will continue to evolve in flexibility to become consistent with developing "best practices" in the field, including the use of a variety of specialist educators in interactive educational professionalism.

Benefits of Cooperative Teaching

Cooperative teaching has significant potential benefits on both immediate and long-term bases and for both students and educators. In the short term, it facilitates the transition of students presently receiving educational programming in segregated educational settings (e.g., ESL students, students with disabilities, and students receiving other specialized services) back into the classroom. This transition, a phenomenon involving greater and greater numbers of students in the schools, is a typical area of difficulty in contemporary inclusion efforts (Reynolds, Wang, & Walberg, 1987; Stainback & Stainback, 1984). The research on integration efforts consistently indicates that such programs are effective when the classroom teachers are able to adapt curriculum and instruction to make it appropriate for all students in the class (Algozzine & Maheady, 1986; Slavin, Leavey, & Madden, 1984; Slavin, Madden, & Leavey, 1984; Smith, Price, & Marsh, 1986; Stainback & Stainback, 1984; Wang & Birch, 1984; Wang & Walberg, 1983). With the support services providers bringing instructional adaptation and individualization skills to the general classroom, the full and successful reintegration of students with a variety of diverse educational needs can be achieved.

In the long term, cooperative teaching facilitates inclusion on a proactive basis. The present system of special programs for students with diverse needs dramatically inhibits support services providers from working with students who have not successfully completed the bureaucratic eligibility maze and been found to be "worthy" of support services. The underlying philosophy of cooperative teaching holds that all students deserve special services when appropriate and needed. In cooperative teaching those students evidencing behavioral, learning, and/or other needs can receive the curricular or instructional changes they need immediately and intensively. This greatly decreases the likelihood of the need for traditional special pull-out services. Gelzheiser (1987) noted that as the general education class thus becomes more individualized, fewer students should be identified as requiring intensive intervention services.

The typical large group general education classroom is characterized by a single educator trying to constantly and simultaneously balance instruction and classroom management. This constant role conflict too often manifests itself in the development and presentation of instruction that is easiest from a management perspective. Unfortunately, this may not be compatible with the development of instructional formats in which students are active rather than passive learners. This is unfortunate in that the research clearly shows that student learning is enhanced when they are actively involved in the learning process, involvement that is most likely in small groups in which substantial conversations flourish (National Education Association, 1985). Cooperative teaching, with its provision of two educators in the classroom, eases the classroom-management burden of the educators, allowing for greater emphasis on creative and student-involved instruction. That is, one educator may concentrate

on instruction of the class while the other maintains primary responsibility for classroom management.

In terms of educator benefits, every practicing school professional is familiar with the frustration of working in isolation, an especially discouraging sensation when some students are not learning. When two educators with discrete and valuable sets of professional skills merge those skills together into a single powerful instructional package, these professional frustrations are tremendously reduced or even eliminated. Over the long term, cooperative teachers report both the acquisition of additional valuable professional skills from their partners and the development of personal supportive friendships. In a survey of general educators and support services providers actively engaged in cooperative teaching efforts, a variety of significant benefits were reported. These included increased job satisfaction, stress and burnout reduction, enhanced job stability, and increased teaching effectiveness (Bauwens, Hourcade, & Friend, 1989).

Approaches to Implementing Cooperative Teaching

Cooperative teaching is an inherently flexible structure. This flexibility makes it possible to implement cooperative teaching in a variety of potential instructional formats, with varying combinations of educators. Three arrangements that have proven to be especially effective are (a) team teaching, (b) complementary instruction, and (c) supportive learning activities. While the three will be described individually for the sake of clarity of presentation, they should not be seen as mutually exclusive. Indeed, at any given time in a classroom in which cooperative teaching is being used, several of these approaches may be used together. Specific implementation procedures will evolve naturally out of the close planning and professional working relationship between the general and special services providers in the proposed cooperative teaching arrangement.

Team Teaching

Team teaching was initially advocated in the 1960s as a way to enhance the overall quality of American educational programming. As was noted then (e.g., Bair & Woodward, 1964), diagnostic, planning, teaching, and evaluative procedures developed by a team of educators are usually stronger and more useful than those developed by a single educator. In the team teaching arrangement of cooperative teaching, the initial presentation of some content is shared between two cooperative teachers, who jointly plan and present academic content to all students. However, at various times each might assume primary responsibility for specific types of instruction or portions of the curriculum (see Figure 3.1).

One way to begin exploring the possible ways cooperative educators might work within a team teaching arrangement is to look at the word *team* as the following acronym.

T = **T**aking turns in delivering portions of the content

E = **E**nriching (e.g., graphics, video clips, humor, additional explanations)

A = **A**sking questions of students/eliciting responses

M = **M**onitoring student learning and responding

For example, during a science lesson a support services provider might follow up content initially presented by a science teacher by showing a short video clip illustrating the concept. Prior to the video she or he can cue the entire class to look for specific terms and illustrations relevant to the immediately preceding lesson ("Enriching"). This might be followed by the general education teacher presenting a follow-up summary of the just-viewed video ("Taking turns"). During this presentation and its subsequent seatwork assignment, the general education teacher and support services provider might separately visit briefly with individual students, asking questions and checking student work to assure that time-on-task (and learning) is occurring ("Asking questions" and "Monitoring"). Team teaching can be an especially effective arrangement when the support services provider

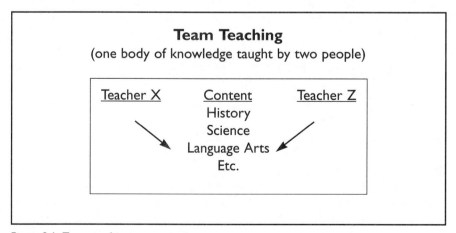

Figure 3.1. Team teaching.

additionally possesses extensive general education competencies.

For example, at the elementary school level, the support services provider may have additional certification in elementary education. At the secondary level, the support services provider may possess certification in a specific academic subject area as well as in his or her unique area of professional specialization.

Complementary Instruction

Many students evidencing school problems, especially at the upper elementary and secondary levels, lack critical school survival skills. Essentially these skills fall into one of three types: thinking skills, learning skills, and acting skills.

Thinking skills involve those competencies required to process information cognitively, to move into such upper levels of Bloom's taxonomy as analysis, synthesis, and evaluation. The mastery of these skills greatly facilitates the acquisition of academic content in the school. An emerging literature base as well as curriculum resources are supporting the feasibility of teaching a variety of students these skills concurrently with the essential subject area content (e.g., de Bono, 1991).

Learning skills (often referred to as *study skills*) include those functional academic survival skills such as taking notes, identifying main ideas in readings or lectures, sharing, summarizing, and other related skills necessary for mastery of a content-oriented curriculum. In the past, such skills were neither directly nor frequently taught to all students, or they were taught only for a prescribed short period of time (often early in the academic year). In addition, these skills often were taught in isolation and not integrated into the ongoing instruction in the class, thus minimizing the probability that the skills would generalize to the academic instruction they were intended to enhance.

Acting skills refer to those social behaviors required for social and academic success in the school. They include soliciting and accepting criticism, giving feedback to others, being more aware of and monitoring one's own behaviors, and so forth. While these skills are especially critical for those students identified as behaviorally disabled, all students can benefit from instruction in these competencies.

In complementary instruction, one educator might maintain primary responsibility for teaching the specific subject matter in the instructional program, while the cooperative teaching partner may assume responsibility for teaching students the how-to skills of thinking, learning, and acting necessary to acquire that subject content and function within the classroom's and school's social systems, and to better succeed in the post-school environment. These skills facilitate the learning and mastery of the content and the success of any social interactions that are inherent in small group active-learning arrangements.

Figure 3.2 graphically illustrates the instructional relationship in complementary instruction between academic content and skills in thinking, learning, and acting. For any given academic content areas, students lacking thinking, learning, or acting skills in these areas will receive the appropriate instruction. That is, students asked to evaluate their work or the work of their classmates may first require some instruction in how to evaluate, a thinking skill. If a test date is approaching, the cooperative teaching partner might provide specific instruction on how to prepare for a test, a learning skill. Finally, if a lesson involves cooperative learning activities that require students to interact with each other, the educator might first teach how to give feedback to others, an acting skill.

For example, a general education teacher at the upper elementary level may be teaching a unit in social studies that includes some classroom lecture and discussion as well as field trips and in-class activities. The cooperative teaching partner might provide additional

---

Complementary Instruction
(one body of knowledge plus infusion of social skills
and/or learning strategy instruction to either facilitate
the learning of the content or enhance participation
in the activity)

Teacher X   Teacher Z

Content + Social Skill and/or Learning Strategy

History + _____ and/or _____
Science + _____ and/or _____
Language Arts + _____ and/or _____
Etc.

Figure 3.2. Complementary instruction.

instruction in skills such as attending, identifying and evaluating main ideas, taking notes, and taking turns to any students in need of such skill development (or indeed, to the entire class as necessary). This complementary instruction might be provided in a short introductory period at the beginning of the overall lesson, at appropriate points throughout the presentation, and in a review at its conclusion.

A critical question is when these skills in thinking, learning, and acting should be taught. A common problem is to simply provide a small amount of instruction in these skills at the beginning of the academic year, with little or no follow-up or reference to these skills thereafter. Given the critical nature of these skills for academic success, such an approach is not justifiable. These skills should be naturally infused in and integrated throughout the academic content, instead of taught as a separate academic area of study. In addition, intensive supplementary mini-lessons should be provided throughout the school year on an as-needed basis. When student errors (either individual or group) can be traced to deficits in thinking, learning, or acting skills, these mini-lessons then should be provided.

A number of complementary instruction procedures can be generated from the word *complementary* as follows:

$$
\begin{aligned}
\textbf{C} &= \textbf{C}\text{AF} \\
\textbf{O} &= \textbf{O}\text{RDER} \\
\textbf{M} &= \textbf{M}\text{AP} \\
\textbf{P} &= \textbf{P}\text{MI} \\
\textbf{L} &= \textbf{L}\text{ISTEN} \\
\textbf{E} &= \textbf{E}\text{RRORS} \\
\textbf{M} &= \textbf{M}\text{ultipass} \\
\textbf{E} &= \textbf{E}\text{SSAY} \\
\textbf{N} &= \textbf{N}\text{OTES} \\
\textbf{T} &= \textbf{T}\text{HINK} \\
\textbf{A} &= \textbf{A}\text{CTion} \\
\textbf{R} &= \textbf{R}\text{AFT} \\
\textbf{Y} &= \textbf{Y}\text{ou DEFEND}
\end{aligned}
$$

CAF stands for "Consider All Factors" (de Bono, 1991). This thinking strategy helps students develop their skills in analysis and evaluation. That is, students are taught to begin these processes by first listing all possible factors that play a role in these processes, mentally prompting themselves both to begin and to continue this task.

ORDER is an assignment-completion strategy in which students learn to "Organize" their material, "Review" the task, "Develop" a calendar to schedule parts of the assignment, "Engage" in each step of the process until complete, and "Review" the calendar frequently to assure progress is continuing. In MAP, students learn to manage their time by "Making" a list of what one is to do; "Asking" oneself which tasks are longest, hardest, or least preferred; and then "Prioritizing" tasks by doing the hardest first.

PMI (de Bono, 1991) stands for "Pluses, Minuses, and Interesting." This thinking strategy helps students to analyze and evaluate tasks and problems by providing them with a structure to do so. Specifically, in PMI students learn to go systematically through a three-step procedure in which they ask themselves which factors or aspects of any given situation were the "plusses," or those things that were good; which were the "minuses," or those things that were weak or negative; and finally which components were "interesting," not necessarily good or bad but nonetheless noteworthy.

The LISTEN strategy (Bauwens & Hourcade, 1989) teaches students to "Look," "Idle" your motor, "Sit" up straight, "Turn" to me, "Engage" your brain, "Now . . . . " Students are taught to correct their errors through the ERRORS strategy. Here students learn to "Examine" their mistakes, "Review" what they know and how they might have erred, "Revisit" their texts and notes where the correct answer can be found, "Organize" new response, "Rewrite" the answer, and "See" if it is correct. In the Multipass system (Schumaker et al., 1981), students are given a content area textbook survey strategy in which they conduct three passes. In the first, they read the chapter title, introductory paragraph, and so on; in the second, they look for and consider contextual cues; and in the last pass, they review end-of-chapter questions.

In the ESSAY response strategy, students learn to "Examine" an essay question, "Separate" it while "Selecting" key words to start a skeletal outline, "Answer" the question, and finally "Yank" out any errors before submitting it. Educators can teach students NOTES, a strategy for note-taking, by going through the following steps. Students learn to first "Name" that day's notes with date and content area; "Organize" the note page into three columns (keywords, information, memory tricks); "Tune" into key words and information; "Embed" that information into the appropriate columns; and then "Select" a way to remember that information and record it in the final column.

Students can acquire critical-thinking skills through THINK, a method by which they learn to "Tell" themselves the question in their own words, "Hammer" out all the possibilities in a brainstorming process, "Inspect" these possibilities and add and modify as appropriate, "Narrow" the potential answers to the strongest, and last (but not least) "Kindly" wait to share the response. To help students more successfully complete homework, educators can teach students the ACTion strategy. Specifically, students learn to "Anticipate" the fun they can have after their homework is done, "Check" and sequence their homework tasks from longest and hardest to shortest and easiest, and then use the "Two-to-one" trick (that is, do two tasks and then one fun thing, or two 15-minute blocks of homework and then one 15-minute fun block, until all homework is done).

RAFT is an essay-writing strategy wherein students learn to write from a viewpoint different than their own (Adler, 1985). Specifically, they are asked to anticipate the "Role" of the writer (someone other than themselves), the "Audience" for whom the essay is to be written, the "Format" (e.g., persuasive, expository), and finally the "Topic." Finally, to develop skills in writing to support an adopted position, students can be taught the You DEFEND strategy (Ellis, 1993), in which they learn to first "Decide" their exact position, "Examine" the reasons behind that decision, "Figure" out the best order for those reasons, "Expose" the position early in the paper, "Note" each reason and its supporting points, and finally "Drive" home the point one last time at the end of the paper.

Specialized complementary instruction can be especially effective in the generalization of these academic and social survival skills to general education settings. All too often, when specialized instruction is delivered in segregated educational settings, students fail to generalize those newly acquired skills to the general classroom (Anderson-Inman, 1986; Brown, Bransford, Ferrara, & Campione, 1983; Gelzheiser, Shepherd, & Wozniak, 1986; Kerr, Nelson, & Lambert, 1987). However, in a cooperative teaching situation where complementary instruction is employed, the student will be more likely to use these enhanced survival skills on a wide basis, since the skills are taught in the same environment in which they are to be used (i.e., the general education classroom) (Alberto & Troutman, 1990).

Supportive Learning Activities

Supportive learning activities are educator-developed student activities that supplement the primary instruction in order to enhance student learning. These active-learning techniques promote substantive conversations, making learning come alive. In the most typical development of supportive learning activities, the general education teacher maintains responsibility for delivering the essential content of the instruction, while the partner is responsible for identifying, developing, and leading the student activities designed to reinforce, enrich, and augment student learning. These supportive learning activities can be used effectively to precede the primary instruction, follow it, or be integrated into it. Throughout these procedures both educators are present and cooperatively monitoring both the primary instruction and the supportive learning activities, though their specific roles will shift to be appropriate to the moment. Figure 3.3 illustrates the relationship of the two educators and their responsibilities in the development and implementation of supportive learning activities.

For example, the two educators might identify that a particular skill or concept in science should be taught. They then would determine which supportive learning activity (or activities) might be most appropriate for reinforcement of the new skill or concept (e.g., small group team discussions, partner work, group investigation projects). One of the two educators would introduce and explain the content to the students. The other educator would then be responsible for the development and implementation of whatever supportive learning activities the two previously had agreed would be most useful for reinforcement of the new content.

Using the letters in the word *supportive*, educators can identify immediately a number of ways in which to develop student activities that supplement the primary instruction, making students more active participants in the educational process. While these proce-

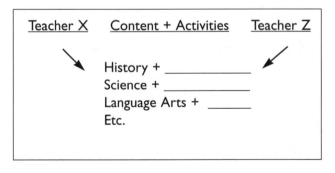

Figure 3.3. Supportive learning activities.

dures certainly can be implemented in traditional one-educator settings, they occur more frequently and easily in cooperative teaching. This is probably due to the fact that the "lead" educator concentrates more on curriculum, freeing the support services provider to target student mastery of that content through the development and timely implementation of supportive learning activities to enhance that mastery. Possible supportive learning activities based on the word *supportive* include the following:

S = **S**imulations (as with computers); **S**tations

U = **U**se of manipulatives

P = **P**ausing (during instruction as well as viewing videos)

P = **P**artners/pairs (students)

O = **O**rganized games in cooperative learning groups

R = **R**eciprocal teaching

T = **T**utoring (peer and cross-age)

I = **I**nside-outside (or pinwheel)

V = **V**oicing values (e.g., via debate)

E = **E**veryone responds

While some of the above are self-explanatory, others may require further information. "Pausing" refers to procedures in which, at a cue from the partner, the lead educator simply stops further instruction (or pauses during the presentation of a videotape). He or she then waits while students think about, analyze, and evaluate the content presented up to that point. This procedure replaces the more typical "Are there any questions?" technique and provides a segue to the next activity.

The other educator then reflects on the content covered to that point and asks the students to integrate and process that information. The advantage to this is that, unlike the lead educator, the partner has been in the role of learner and thus may have a better sense of when to pause and integrate. Pausing at such points in the presentation of material has been found to significantly enhance student acquisition of material and has been specifically proposed as an effective teaching practice applicable to secondary mainstreamed students (Ruhl, Hughes, & Schloss, 1987). This procedure results in higher and more complete levels of student learning than does the more frequent type of educator pause/transition, "Does anyone have any questions?"

In "Partners/pairs" activities, two students participate in new learning activities as equals, taking turns as they work on assignments. "Reciprocal teaching" is a powerful instructional arrangement in which small groups of students (two to three students) take content previously taught them, put it into their own words, and then take turns reteaching it to each other. In "Tutoring" procedures (both peer and cross-age), one student is clearly the teacher while the other is the student.

"Inside-outside" (or pinwheel) is a drill-and-practice procedure involving 6, 8, or 10 students in 3 x 3, 4 x 4, or 5 x 5 physical configurations, as shown in Figure 3.4. (The specific configuration can be repeated to include all students in the class simultaneously.)

For example, in a 5 x 5 configuration (as illustrated in Figure 3.4), five students stand back to back as the "inside." Five other students ("outside") are arranged so that each faces one of the inside students. (While the following explanation of "Inside-outside" is based on spelling, the procedure itself can be used with almost any content area and grade level.) If the students are working on spelling, for example, they may have 20 words to study. The five inside students have the responsibility to review 4 of the 20 words from the list prepared on an index card. Each inside student gives his/her outside

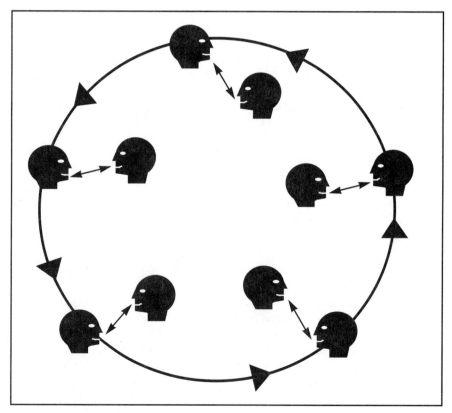

Figure 3.4. Pinwheel drill-and-practice procedure.

partner each of the 4 words to be spelled. If the outside partner spells a word incorrectly, the inside student corrects it. After each dyad has completed its assigned 4 words, the educator cues the outside students to rotate ("pinwheel") one position to the right, so that each student has a new partner—and a new set of 4 spelling words. After each outside student has worked with each of the inside students, they switch roles so that the outside students move to the inside and vice versa, with the rest of the procedures then repeated.

"Everyone responds" is one way to constantly monitor individual progress during lessons within a large group context. In a primary-level lesson on problem solving, one of the educators might pose a practical mathematical story problem and ask the class to "think, write, share, and show" the appropriate arithmetic process to solve the problem. Each student then writes the correct arithmetic sign (or selects the prewritten card) and chats briefly with a partner. On cue all students display their cards as a group to the educators, who both check and offer feedback.

The procedures involved in supportive learning activities differ from those in complementary instruction in that in the latter, one educator teaches the specific academic content of the curriculum (the *what* of learning), while the other maintains responsibility for teaching students the academic or survival skills necessary to acquire that content (the *how* of learning). In the supportive learning activities approach, one educator introduces the essential academic content of the lesson, while the other develops supplementary activities designed to supplement and enrich that specific academic content.

Combining Arrangements

As suggested earlier, any given lesson delivered via a cooperative teaching structure may incorporate more than one of these three teaching arrangements. Such decisions typically are made on a case-by-case basis by the participants themselves. Factors to be considered in these decisions might include the following.

1. What are the unique sets of skills each educator can bring to that particular lesson?

2. What is each educator's familiarity and comfort with the specific content to be taught and the ways in which it can be taught?

3. What difficulties have students previously experienced with similar material, and what cooperative teaching arrangements have been most effective in responding to those difficulties?

4.   What sorts of cooperative teaching arrangements have been (or are likely to be) most effective with this particular group of students?

5.   How user-friendly (or accessible) is the material to students? (Characteristics of curricular materials such as readability; density or complexity of the concepts; inherent interest level of the material; and format, structure, and layout all influence the type and degree of cooperative teaching arrangements that should be implemented in any given lesson.)

6.   How critical is each piece of that particular lesson? (The portions determined to be most critical might then be backed up through the selected use of cooperative teaching arrangements.)

Two practical school examples may clarify how combinations of cooperative teaching arrangements can enhance the effectiveness of instruction. Figure 3.5 graphically illustrates how all three cooperative teaching arrangements were integrated into a U.S. history lesson. Prior to that lesson, the history teacher had met with the school's

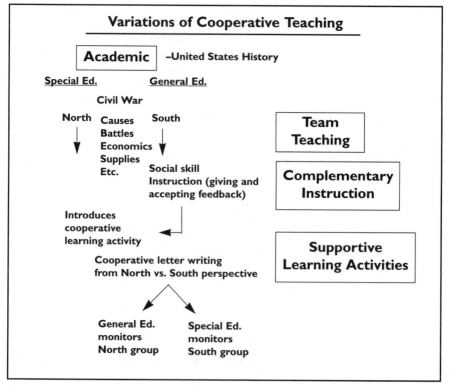

Figure 3.5. Variations of cooperative teaching: U.S. history lesson plan.

special educator, and the two had determined that both were adequately familiar with the academic content of that lesson. In addition, the history teacher was skilled in structuring cooperative learning activities, while the special educator was effective in social skills instruction. In the past they had found that students had difficulty obtaining information (especially such basic and fundamental concepts as causes of the Civil War) from the textbook, and the two educators felt this information was among the most critical for that lesson. With these considerations in mind, they developed the following lesson, which incorporated the three cooperative teaching arrangements of team teaching, complementary instruction, and supportive learning activities.

To begin with, each of the educators delivered part of the academic content (team teaching). Specifically, the special educator described to the students how the unit would be cooperatively taught, at which point the history teacher introduced the unit she had taught alone in the past. She then discussed critical information such as causes, economics, supplies, and battles from the South's perspective, while the special educator did the same from the perspective of the North. He then delivered a mini-lesson on social skills, specifically teaching students how to best give and accept feedback to and from others in their cooperative learning groups (complementary instruction).

The history teacher then introduced a supportive learning activity in which groups of students assumed the perspective of ordinary citizens from either the North or South and wrote letters to their counterparts from the other side explaining their beliefs and questioning those of the other group (the aforementioned RAFT strategy). (These letters could be written individually or as a group project, depending upon the individual needs of the specific students involved.) During this activity both educators monitored the work of the two groups, making sure that all students eventually switched perspectives from North to South (or vice versa), either during that lesson or in the next lesson (supportive learning activities). Finally, the special educator asked students to process what they had learned about the Civil War, using the PMI strategy ("Pluses, Minuses, and Interesting"), while the history teacher finished with final closing points.

Similarly, Figure 3.6 illustrates a cooperatively taught science lesson. In this example, the general education teacher had met with the Chapter 1 teacher. The two of them had determined that the general education teacher was more comfortable with the content in science instruction and developing lesson-closing procedures, while the Chapter 1 teacher was especially skilled at direct instruction proce-

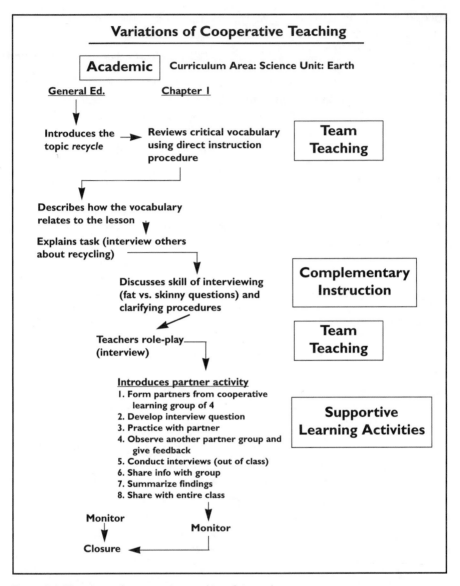

Figure 3.6. Variations of cooperative teaching: Science lesson.

dures and social skills instruction and arrangements. Both were competent and comfortable in role-playing and instructional monitoring procedures. (Access to unique instructional procedures such as role-playing are made possible in cooperative teaching, where two instructors are in the classroom simultaneously.)

In the past, the educators in the example had found that their students learned ecological concepts most thoroughly when those concepts first were introduced by the educators as they relate to the students' own experiences and then were followed by active student involvement. In this particular lesson, the general educator introduced the term *recycle* and gave examples that students were familiar with through their own community's and school's recycling programs. The Chapter 1 teacher then made sure that all students understood the new vocabulary and related concepts, providing direct instruction as necessary to achieve this. The general education teacher then continued, making the transition from those words and concepts to the instructional activity for that lesson, an interview activity with citizens in the community. The Chapter 1 teacher explained how interviewing is done, specifically explaining to the students about "fat" versus "skinny" questions (i.e., open-ended versus close-ended questions).

Prior to having students practice interviewing with each other, the two educators role-played sample interviews, modeling for all students appropriate questioning procedures and topics. The two educators then asked the students to move into their (preassigned) cooperative learning groups of four, where each group was responsible for developing questions on topics it considered important. While the two educators simultaneously monitored each group, the students in each group practiced interviewing each other, with feedback from other students and the educators provided as appropriate.

After their interview skills had been developed through this practice activity, each student was assigned the individual 5-minute homework task of taking the series of recycling questions the group had developed and interviewing a community citizen (e.g., neighbor, grocery store employee). The next day the students used the discussion time for each cooperative learning group to summarize the data from the interviews and prepare a report for their classmates regarding their cumulative interview results. Both educators were available (as necessary) to help students in their group summarize and present their results, and to provide wrap-up activities.

Conclusions

Cooperative teaching can have significant beneficial effects in that its team approach enables educators to avoid the stress and burnout that often result from working in the unique psychological climate of isolated education settings (Crane & Iwanicki, 1986). By working within an integrated educational setting that contains two (or more) sets of professional education skills and knowledge, educators may enhance their overall job satisfaction and stability. For example, Scott and Smith (1988) found that educators who work in collaborative school environments reported enhanced levels of enjoyment of work and also perceived themselves as more effective in the delivery of instruction.

In a successful construction project, by the conclusion of the blueprints-development stage the experienced building contractor can review the blueprints and get a good sense of how the actual finished project likely will look. Similarly, this chapter has outlined basic blueprints for developing cooperative teaching arrangements, specifically laying out plans for three possible structures.

In the first of these, team teaching, a common body of knowledge is a shared instructional responsibility between two cooperative teachers, often a general educator and a support services provider (for example, a special educator or a Chapter 1 teacher). In supportive learning activities, one educator has the primary responsibility for the initial delivery of core content, while the other develops and initiates student activities that supplement the primary instruction to enhance student learning. The final structure under cooperative teaching, complementary teaching, involves one of the educators (often the general educator) presenting the core content, while the other (often the support services provider) teaches students the academic or social survival skills necessary to learn the material and also to function more effectively within the classroom's social systems.

In any remodeling project, after the blueprints have been developed, the next step is to identify the specific subcontractors who can take on and successfully complete each part of the plan. Chapter 4 provides basic procedures for identifying the educational subcontractors or partners in cooperative teaching most likely to have success in the cooperative teaching remodeling project and then provides effective suggestions for helping them to begin cooperative teaching.

Chapter 3 Activity
Concerns-Based Adoption Model (CBAM)

The most common initial response by most people when confronted with the possibility of change in their lives is concern. This apprehension about change is as true of educators as it is of anyone. Rather than trying to hide these concerns, one should instead seek to learn more about these initial misgivings. This first stage of self-analysis then gives each person an objective beginning point from which to begin adapting to the new idea or procedure.

One approach that has proven to be especially fruitful in this self-analysis is the Concerns-Based Adoption Model (CBAM) (Hord, Rutherford, Huling-Austin, & Hall, 1987). The CBAM allows individuals to assess their level of concern regarding potential educational innovations. The results are organized into seven levels, which are then grouped under three major loci of concerns as follows.

Locus of Concern	Levels of Concern (within each locus)
SELF	Awareness
	Informational
	Personal
TASK	Management
IMPACT	Consequences
	Collaboration
	Refocusing

This adaptation of the CBAM allows educators to assess their concerns about the implementation of cooperative teaching in their schools.

The first of the three loci of concern is Self, which is further broken down into three levels. The first of these begins with concerns at the Awareness level. At this level people either may not know about the innovation or are not interested. At the Informational level, respondents are interested in gaining additional knowledge about the proposed changes. The third level of the Self locus is the Personal level, in which the person is interested in the specific impact the proposed change(s) will have directly upon him or her.

At the second locus of concern, Task, there is one level: Management. This is where pragmatic concerns such as time, ability, and resources are identified.

The third locus of concern is Impact. The three levels here start with Consequences, in which respondents note the possible effects the change will have on students. In the second level, Collaboration, individuals identify possible concerns about the impact of the change on their working relationships with other professionals. Finally, at the highest level, Refocusing, educators note their interest in adapting and individualizing the proposed changes specific to their unique needs and characteristics.

While the three loci of concerns have no specific hierarchical arrangement, the individual levels of concern within each do have a definite sequence. For example, within the Self locus of concern, professionals at the Awareness level are at an earlier point of adjustment and thus have different profiles and needs than those at the Personal level.

The Instrument

The following self-assessment instrument was adapted and extensively field-tested to allow school professionals to identify for themselves their own levels of concern regarding cooperative teaching. In completing the evaluation, remember that the purpose of this activity is to facilitate one's own personal and professional growth. This is best achieved through responses that are as accurate as possible.

Cooperative Teaching: Levels of Concern

This questionnaire is designed to determine your thoughts and perceptions about cooperative teaching. Some items on the questionnaire may appear to be of little relevance to you at this time. For those items, please circle zero on the scale. Other items will represent concerns you have in varying degrees of intensity and should be marked on the higher side.

Scoring Key

This statement is absolutely true to me at this point in time = 6
This statement is very true to me at this point in time = 5
This statement is moderately true to me at this point in time = 4
This statement is somewhat true to me at this point in time = 3
This statement is slightly true to me at this point in time = 2
This statement is not at all true to me at this point in time = 1
This statement is irrelevant to me at this point in time = 0

Please respond to the items below in terms of your present feelings about cooperative teaching.

Item	Rating Scale
1. I am concerned about students' attitudes toward cooperative teaching.	0 1 2 3 4 5 6
2. I now know of some other approaches that might work better.	0 1 2 3 4 5 6

	Rating Scale
3. I don't even know what cooperative teaching is.	0 1 2 3 4 5 6
4. I am concerned about not having enough time to organize myself each day.	0 1 2 3 4 5 6
5. I would like to help other faculty in their use of cooperative teaching.	0 1 2 3 4 5 6
6. I have a very limited knowledge of cooperative teaching.	0 1 2 3 4 5 6
7. I would like to know the effect implementing cooperative teaching will have on my professional status.	0 1 2 3 4 5 6
8. I am concerned about conflict between my interests and my responsibilities.	0 1 2 3 4 5 6
9. I am concerned about revising my use of cooperative teaching.	0 1 2 3 4 5 6
10. I would like to develop working relationships with both our faculty and outside faculty using cooperative teaching.	0 1 2 3 4 5 6
11. I am concerned about how cooperative teaching affects students.	0 1 2 3 4 5 6
12. I am not concerned about cooperative teaching.	0 1 2 3 4 5 6
13. I would like to know who will make the decisions in the cooperative teaching approach.	0 1 2 3 4 5 6
14. I would like to discuss the possibility of using cooperative teaching.	0 1 2 3 4 5 6
15. I would like to know what resources are available if we decide to adopt the cooperative teaching approach.	0 1 2 3 4 5 6
16. I am concerned about my inability to manage all that cooperative teaching requires.	0 1 2 3 4 5 6
17. I would like to know how my teaching or administration is supposed to change.	0 1 2 3 4 5 6
18. I would like to familiarize others with the cooperative teaching approach.	0 1 2 3 4 5 6
19. I am concerned about evaluating the impact of cooperative teaching on students.	0 1 2 3 4 5 6
20. I would like to revise the instructional approach to cooperative teaching.	0 1 2 3 4 5 6
21. I am completely occupied with other things.	0 1 2 3 4 5 6
22. I would like to modify our use of cooperative teaching based on the experiences of our students.	0 1 2 3 4 5 6
23. Although I don't know about cooperative teaching, I am concerned about its use.	0 1 2 3 4 5 6

	Rating Scale
24. I would like to excite my students about their part in cooperative teaching.	0 1 2 3 4 5 6
25. I am concerned about time spent working with nonacademic problems related to cooperative teaching.	0 1 2 3 4 5 6
26. I would like to know what the use of cooperative teaching will require in the immediate future.	0 1 2 3 4 5 6
27. I would like to coordinate my effort with others to maximize the effects of cooperative teaching.	0 1 2 3 4 5 6
28. I would like to have more information on time and energy commitments required by cooperative teaching.	0 1 2 3 4 5 6
29. I would like to know what other educators are doing in the area of cooperative teaching.	0 1 2 3 4 5 6
30. At this time, I am not interested in learning more about cooperative teaching.	0 1 2 3 4 5 6
31. I would like to determine how to supplement, enhance, or replace cooperative teaching.	0 1 2 3 4 5 6
32. I would like to use feedback from students to change the program.	0 1 2 3 4 5 6
33. I would like to know how my role will change when I am using cooperative teaching.	0 1 2 3 4 5 6
34. Coordination of tasks and people is taking too much of my time.	0 1 2 3 4 5 6
35. I would like to know how cooperative teaching is better than what we have now.	0 1 2 3 4 5 6

Scoring

Each of the seven individual levels has five questions on the instrument that specifically target that level. After responding to each of the 35 items, please transfer the rating for each item to the score sheet and add up the scores for each level as shown. (The item numbers from the instrument appear under the appropriate blanks.)

Cooperative Teaching: Levels of Concern Score Sheet

Self

Awareness	___ +	___ +	___ +	___ +	___ =	_____
(test items)	3	12	21	23	30	Awareness total

Informational	___ +	___ +	___ +	___ +	___ =	_____
(test items)	6	14	15	26	35	Informational total

Personal		+		+		+		+		=	
(test items)	7		13		17		28		33		Personal total

Task

Management		+		+		+		+		=	
(test items)	4		8		16		25		34		Management total

Impact

Consequences		+		+		+		+		=	
(test items)	1		11		19		24		32		Consequences total

Collaboration		+		+		+		+		=	
(test items)	5		10		18		27		29		Collaboration total

Refocusing		+		+		+		+		=	
(test items)	2		9		20		22		31		Refocusing total

Interpretation

While there is not a fixed, cut-and-dried system to translate the results of this instrument into specific prescriptions, the following information can help educators become better prepared to respond to the changes inherent in implementing cooperative teaching. Within the Self locus of concern, educators whose scores are highest at the first level, Awareness, are indicating that up to this point they have heard little about the proposed changes. Such individuals might seek out and talk with colleagues who know about cooperative teaching, making sure they receive basic information without being overwhelmed by too much.

Professionals with high scores at the Informational level have heard about the change but at present do not know a great deal about it and thus are in need of more information. These educators might visit sites where these arrangements have been successfully implemented, in particular looking to see how these practices relate to their current work.

High scores within the Personal area indicate that the respondent is especially concerned with what sort of individual effect the change will have upon his or her daily functioning, or how he or she can expect to be affected by the change. These educators should understand that such concerns are common and legitimate. One way to alleviate concerns here is to meet informally with educators who presently are active in cooperative teaching. In all likelihood these school personnel experienced similar concerns and can explain how their personal concerns diminished over time as they gained experience and success with the program.

Educators recording high scores in the area of Management within the Task locus of concern are saying that they need practical how-to information. These educators should concentrate on "nuts and bolts" aspects, meeting with other educators to generate specific answers to immediate questions and problems.

The final three sets of data come from the Impact locus of concern. High scores in the first of these, Consequences, indicate the respondent is most interested in the direct results of implementing cooperative teaching. These individuals should make special efforts to visit programs where cooperative teaching has been well-established for some period of time, so that the effects and results can be clearly seen.

School personnel with high scores in the Collaboration level of concern are indicating that they have implemented and been successful with cooperative teaching. Because of that success, they are now most interested in "spreading the news" to other professionals. These individuals are the obvious choice for helping to provide inservice training activities to those just beginning these new professional relationships. One especially useful system is to have several of these professionals work together cooperatively to plan training activities and offer technical assistance.

Finally, respondents with high scores in the Refocusing level of concern represent the most sophisticated implementers of cooperative teaching. These individuals have successful experiences with successful implementation during which they likely have identified procedures through which they might customize and revise the approach to work even more effectively. School professionals at this level should seek out and solicit the resources they need to make the changes necessary to make the system work even better. They also should continue the constant process of reexamination of what they are doing in the schools, why they are doing it, and the present and future impact of this work.

References

Adler, S. (1985). *Report of the Montana Writing Project*. Helena: Montana State Department of Education.

Alberto, P. A., & Troutman, A. C. (1990). *Applied behavior analysis for teachers*. New York: Macmillan.

Algozzine, B., & Maheady, L. (1986). When all else fails, teach! *Exceptional Children, 52*, 487–488.

Anderson-Inman, L. (1986). Bridging the gap: Student-centered strategies for promoting the transfer of learning. *Exceptional Children, 52*, 562–572.

Bair, M., & Woodward, R. G. (1964). *Team teaching in action*. Boston: Houghton-Mifflin.

Bauwens, J., & Hourcade, J. J. (1989). Hey, would you just LISTEN? *TEACHING Exceptional Children, 21*, 61.

Bauwens, J., Hourcade, J. J., & Friend, M. (1989). Cooperative teaching: A model for general and special education integration. *Remedial and Special Education, 10*(2), 17–22.

Brown, A. L., Bransford, J. D., Ferrara, R. A., & Campione, J. C. (1983). Learning, remembering and understanding. In J. H. Flavell & E. M. Markman (Eds.), *Handbook of child psychology* (4th ed., Vol. 3, pp. 77–166). New York: Wiley.

Crane, S. J., & Iwanicki, E. F. (1986). Perceived role conflict, role ambiguity, and burnout among special education teachers. *Remedial and Special Education, 7*(2), 24–31.

de Bono, E. (1991). *The CoRT thinking program.* Wood Dale, IL: SRA.

Ellis, E.S. (1993) A learning strategy for meeting the writing demands of secondary mainstream classes. *The Alabama Council for Exceptional Children Journal,* Volume 10 (*1*), 31–38.

Federal Register (1977, August). (Vol. 42, pp. 42474–42515), Washington, DC: U.S. Government Printing Office.

Gelzheiser, L. M. (1987). Reducing the number of students identified as learning disabled: A question of practice, philosophy, or policy? *Exceptional Children, 54,* 145–150.

Gelzheiser, L. M., Shepherd, M. J., & Wozniak, R. H. (1986). The development of instruction to induce skill transfer. *Exceptional Children, 53,* 125–129.

Hord, S., Rutherford, W., Huling-Austin, L., & Hall, G. (1987). *Taking charge of change.* Austin, TX: Southwest Education Development Laboratory.

Johnson, D. W., & Johnson, R. T. (1986). Mainstreaming and cooperative learning strategies. *Exceptional Children, 52,* 553–561.

Kerr, M. M., Nelson, C. M., & Lambert, D. L. (1987). *Helping adolescents with learning and behavior problems.* Columbus, OH: Merrill.

National Education Association. (1985). *Nine principles of education.* Washington, DC: Author.

Reynolds, M. C., Wang, M. C., & Walberg, H. J. (1987). The necessary restructuring of special and regular education. *Exceptional Children, 53,* 391–398.

Ruhl, K. L., Hughes, C. A., & Schloss, P. J. (1987). Using the pause procedure to enhance lecture recall. *Teacher Education and Special Education, 10*(1), 14–18.

Schumaker, J. B., Deshler, D. D., Denton, P., Alley, G. P., Clark, F. L., & Warner, M. M. (1981). *Multipass: A learning strategy for improving reading comprehension* (Tech. Rep. No. 33). Lawrence: University of Kansas, Center for Research on Learning.

Scott, J. J., & Smith, S. C. (1988). *From isolation to collaboration: Improving the work environment of teaching.* Elmhurst, IL: North Central Regional Educational Laboratory.

Slavin, R. E. (1987). *Cooperative learning: Student teams.* Washington, DC: National Education Association.

Slavin, R., Leavey, M., & Madden, N. (1984). Combining cooperative learning and individualized instruction. *Elementary School Journal, 84,* 410–422.

Slavin, R., Madden, N., & Leavey, M. (1984). Effects of cooperative and individualized instruction on mainstreamed students. *Exceptional Children, 50,* 434–443.

Smith, T. E., Price, B. J., & Marsh, G. E. (1986). *Mildly handicapped children and adults.* St. Paul, MN: West.

Stainback, W., & Stainback, S. (1984). A rationale for the merger of special and regular education. *Exceptional Children, 51,* 102–111.

Wang, M., & Birch, J. (1984). Effective special education in regular classes. *Exceptional Children, 50,* 391–399.

Wang, M., & Walberg, H. (1983). Adaptive instruction and classroom time. *American Educational Research Journal, 20,* 601–626.

....

4 Getting Construction Underway
Implementing Cooperative Teaching

....

"A journey of a thousand miles must begin with a single step."
—Lao-Tzu

With blueprints and associated plans finally completed and in hand, home remodelers move into the "hammer and nails" phase of their remodeling project, actually beginning the physical construction of their new structure. The building materials involved in this phase of a home remodeling project include things such as lumber, plaster, nails and screws, and paint.

Likewise, those involved in the collaborative remodeling of the schoolhouse must identify, obtain, shape, and assemble the building materials necessary for their remodeling project. In the schoolhouse remodeling project the materials and resources required will be things such as time, scheduling, and administrative support. These three things are most frequently mentioned by educators as the most significant resources they need. Additionally, limitations of these resources are usually reported by professionals in the schools as the primary reasons why it is not possible for them to collaborate more extensively with their colleagues (Bauwens, Hourcade, Ehlert, & Schrag, 1992). This chapter presents these three resources as malleable assets that can be obtained and shaped to help rebuild a more effective and "livable" schoolhouse.

The Nature of Time

The notion of time is a fascinating yet ultimately elusive one. Like the air around the earth, people are constantly immersed in time while generally giving it next to no thought (except to wish for more of it when it appears to be in short supply). The concept of time remains an abstract and theoretical one. One cannot see, hear, feel, taste, or otherwise physically perceive time. Although people live with time at every moment throughout their lives, it remains a concept that ultimately escapes definition.

When people do consider the concept of time, it is usually in the sense of a resource. However, when compared to other resources over which educators usually have some control (e.g., money, paper, materials), time has a unique quality. Unlike other resources, time cannot be stockpiled or saved for later use. Time is irreversible and irreplaceable, moving at a fixed and invariable rate, regardless of whether one wishes to spend it or save it.

Imagine one had a bank account into which $86,400 was deposited every day. In addition, further imagine that the total of whatever residual amount had not been spent was canceled every evening. In such a situation, the only reasonable thing to do would be to withdraw and spend every cent every day. Similarly, each person has a "time account" into which 86,400 seconds are deposited each morning, all of which are gone by the evening. Whatever amount of that total has not been invested in productive use is lost forever (Drawbaugh, 1984).

The term *time management*, though used herein and extensively elsewhere, is something of a misnomer. The passage of time is actually beyond the ability of people to control or manage. It passes regardless of the actions or inactions of people. Thus, instead of managing time, it may be more accurate to speak of managing one's own behaviors with respect to time (Mackenzie, 1972) or evaluating one's own use of time. There is little question that, as educators begin to work collaboratively in the schools, their schedules and uses of time will change dramatically. In addition, the single most essential ingredient in any school reform effort usually is reported to be time (e.g., Fullan & Miles, 1992; Louis, 1992; Raywid, 1993). Especially early on, the pursuit of time to plan and implement cooperative teaching will be paramount. In order to better understand how this limited resource might be used more effectively, one must begin with an assessment of present patterns of time use.

Assessing Time Usage

Any financially successful home remodeler must keep a careful inventory of materials that are being used on the job, which also enables predictions about materials that will be needed in the near future. In their school remodeling efforts, however, many educators fail to do the equivalent in assessing their use of time. Two ways in which this might be done include time logs and time questionnaires.

Time logs. Professionals in the schools have a near-universal sense that time slips away from them ever more rapidly. Often these educators have little idea of where this time is going. One way school professionals can begin to understand how time is being used is to keep a daily time log. While almost every educator has some general sense of how his or her time is being used, when one actually records specific times and specific activities for a period of days a very different picture often emerges.

In its most basic form, a time log lists two columns: one for time, and one for activity. Starting with awakening, one records what time it is and what one is doing. When that activity is completed and a new one started, the new time and new activity are recorded, and so on. Alternatively, a time log might contain preexisting blocks of time (for example, 15-minute blocks). In each block the educator can record each activity occurring during that block. (A sample time log is listed in Appendix A.)

When educators actually complete time logs for several days, they typically are surprised to find how much time is spent on activities they seldom think about and how little time is devoted to those functions that they anticipated to make up the largest part of their work and lives. To make the discrepancy between anticipation and reality even more dramatic, some educators have found it effective to first identify and list the activities they believe are the most important parts of their lives and record the amount of time they estimate they presently spend on each of these. After this predictive time log is completed, they then undertake an actual time log and compare the predicted usage pattern with the actual recorded pattern. In doing this many educators have found the following surprise results (Drawbaugh, 1984).

(a) Much time is spent on routine tasks and activities of low priority.

(b) Little time is spent in planning and working toward established goals.

(c) Uncommitted time during the typical school day is limited to about one hour.

(d) Time is wasted in roughly the same way each day and each week.

Time questionnaires. Another way that professionals in the schools can begin to gain some sense of the degree to which they are using time productively is to complete a time questionnaire, such as the one provided as this chapter's concluding activity. While the data provided from time logs and time questionnaires may vary, each of these assessment instruments essentially allows one to evaluate how wisely (or how poorly) time presently is being used.

Identification of "time robbers." The last step in this assessment of present patterns of time use is to identify those specific factors that are the most significant wastes of time. Almost always, professionals in the schools can find unexpected factors that seem to be consuming disproportionate amounts of time.

One way to approach this is to see these time robbers as coming from two sources: external and internal (Mackenzie, 1972). The external sources (that is, those that are beyond the educator's control) are often easier to identify first. They include functions such as meetings, paperwork, unscheduled activities, and so forth. If educators perceive that their time-management problems are attributable primarily to external causes, they may see themselves as helpless pawns being manipulated by forces beyond their control. This leads to little improvement. However, the reality is that educators do indeed have great control over the majority of time robbers, because they are generated internally. This makes it possible to implement truly significant and productive changes.

When school professionals sit down to do more exhaustive and in-depth self-analyses of their own daily schedules, these internally generated time wasters (those evolving from the educator) can be easily identified. They include problems such as lack of planning, procrastination, lack of organization, inability to say no, refusal to delegate work to others, and personal and outside activities. It is quite human to look to others and conditions outside oneself for the reasons why one's time seems to slip away unproductively. However, when school professionals can step back and objectively analyze their unique situations to see how much time is managed inefficiently due to these internally generated factors, they then will have taken a significant step in using this invaluable and nonrenewable resource more wisely and efficiently.

Preexisting constraints on time. Most professionals within the schools have certain preexisting structural limitations upon their time. Daily schedules for educators include more than instruction of students. Most school professionals are expected to be at the school by a certain time before classes start and to remain a certain amount of time after they end. On certain occasions educators are asked to come in especially early or stay especially late (typically without additional compensation).

However, these structural limitations may be less restraining than they appear at first glance. Bartholomew and Gardner (1982) calculated that educators spend an average of 45.9 hours per week on all teaching duties. They also noted that educators directly control at least 2 hours of each of their 8-hour workdays and also directly control the 60 nonteaching days per year (weekdays through the summer). These hours combine to yield educators a total of 852 hours per year (more than 100 eight-hour days) over which they have direct control. (The question of whether educators are paid for professional activities during the summer aside, the reality is that this time is indeed available for such use.)

Finding Planning Time

School professionals beginning the move into cooperative teaching frequently are concerned with finding the planning time that will be required. In becoming more creative in analyzing how their schools presently function and how they might function in the future under a restructured collaborative system, educators are identifying ways in which time can be freed up for ongoing planning and continuing review of their cooperative teaching (Raywid, 1993). Flexible scheduling can help to unlock blocks of time that then can be used for the development of cooperative teaching (Raywid, 1992).

For example, several states have converted several instructional days per year into staff development days (Raywid, 1993). If these are kept flexible, educators can develop collaborative programs at these times. In other states and districts, each school day has been lengthened by 20 to 30 minutes, with equivalent early dismissal of students on Fridays. School professionals then use this time for planning, including planning for cooperative teaching. Some districts that have required students to complete community service projects as part of their school programs have found that these student placements freed blocks of instructional time that then could be used for educator planning (e.g., Raywid, 1993).

Some schools have instituted regular assemblies conducted by the principal, assistant principal, or community volunteers. In these programs large sections of the student population are accompanied by the school's aides and administrators who take attendance and monitor the students during the assembly and then escort them back to their classes afterward. During this time the rest of the school's professional staff arrive early and go directly to their planning meetings, using this block of time to develop their collaborative programs.

The use of paraprofessionals for direct instructional purposes is becoming increasingly common in districts where such school personnel are conceptualized and prepared as "educational assistants" or "teacher assistants." While some districts argue that such a use of paraprofessionals is not allowed under law, an analysis of federal legislation reveals no such prohibition. In these schools the educational assistants provide an increasingly larger share of the direct instruction to students, while the school professionals use this additional time for their instructional planning, including their planning for cooperative teaching.

In larger schools and districts, increasing class size by one or two students can provide a pool of resources adequate to provide teams of regular substitutes to fill in for educators on a regular and scheduled basis. The released educators then use this released time for their cooperative teaching planning and review (Raywid, 1993).

Some educators involved in cooperative teaching have found that scheduling a common daily lunch period and a common preparation period immediately thereafter can yield a shared hour and a half daily (Raywid, 1993). Year-round schools with 3-week intersessions between quarters allow collaborating educators intensive 2- or 3-day planning meetings (Raywid, 1993). The occasional combining of classes for activities equally appropriate and applicable to all students (for example, viewing of videotapes or selected cable programming to enrich content) also can release educators from direct instructional responsibilities so that they can plan their cooperative teaching efforts (Watson, Buchanan, Huyman, & Seal, 1992). The current explosion of technologically based instructional delivery systems holds great promise for such possibilities.

As instruction is creatively rethought, other possibilities emerge. The implementation of cooperative learning arrangements and peer tutoring (once well-established and up and running) can free up significant amounts of educator time that was previously spent in direct instruction for overall student monitoring and cooperative program planning. Cross-age tutoring programs (for example, 20-minute oral-reading periods several times a week) can provide educators the opportunity to get together while student activities are monitored by support staff.

In addition, many nonschool personnel are becoming involved in the instructional process in the schools. These include volunteers such as retired educators, professionals from the business community, state employees, parents, and many others. Most universities have an abundance of students majoring in education (and other disciplines) who find the opportunity to obtain credit for education practica experiences worthwhile and necessary. The increasing emphasis of most college and university teacher-preparation programs on early and frequent practical experiences in the schools provides school professionals with a potential abundance of university student instructors who can teach students directly while providing educators with the time necessary to plan their cooperative teaching.

While certainly these individuals must be monitored in their work with students, especially early on, the investment of the school professionals' time in this effort can be repaid severalfold as that volunteer gains the skills necessary to free up the educators for other tasks. For example, a volunteer might assume instructional responsibility for monitoring group work while the cooperating teachers meet in a quiet area of the classroom for several minutes.

In short, the ways in which educators can use their time more effectively, and thus have the time to plan for cooperative teaching, is limited only by the creativity they have in analyzing how instruction is presently carried out in the schools and in identifying other ways in which that instruction might be done. If indeed there is a shortage of anything, it may be a shortage of knowledge of how to tap more effectively into educators' analytical skills and creativity, not a shortage of time.

Using Planning Time Efficiently

No home remodeler can make a profit unless he or she plans the use of material in a way that makes maximum use of materials such as lumber and plaster. Similarly, finding the time to meet and plan for cooperative teaching, while a necessary first step, does not in and of itself ensure that the planning time will be used well. In fact, by some estimates half of all time spent in meetings is wasted (Mackenzie, 1972).

Efficient meetings do not happen automatically. There are a number of strategies that can make meetings more productive.

Establish an agenda. This is perhaps the single most important step in making sure a meeting concludes with the expected products or results. The agenda should include a point-by-point outline of exactly what the educators should accomplish at that meeting, as well as the known factors that might influence each of these. The points to be covered should be worded in question form, which encourages all participants to think about answers.

These points should be listed in the exact order in which they are to be covered. If one person has special responsibility for any point, list that person's name by that point. A typical agenda used by educators to develop and implement cooperative teaching is shown in Figure 4.1.

With ongoing meetings, there may be a number of common points that are reviewed every week, every 2 weeks, or whatever. The continuing inclusion of these points in meeting agendas allows the professionals involved to maintain constant quality control and to

1. Reflection: How did we do last week?

   a. What were the best things that happened in our cooperative teaching this past week?

   b. What did either of us make mental notes to talk about improving?

2. Goal-setting: What could we do, and what should we do, this next week?

   a. What are the possible things we might do?

   b. Which of these things will best help us to effectively teach all students?

3. Resources: Based on the goals we've set for this next week, what are the resources we'll need to achieve these goals?

   a. What are the physical resources (materials, equipment, and so forth) that will be required?

   b. What are the personnel resources that will be required?

4. Responsibilities: Which of us will be responsible for which goals and activities?

Figure 4.1. Agenda for a cooperative teaching meeting.

catch and resolve small problems before they escalate. Perhaps the single most important point to review regularly is the quality of the interactions between educators implementing cooperative teaching. That is, in addition to reviewing the curriculum, the teaching partners also must discuss the quality and quantity of their relationship and instruction. This new feature of cooperative teaching (sensitivity to the relationship one has with colleagues as well as students) is easy to overlook. (This critical skill is further explored in Chapters 6 and 7.)

Stay with the agenda. It's difficult to imagine house remodelers coming to work at a remodeling site, beginning their work by reviewing the architectural plans, and then deciding to ignore them for the rest of the day. The inevitable chaos that would result is predictable. Yet most educators have participated in exactly this sort of situation.

Almost all school professionals have been at meetings where the discussion seemed to meander and wander aimlessly. At these meetings individual participants bring up possibly interesting tangential points that nevertheless disrupt the continuity of the meeting, cause the entire meeting to drift off, and ultimately result in the meeting failing to accomplish its goals. In participating in meetings to develop collaborative programs, educators should be aware of this tendency and be alert to introduced points and topics that fail to advance the meeting's agenda.

After each point is discussed and resolved, it should be checked off, with all participants taking notes on the agreed-upon actions to be taken. In addition, one person should restate and summarize the decisions made and conclusions reached before the meeting ends. This assures that all leave with a common sense of accomplishment, purpose, and direction. Alternatively, one person can keep a record of decisions reached, using carbon paper, a computer, or a copy machine to distribute results to his or her partner(s) before departing.

Establish priorities. To ensure that the most important items are covered, the agenda preparer should use the classic newspaper "reverse pyramid" ordering style. That is, the most important item to be discussed and resolved should lead off the agenda, the second most important item should be discussed second, and so on. This "toploading" of the agenda, with the most important items first, ensures that the meetings address and effectively resolve the most important questions identified at that time.

Set time limits. Different items on the agenda likely will require differing amounts of time. One way to control the too-frequent development of spending 30 minutes on some minute detail, leaving only 10 minutes for more important items on the agenda, is to have time limits for discussion on each item as well as a time limit for the overall meeting. A predetermined timekeeper should regularly remind the attendees how much time is left for any given item and how much time remains for the entire meeting.

Control interruptions. It's usually best to meet in a relatively out-of-the-way location, a quiet corner that is not highly visible. This helps to minimize interruptions (which typically are for insignificant, "could have waited" things). In addition, the commitment to cooperative teaching must be clear to all. Cooperating educators must be adamant about not being interrupted during their planning times and resist attempts by others to do so. Each professional in the school must control his or her own time.

Be on time, start on time, end on time. It's unfair to all involved for a person to be late for meetings, as that precious resource of time is then essentially wasted for those who were professional enough to be on time. A school professional who is consistently late for meetings is sending an unspoken communication, "My time is more important than your time" or "I do not consider this meeting, or the rest of you, important." While occasional lateness is no cause for concern, chronic tardiness for meetings must be resolved.

One way to do this might be to target this problem as an issue to cover at the next meeting. In this discussion the on-time partner must be able to communicate effectively to the tardy offender the specific sorts of problems (both functional and interpersonal) that the behavior is causing. The two might then seek to find a "win-win" resolution for the situation.

In addition, during the informal moments at the beginning of meetings it's important that people take a few moments to reestablish social contact with each other, especially after not having seen each other for a while. However, this should not take up more than a few minutes. While it's certainly to be hoped that collaborating educators enjoy each other's company, these meetings cannot remain productive if they become social get-togethers.

Ending on time emphasizes to all the importance of controlling the use of time. It also helps to communicate the idea of time as a resource to be managed.

Plan the next meeting. As a routine item on the agenda educators should include planning the next meeting: time, place, and what is to be accomplished. Educators should take advantage of these rare opportunities to work together by taking a few minutes to plan ahead so that future meetings will be equally productive.

Developing Schedules

The scheduling of the professionals involved in cooperative teaching has been described as the plan of action to implement a school's newly found philosophy of professional collaboration (Adams &

Cessna, 1991). Scheduling difficulties are also the most frequently reported barrier to collaboration (Bauwens, Hourcade, Ehlert, & Schrag, 1992). These difficulties are resulting from a radical paradigm shift that is requiring educators to rethink the very nature of their jobs.

Given the significant structural changes inherent in the implementation of cooperative teaching, it will be necessary to make major shifts in the way the school's professional personnel are utilized throughout the day. In cooperative teaching, support services providers (who historically have worked via a pull-out approach independently from their general education colleagues) now will be spending the majority of their professional workdays working directly with other educators within general education classrooms.

Scheduling Considerations for Support Services Providers

In cooperative teaching support services providers (e.g., a school counselor, special educator, psychologist, speech–language therapist, school social worker, gifted/talented facilitator) typically go into general educators' classes for varying periods of time. In developing schedules for their work with their general education partners, these support services providers first should consider the following questions:

1. How much does the support services provider wish to participate in cooperative teaching, especially initially? This is perhaps the single most important question. Some are eager to become heavily involved. Others are more comfortable beginning in small doses.

2. How much time do they have available for cooperative teaching? Often support services providers have a variety of other duties (e.g., counseling, therapy, testing, meetings). While many of these duties can be restructured, others simply must be worked around.

3. How many support services providers are available to (and would like to) participate in cooperative teaching? When many of these professionals are involved in cooperative teaching, transdisciplinary support for general education teachers becomes more quickly accepted and readily available. In addition, under such conditions, each of these different support services providers begins to acquire the other's unique professional skills as well.

4. In which classrooms are the students who might benefit most from cooperative teaching? (In other words, how many

general education educators will be involved initially, and how many might be involved ultimately?) Some schools will cluster such students with just a few educators, while others subscribe to a "natural proportions" philosophy, in which students with special needs are dispersed throughout all classes. While the former option may enhance the ease and efficiency of services delivery, many educators have come to see this segregation as the equivalent of "educational ghettos."

5. To what degree is the school's regular curriculum and material appropriate for students with special needs? How much adaptation and modification of this curriculum (and accompanying materials) will be required? This determines to a large extent the amount of time the support services provider will be engaged in active preparations for cooperative teaching.

6. What are the wishes of the students with special needs? Many times, especially in middle school and high school, these students feel singled out and isolated when it is time for them to leave the general classroom and go to the "special" room and teacher. Such feelings can be minimized through extensive in-class cooperative teaching.

7. How much support is needed by the students? This is one of the most critical determinations in developing a cooperative teaching schedule. As a general rule, the greater the student needs, the more time the support services provider might be expected to be in that general education classroom. At the rare extreme, some classrooms with one or more students with severe disabilities might have a support services provider in the room for the entire school day. Conversely, classes with students with mild needs may have a support services provider working in the room for only a brief period, and not necessarily on a daily basis.

8. What are the general education teacher's wishes and comfort level with cooperative teaching? Some may wish to participate extensively, while others may prefer minimal levels, especially at first. Needless to say, this pre-implementation consideration should be thoughtfully discussed early on, with both partners able to self-disclose their true feelings about this new way of teaching.

9. What are the wishes of the parents of the students with special needs (in terms of the types of educational programs they would like their students to receive)? Many parents actively participated in the historical battles to win specialized services for their children (e.g., pull-out programs with specialized resource rooms). Understandably, some may be reluctant to give up such programs for the unknowns

involved in cooperative teaching. Other parents are at the forefront of inclusion efforts for their children with disabilities and will actively support and promote cooperative teaching, which they see as supportive of inclusion efforts and programs (Heinrich, 1992).

Scheduling Considerations for General Educators

1. Most importantly, does the general education teacher agree that all students can learn? In many ways, traditional pull-out and segregated special education grew because of the absence of this belief. Successful cooperative teaching requires the fundamental belief that all students can learn.

2. How much does the general educator wish to participate in cooperative teaching, especially initially? At least at first, some general educators may feel defensive about other educators entering "their" rooms. In the past, the infrequent professional visit to the classroom typically was to evaluate the educator, leaving the educator with, at best, mixed feelings about visitors. Others will pragmatically welcome any additional educational support in the classroom.

3. How much support does the general education teacher need or want? Some educators will possess knowledge and skills necessary to teach a wide variety of students, while others may lack coursework, experience, or the disposition to teach increasingly academically diverse groups of students.

4. How flexible can the educator be? Working with a second professional inherently requires more flexibility than does working alone. After years of having sole responsibility for developing classroom schedules, some educators may find that they are uncomfortable moving into the more flexible scheduling that cooperative teaching often requires.

5. How will parents of all students in the classroom feel about the implementation of cooperative teaching in the classroom? In the experience of many schools, parents of students with special needs are becoming more receptive to the idea of inclusion, including the provision of support services via cooperative teaching in the general education classroom (Stainback & Stainback, 1992).

Scheduling Considerations for Both Cooperative Teaching Partners

As general educators and support services providers start to develop a schedule for their new cooperative teaching arrangement, they must jointly consider a number of general questions. These include the following (Adams & Cessna, 1991):

1. What are the needs of *all* students in the school?
2. What curricula, instruction, and instructional arrangements can best meet all student needs in the general classroom?
3. What resources (human and otherwise) are available in the school that can be incorporated into the educational program? What outside resources (e.g., university faculty and students, consultants, parents and other adults) might be drawn in as needed?
4. What are the supports that general education teachers require to best meet the needs of all their students in appropriate settings throughout the day?
5. What are the unique strengths of the individual educators involved in cooperative teaching, and how can scheduling best utilize these?

The eventual schedule that evolves should reflect consideration of these questions. Its primary function should be the meeting of student needs. Perhaps needless to say, these schedules will have to be characterized by flexibility. While some cooperating educators might be more comfortable (especially initially) with a fixed schedule, the acknowledgment early on that any schedule must be fluid and subject to frequent change as appropriate will help facilitate the development and subsequent revisions of the most effective cooperative teaching plan possible.

Types of Schedules

Those educators who have been most successful in cooperative teaching have found it easiest to begin simply. In planning for their cooperative teaching, the partners first should determine how much time per day will be spent in cooperative teaching and how many days per week will be involved.

Dyadic stable schedules. The least complicated cooperative teaching arrangements include one support services provider working with one general educator (a dyad). Their schedule for cooperative teaching is fixed (a typical example is every day for a particular period). Figures 4.2 and 4.3 illustrate dyadic stable schedules, one for a daily schedule and one for a 3-day-a-week schedule.

Dyadic stable schedules, especially daily schedules, do offer several advantages. Their consistency is often easier for both students and educators. There is less possibility for confusion, as carryover and follow-up is consistent. Downtime during which the support ser-

	Monday	Tuesday	Wednesday	Thursday	Friday
8–9:00	X	X	X	X	X
9–10:00	X/I	X/I	X/I	X/I	X/I
10–11:00	X	X	X	X	X

(*X* represents the general educator in the general education classroom; *I* represents the support services provider in the general education classroom.)

Figure 4.2. Cooperative teaching schedule: Daily basis.

	Monday	Tuesday	Wednesday	Thursday	Friday
8–9:00	X	X	X	X	X
9–10:00	X	X/I	X/I	X/I	X
10–11:00	X	X	X	X	X

(*X* represents the general educator in the general education classroom; *I* represents the support services provider in the general education classroom. Many cooperative teaching partners have found Mondays and Fridays too unsettled and variable to work consistently.)

Figure 4.3. Cooperative teaching schedule: Clustered basis.

vices provider must get up to speed, catching up on what has been accomplished since the last time she or he was in the room, is minimized. The daily schedule also makes educator planning easier and facilitates the development of solid professional relationships. Finally, the daily presence of both educators reduces the potential for the support services provider to be perceived as a visitor to the general education classroom.

However, there also exists the possibility of some burnout and boredom, since the cooperative teaching partners are together day after day after day. A certain degree of complacency and staleness may occur. Also, the participants may find themselves becoming dependent upon each other, rather than learning to carry out certain tasks independently. The support services provider will be able to work only with a small number of students and general educators.

Finally, some students may become dependent upon these intensive levels of support services instead of acquiring more independent learning skills.

Cooperative teaching schedules set up on a clustered basis also offer advantages and disadvantages. The cluster schedule allows general educators to receive the in-class support and technical assistance necessary to meet the diverse and changing needs of all students in the classroom without becoming overly dependent upon the support services provider. The support services provider then can distribute his or her time more widely among other general educators and classrooms.

Disadvantages of the cluster schedule include the fact that the support services provider does not learn about the students in the class as rapidly. In addition, there needs to be a certain amount of catch-up each time the support services provider reenters the classroom. Students are not able to receive specialized services on a daily basis, and there undoubtedly will be occasions when the support services provider is not there when his or her special skills would be useful. Nondaily appearances of the support services providers make them appear more like special visitors, not equal teach-ing partners. Planning may be more difficult and require more time, as lessons that require the work of both educators must be planned for those days when both are scheduled to be in the classroom together.

Rollover schedules. As the support services provider becomes more comfortable with the implementation of a cooperative teaching arrangement in a general education classroom, she or he likely will wish to expand cooperative teaching to more than one general classroom and more than one general educator. Figure 4.4 illustrates this rollover concept.

	Monday	Tuesday	Wednesday	Thursday	Friday
8–9:00	X	X	X	X	X
9–10:00	X/I	Y/I	X/I	Y/I	X/I
10–11:00	X	X	X	X	X

(X represents the first general educator in the first general education classroom; I represents the support services provider in the general education classroom; Y represents a second general educator in a second and different general education classroom.)

Figure 4.4. Cooperative teaching schedule: Rollover basis.

The rollover concept does provide one very significant advantage. This schedule allows the support services provider to work with a greater number of general educators and students, allowing access to his or her specialized skills by a much larger group of colleagues and students. More general educators can acquire the specialized skills the support services provider brings to the general education classroom. In addition, more students will be able to receive these specialized services. These advantages should not be dismissed easily. Having the support services provider come in on certain days helps break the monotony that invades many general education classrooms. By being exposed to different teaching styles students may well acquire more sophisticated learning strategies that will then generalize to other learning environments in the future. In addition, many educators have found that with support services provided less frequently, students develop cooperative learning arrangements, learning to help and be interdependent upon one another.

Disadvantages of rollover schedules include the fact that the support services provider has less time for his or her traditional duties (e.g., special educators have less time for pull-out activities; speech and language therapists have less time for direct therapy). Planning is also made more complex and difficult. The more colleagues with whom one works, the more individual styles one must learn to accommodate. Help for general educators is available only at certain times and on certain days, making their planning more difficult. Some students, general educators, and support services providers may find the switching back and forth disconcerting and even disruptive. Some general education classrooms and some students may well need the support services provider on a daily basis, who may develop a sense of being stretched too far and spread too thin to be effective. (One solution is simply to have *all* support services providers working with *all* general educators.)

Most home owners would prefer to work with creative architects and home remodelers who can provide them with a number of possible directions in which to take their project. As is the case with many aspects of cooperative teaching, scheduling formats are limited only by the creativity of the cooperative teaching partners. While hourlong blocks are included in the aforementioned examples for simplicity's sake, in reality the amount of time spent in cooperative teaching may be as little as 20 to 30 minutes or, conversely, may extend to most or all of the school day.

The specific amounts of time are determined in part by student needs and in part by the level of skills (both present and emerging) in the general educator. As the general educator is exposed to and acquires specialized skills from the support services provider, the support services provider is then freed to move on to other general education classrooms.

Administrative Support

When professionals in the schools are asked to explain the success or failure of innovative projects they have implemented, one of the most frequently reported variables is the presence or absence of administrative support. There is a consensus in the professional literature that administrative support is a critical factor associated with the success (or lack thereof) of change projects (Arends, 1982; Manasse, 1984). For example, Montgomery (1990) concluded that programs in which support services providers collaborate with general educators require "considerable support" from the school principal, and perhaps from district-level administration as well. This idea of the necessity of administrative support, though frequently reported, is only beginning to be analyzed and defined.

In considering the issue of administrative support, all professionals participating in cooperative teaching programs must see that support is a two-way street and operates on a reciprocal basis. That is, administrators must see that their efforts to support educators in implementing cooperative teaching are acknowledged and appreciat-

ed. As these school professionals receive support from their administrators, they must make sure that the administrative support is returned. This combination of "top down" and "bottom up" support will facilitate comprehensive systems change most effectively.

The School Principal

In most schools the principal serves as the clear primary administrative figure. As Wyant and Bell (1981) noted, any significant school changes must have the principal's endorsement in order to succeed.

Principals are subject to a number of pressures from both inside and outside the school district, many of which teachers and other school professionals typically remain unaware. An additional problem is that often educators attribute a great deal of power to principals, not realizing the very significant formal (and especially informal) restrictions on a principal's options. Most effective principals quickly learn that simply asking or telling staff to do a certain thing, or to act a certain way, is an ineffective way of ensuring that those changes do indeed come about. (Chapter 8 explores administrators and administrative support in more detail.)

There are several administrative indicators that suggest that an innovation such as cooperative teaching will be successful (Montgomery, 1990). One of the most significant is a principal who knows the school's curriculum well and is involved actively in measuring the impact of that curriculum upon students' learning. The principal must be committed to ensuring that all students in the school have access to that curriculum. Principals who have shown a belief and a willingness to participate in staff training and retraining also are likely to facilitate the development and implementation of collaborative structures in their schools. Finally, principals who in the past have openly espoused the philosophy of shared educational responsibility (that all students, including those receiving special education services, are "everybody's kids") and who have taken care to establish a school culture based on this principle are most likely to help restructure their schools to enable educators to participate in cooperative teaching.

A potential complication is reported by Wyant and Bell (1981), who observed that the problems of principals are compounded when specialists and associated resource persons work within, and are incorporated into, the school's overall functioning. The presence of change agents from special education (and elsewhere in the school) may send a message to the principal (and others) that the school's status quo is troubled and that the principal alone is unable to correct the situation. In such a scenario the principal may sense a challenge to his or her authority or overall administrative competence and respond by effectively undermining the implementation of any proposed changes.

Developing Administrative Support

As Montgomery (1990) noted, the initial hurdle to any change is inertia. The "we've never done it that way before" syndrome is typical, usually appearing early in the process of seeking administrative support. She additionally concluded that administrators are haunted by two great fears: that they will lose control of a program and that money and resources will be mismanaged.

One reason administrative eyebrows go up when innovative proposals are suggested is that budgets typically are built upon existing service models, not on novel approaches. This almost inevitably results in understandable financial concerns when unpredictable innovative approaches are proposed. Given that in most districts resources for the support services providers are based upon the number of students technically identified as requiring specialized educational programs, some principals will be reluctant to approve projects that actually might serve to reduce the amount of this funding. (This may well be the case in the short term, until funding models once again catch up with service delivery systems as they have in the past.)

In addition, even the most eager innovators will readily acknowledge to administrators that not all the answers are known at first. Such a position, though professionally honest, is nevertheless an understandable source of concern for principals. Educators implementing cooperative teaching must help the school principal to see the necessity for an initial period of experimentation to identify those features of support services that will respond most effectively to that particular school's unique needs. While principals and other stakeholders should be kept abreast of the status of the program, full-scale evaluation of cooperative teaching should not come until after this initial period is completed.

As educators seek to implement cooperative teaching, there are a number of ways they can elicit the administrative support necessary for the program's success (Montgomery, 1990). To begin with, cooperating educators should alert the principal well in advance of the proposed changes. The support services provider might point out to the principal that this new arrangement will increase the visibility and productivity of the support services provider. This explanation probably should be done in a short, one-page description, giving the specifics of how cooperative teaching will function. The explanation can be given most clearly through a who, what, where, when, why, and how format. In addition, the support services provider should let the principal know that all parents of the students impacted by the change will be aware of the program, so that the principal is not on the defensive or uninformed should parental questions arise. Many educators implementing cooperative teaching have found it useful to write letters to all parents of students in the class, regardless of whether or not those students had received support services in the past, explaining the arrangement. (A sample letter is included in Figure 4.5.)

The cooperating educators should share frequent, brief, written update reports with the principal concerning their cooperative teaching, especially early on. (These notes to the principal also make it easier for the cooperating educators to self-reflect.) While these progress notes should highlight advantages, possible problems also should be noted. School professionals will find that good principals usually

---

Dear Parents:

As some of you know, in the past here at Barr School, whenever students received specialized educational services they almost always left their regular classroom to receive their special programs. However, today there is much research that finds that students do not make as much progress this way as they might with other approaches.

This school year we will begin a different, and what we believe will be a better, approach to educating all our students, including those who need extra support. In our new cooperative teaching arrangement a variety of staff professionals will be coming into the general classrooms to work with the students' teachers so that they can combine their skills to teach all students. We believe that this approach will help **all** of our students succeed better in the general class and also will help the students with special needs feel less isolated.

If you are the parent of a student presently receiving special services, please contact your child's teacher at 555-5678. He or she will explain the program in more detail and work with you to make the necessary changes in your child's program. We also have a video available for checkout that will show you this exciting program in action at another school. We are excited about this new approach at Barr School and invite you to come and see the program in action.

Sincerely,

Jim Patent
Principal

Lori Carnick
Teacher

Figure 4.5. Sample letter to parents.

have solid problem-solving skills, and cooperating educators should take advantage of this to help identify solutions to unforeseen dilemmas. In addition, the solicitation of the principal's skills in this problem-solving activity has the salutary effect of increasing the principal's personal and professional investment in the ultimate success of the cooperative teaching.

Cooperating educators should resist telling colleagues about the program early on, instead waiting until it has been firmly established. The school's staff will likely be more interested in hearing about what is actually going on at the time than in receiving an advance presentation of what one intends to do. For example, one would not hold a housewarming party for a remodeling project while the walls were unpainted and the roof incomplete!

Rather than giving all colleagues at school information about their cooperative teaching, the involved parties might place information about it on a common bulletin board. Like most other people, educators read only what they want to read and only when they want to read it.

Cooperating educators should try to maintain a data base that supports the effectiveness of the collaborative intervention. A brief numerical or statistical summary of the accomplishments of the collaborative effort provides principals with a report that is easily understood by their superiors. (Chapter 5 explains in more detail how evaluation of cooperative teaching might be done.)

The support services providers should go out of their way to become integrated with the school's staff as a whole. This includes volunteering for committees (especially those not related to special services), correcting papers, helping with the school newspaper, and so forth. Such actions demonstrate clearly to the rest of the school staff that all educators are there for all students.

Once collaborators have shown the principal the advantages of this approach, the principal may well be in support of the program. However, even though the principal may support cooperative teaching, he or she may be unsure of how to demonstrate that support.

Expressions of Administrative Support

Many principals may not be aware of the variety of ways in which they can show support for proposed changes in how education is provided to all students in a school. Certainly the types of support administrators provide to professionals implementing cooperative teaching are as varied as the administrators themselves. Yet certain categories or types of administrative support have been identified (e.g., Arends, 1982).

Perhaps one of the most important initial types of support a principal can offer cooperating educators is a clear vision of what the school can become and the role of each professional in that school in making that vision a reality (Manasse, 1984). An administrator's essential understanding of the philosophical underpinnings of cooperative teaching and the foresight to see how this can be brought to reality make it easier for educators to sense support from administration. This administrative vision includes the development of an agenda of planned actions (in essence the development of the architectural plans that clearly illustrate the newly remodeled schoolhouse) and a schedule of construction.

Ideas concerning organizational problems, and solutions to those problems, are received differently and with greater attention when seen as coming from individuals in positions of authority. To this end, clear and ongoing verbal and nonverbal support from a principal or other school authority figure can have great impact on the likelihood of a project's success. The frequent demonstration of support through public actions such as verbal comments, short written notes, and literal pats on the back shows that the principal is thinking about the project and that he or she is excited about it and anticipates that others will be excited as well.

Another component of administrative support targets the inherent instability automatically introduced into a preexisting system when an innovation is implemented. Both staff members associated with the innovation and those not directly associated with it will look to the school authority figure to clarify the roles of the professionals in the school, especially those most directly associated with the proposed changes. This role clarification also extends to the school authority figure, who must be clear about his or her new role vis-à-vis the innovation as well as about his or her ongoing responsibilities.

One of the most frequent roles an administrator faces in the implementation of a new program is that of defender of the changes. This ranges from facing direct hostility and resistance from staff members heavily invested in the present system to helping innovators cut through bureaucratic red tape. In the absence of such support those at the forefront of innovations will find themselves beaten down.

Finally, perhaps the strongest expression of support for change is allocation of resources of value by the school authority figure. These resources may include release time and planning time; space (especially space with symbolic value, such as space that is large or physically close to the administrator); money; status; suggestions for scheduling; staff development opportunities; freedom to experiment; and dedicated time from, and access to, the administrator. All these make it clear that the project enjoys administrative support.

It is important to note that the majority of these administrative displays can be seen as small, bureaucratic matters: allocation of space, pats on the back, and so forth. This does not diminish the crucial role they play in the acceptance and ultimate success of innovative projects. The skillful administrator recognizes their symbolic importance and uses that to advance the innovation.

Conclusions

At the risk of oversimplifying the process of change, most educators who have implemented cooperative teaching successfully have done so by deliberately beginning small. That is, rather than starting by attempting to dramatically reshape their entire school, they initially sought to incorporate occasional periods of cooperative teaching into their work. As they gained familiarity with and experience in cooperative teaching, they expanded their efforts, eliciting administrator support as their growing successes were noted.

One way to conceptualize how changes such as cooperative teaching are implemented in the schools is to consider again a home remodeling project. A group of individuals from diverse backgrounds and perspectives jointly develop the architectural plans. The building materials then are brought to the job site and shaped and cut to fit the new plans.

The workers then begin their individual jobs simultaneously. Some workers work on the flooring, others work on the walls and associated electrical outlets, and still others work on the ceiling and roof. Thus the remodeling project is carried out from neither a pure top-down nor a pure bottom-up approach. These processes are carried out simultaneously.

Similarly, the development and implementation of cooperative teaching in the schools is most likely to be successful when it is neither solely top down (implemented by direct administrative decree in the absence of educator input) nor bottom up (educators attempting cooperative teaching in the absence of administrative interest, input, or support). When administrators carry out their ceiling work as educators reconstruct walls and outlets, the project is completed quickest and with the greatest sense of unified purpose.

Chapter 4 Activity
Time-Management Survey

Each of the following questions is designed to help identify normal time use patterns. Please circle the number that best indicates normal practice. This self-assessment will show those areas where time management is effective, as well as those areas that still need attention. (A few of the questions may not be applicable to a particular situation. In such cases, "NA" should be circled to indicate that the question is not applicable.)

Scoring key:
Always or Yes = 1
Usually = 2
Sometimes = 3
Rarely = 4
Never or No = 5
Not Applicable = NA

1. Do you have a clearly defined list of objectives in writing?

    1   2   3   4   5   NA

2. Have you recorded your actual time use any time within the past year?

    1   2   3   4   5   NA

3. Do you write out your objectives and priorities each day?

    1   2   3   4   5   NA

4. Do you spend time each day reviewing your daily objectives and priorities with any colleagues who will be affected by them?

    1   2   3   4   5   NA

5. Can you find large blocks of uninterrupted time when you need it?

    1   2   3   4   5   NA

6. Have you eliminated frequently recurring crises from your job?

    1   2   3   4   5   NA

7. Do you refuse to answer the telephone when engaged in important conversations?

    1   2   3   4   5   NA

8. Do you plan and schedule your time on a weekly and daily basis?

    1   2   3   4   5   NA

9. Do you use travel and waiting time productively?

    1   2   3   4   5   NA

10. Do you delegate as much as you could to others?

    1   2   3   4   5   NA

11. Do you prevent your aide from delegating his or her tasks and decisions upward to you?

    1   2   3   4   5   NA

12. Do you use your aide as well as you could?

    1   2   3   4   5   NA

13. Do you take time each day to sit back and think about what you're doing and what you're trying to accomplish?

    1   2   3   4   5   NA

14. Have you eliminated one time waster within the past week?

    1   2   3   4   5   NA

15. Do you feel really in control of your time and on top of your job?

    1   2   3   4   5   NA

16. Is your desk and office well organized and free of clutter?

    1   2   3   4   5   NA

17. Can you successfully cope with stress, tension, and anxiety?

    1   2   3   4   5   NA

18. Have you successfully eliminated time waste in meetings?

    1   2   3   4   5   NA

19. Have you learned to conquer your tendency to procrastinate?

      1   2   3   4   5   NA

20. Do you tackle tasks on the basis of importance and priority?

      1   2   3   4   5   NA

21. Have you discussed time-management problems with your aide within the past month?

      1   2   3   4   5   NA

22. Do you resist the temptation to get overly involved in your aide's activities?

      1   2   3   4   5   NA

23. Do you control your schedule so that other people do not waste their time waiting for you?

      1   2   3   4   5   NA

24. Do you resist doing things for others that they probably could and should be doing for themselves?

      1   2   3   4   5   NA

25. Are you reluctant to interrupt your aide or colleagues unless it is really important and can't wait?

      1   2   3   4   5   NA

26. Do you meet deadlines and finish all your tasks on time?

      1   2   3   4   5   NA

27. Can you identify the few critical activities that account for the majority of your results in your job?

      1   2   3   4   5   NA

28. Have you been able to reduce the amount of paperwork and/or the amount of time it consumes?

      1   2   3   4   5   NA

29. Do you effectively control interruptions and drop-in visitors rather than allowing them to control you and your time use?

      1   2   3   4   5   NA

30. Are you better organized and accomplishing more than you were 6 months ago?

      1   2   3   4   5   NA

31. Are you able to stay current with all your reading?

      1   2   3   4   5   NA

32. Have you stopped taking work home in the evenings and on weekends?

      1   2   3   4   5   NA

33. Have you mastered the ability to say no whenever you should?

      1   2   3   4   5   NA

34. Are you spending enough time training and developing your aide?

      1   2   3   4   5   NA

35. Do you feel that you have enough time for yourself for recreation, study, community, or family activities?

      1   2   3   4   5   NA

Total Score _____

Scoring Guide: All circled numbers should be added up to find a total score. The lower the score, the better one's use of time is. The higher the score, the more indication there is that there are improvements one could and should be making to improve management of time.

References

Adams, L., & Cessna, K. (1991). Designing systems to facilitate collaboration: Collective wisdom from Colorado. *Preventing School Failure, 35*, 37–42.

Arends, R. I. (1982). The meaning of administrative support. *Educational Administration Quarterly, 18*, 79–92.

Bartholomew, B., & Gardner, S. (1982). *Status of the American public school, 1980–1981*. Washington, DC: National Education Association.

Bauwens, J., Hourcade, J. J., Ehlert, B. J., & Schrag, J. (1992). *Restructuring America's schools through collaboration: Barriers and solutions*. Unpublished manuscript, Boise State University, Boise, ID.

Drawbaugh, C. C. (1984). *Time and its use: A self-management guide for teachers*. New York: Teacher's College Press.

Fullan, M., & Miles, M. (1992). Getting reform right: What works and what doesn't. *Phi Delta Kappan, 73*, 745–752.

Heinrich, M. (Director). (1992). *All kids belong: Sarah's story* [Videotape]. Portland, OR: Multnomah Education Service District.

Louis, K. S. (1992). Restructuring and the problem of teachers' work. In A. Lieberman (Ed.), *The changing contexts of teaching. 91st yearbook of the National Society for the Study of Education* (Vol. 1., pp. 138–156). Chicago: The National Society for the Study of Education.

Mackenzie, R. A. (1972). *The time trap: How to get more done in less time*. New York: McGraw-Hill.

Manasse, A. L. (1984). Principals as leaders of high-performing systems. *Educational Leadership, 41*(5), 42–46.

Montgomery, J. K. (1990). Building administrative support for collaboration. In W. A. Secord (Ed.), *Best practices in school speech-language pathology* (pp. 75–79). San Antonio, TX: The Psychological Corporation.

Raywid, M. A. (1992). *Making time to do reform*. Unpublished manuscript, University of Wisconsin, Wisconsin Center for Education Research, Madison.

Raywid, M. A. (1993). Finding time for collaboration. *Educational Leadership, 51*(1), 31–34.

Stainback, S. S., & Stainback, W. (1992). Schools as inclusive communities. In W. Stainback & S. Stainback (Eds.), *Controversial issues confronting special education: Divergent perspectives* (pp. 29–44). Boston: Allyn and Bacon.

Watson, A., Buchanan, M., Huyman, H., & Seal, K. (1992). A laboratory school explores self-governance. *Educational Leadership, 49*(5), 57–60.

Wyant, S. H., & Bell, W. E. (1981). Diagnosing and dealing with barriers to change. In M. P. Gaasholt & N. G. Haring (Eds.), *Organizing for change: Inservice and staff development in special education* (pp. 1–36). Seattle: University of Washington, Program Development Assistance System.

5

Inspecting the Job
Evaluating Cooperative Teaching

"The facts will eventually test out all theories, and they form, after all, the only impartial jury to which we can appeal."
— Jean Louis Rodolphe Agassiz

After first deciding to remodel a house, home owners usually spend hours reviewing potential plans and blueprints, ultimately selecting those that appear best suited for their purposes. As the work progresses, with some walls coming out while others are con-

107

structed, new framing and flooring being added, and so on, all the involved participants frequently pause to look at and evaluate the work accomplished to that point, trying to envision how each step will contribute to the overall project. Upon completing their remodeling project, home owners and remodelers usually take great pride in stepping back and admiring their work, "oohing" and "aahing" over it, and imagining how the new structures will improve their quality of life.

In some cases, however, after moving into the newly remodeled house, the occupants find the results unsatisfactory. Traffic patterns may be awkward, the newly renovated rooms may feel more crowded than anticipated, there may be too much or too little light, and so forth. In short, a variety of unexpected results can lead to dissatisfaction with the project's outcome. While some of these developments may be inevitable, many others can be avoided by checking throughout the construction process to make sure that all dimensions are implemented as they were planned, the correct predetermined materials are indeed used, and so forth. In fact, in most locales, before occupants can move into a remodeled project, an inspector must come in to review the completed project to ascertain its quality.

One way to minimize unexpected and unpleasant developments in the rebuilding process is to have clearly determined beforehand exactly what outcomes are desired and what jobs, features, and specifications are necessary to yield those outcomes. This information then serves as a point of comparison for the ongoing construction, with regularly scheduled checks continuing along the way to make sure that all is progressing as planned. As educators remodel the schoolhouse through the implementation of cooperative teaching, they also must begin with a clear sense of what it is they hope and anticipate this approach can accomplish. The potential outcomes and advantages might include benefits for all students, for the overall educational system, for educators in the school, and for parents and the general public. Each of these potentially critical dimensions are discussed in this chapter, with suggestions offered for the evaluation of each.

Understanding Program Evaluation

McLaughlin and McLaughlin (1993) outlined a strong conceptual framework for thinking about evaluation. As they noted, evaluation is

a process through which information is collected that allows people to make comparisons with some predetermined set of criteria or standards. This process is most useful if several points are kept in mind from early on in the development of an evaluation program.

First, evaluation must be designed with a specific purpose (or purposes) clearly in mind from the beginning. The essential purpose for any evaluation is determined by answering at least two questions:

1. Who are the potential consumers of the information to be generated by the evaluation?

2. What is it they should know?

In schools where personnel are preparing to implement cooperative teaching, there are a number of potential consumers of data collected on the impact of this innovation. Some possible users of this information might include:

- parents
- educators at that school involved in cooperative teaching
- educators at that school not involved in cooperative teaching
- educators at other schools who are not presently involved in cooperative teaching but are considering whether to become involved
- educators at other schools who have adopted cooperative teaching

- professors in teacher preparation programs at universities
- staff development professionals and educational consultants in school districts or educational support centers
- school building administrators
- state department of education staff and administrators
- school district administrators
- educational researchers

Each of these potential groups likely has different questions they would like answered through evaluations of cooperative teaching. Without the initial determination of the potential interested users of evaluative data and how the evaluation might be designed to try to meet the diverse needs of all these groups, subsequent use of the information will be limited.

A second point is the closeness of the relationship of the overall program that is being evaluated with the design of the evaluation procedures. Many professionals involved in program evaluation report afterwards that they are unable to decide how best to apply the results of their evaluation procedures to subsequent decisions about their programs. This common difficulty can be minimized by ensuring that the evaluation design incorporates (and is based on) the essential underlying theory of the approach to be reviewed and on how the specific mechanics of that theory are translated into actual practice. Thus, in evaluating cooperative teaching one might anticipate that the evaluation will include the collection of data on the relationship between the cooperative teaching partners as well as the overall educational effectiveness of the arrangements.

A third point is the realization that changes in the evaluation procedures likely will be necessary once the evaluation has begun. As data are collected, new questions may begin to emerge, and unanticipated problems with the evaluation procedures may become apparent. If all involved parties realize that the evaluation procedures are likely to change over time, and if they continue to communicate with each other about evaluation in their cooperative teaching, those inevitable changes will be less stressful.

These basic points begin to form the essential first phase in any process of evaluation. Keeping them in mind, it is then possible to begin considering how best to evaluate cooperative teaching. The following section provides a practical guide for developing evaluation procedures for cooperative teaching.

Evaluating Cooperative Teaching

The evaluation procedures for cooperative teaching should be based on the specific issues that led to the proposal to implement it in the first place. These issues will be as varied and individualized as the schools or educators themselves.

One way to begin thinking about evaluating the impact of cooperative teaching is to think again about how home owners might evaluate their home remodeling project. The home owners might check to make sure that each part of the job is being done as planned and also might check the specific results after each job is completed. In other words, during the actual construction phase of the project, the home owner might determine whether each of the different subcontracted jobs (e.g., electrical, flooring, painting) is being done as per the previously agreed-upon specifications. In addition, after the work has been completed, the home owner will likely check to see that the results (e.g., dimensions, specifications) that were decided upon beforehand actually were achieved. Thus the specific jobs or processes that are required throughout the project are evaluated, followed by an after-the-fact evaluation of the results or outcomes.

In addition to the evaluation of both processes and outcomes, as the work progresses and is completed the home owner may be involved in measuring such things as wall thickness, quality ratings and numbers of coats of the paint being used, number of outlets installed, and so forth, checking to see that the specifications are being met. In addition to this objective data, however, the home owner usually develops a subjective sense of whether the colors he or she selected actually feel as pleasant as was expected, whether the window size is providing the sense of airiness that was hoped for, and so forth.

Thus, one way to think about evaluating cooperative teaching is to conceptualize a 2 x 2 matrix with four cells containing possible types of information. One of the two dimensions includes two specific aspects: (a) the processes that are being used in the program and (b) the outcomes of those processes. The other dimension includes the two forms of the information that might be collected: objective information (conclusions based on impersonal data) or subjective information (conclusions based on personal perceptions). Figure 5.1 graphically illustrates this 2 x 2 matrix, which yields four possible types of data about cooperative teaching:

- objective analyses of the processes involved

(list continues)

- objective analyses of the outcomes
- subjective analyses of the processes involved
- subjective analyses of the outcomes

Objective Versus Subjective Information

At an early point in evaluating cooperative teaching, evaluators will be faced with a decision with significant and far-reaching consequences. Should the evaluation be based on objective (impersonal, data-based) information, subjective (personal perception) information, or some combination of both? Each has potential advantages; thus, comprehensive evaluation procedures might choose to incorporate both types of information.

Objective information consists of observable data not subject to personal opinion or impression. For example, in evaluating the planning component of cooperative teaching, evaluators might learn that the cooperative teaching partners had met every week for the last 3 months. These data would be identical for both participants as well as for any observer and are only minimally subject to personal interpretation (i.e., "Are you counting that as a meeting? I thought we were just chatting!"). Additional types of objective data might include such things as the number of hours the two educators actually spent cooperatively teaching in the same classroom; standardized test scores of students in classrooms where cooperative teaching was implemented compared to those not so taught; time spent in training for cooperative teaching; amount of money spent to support cooperative teaching; and so forth.

		Types of Data	
		Objective	Subjective
Dimension Evaluated	Processes	objective processes	subjective processes
	Outcome	objective outcomes	subjective outcomes

Figure 5.1. Types of information that might be gathered to evaluate the effects of cooperative teaching.

Subjective information, while at times less clear-cut, may offer some of the necessary interpretative "fleshing-out" of more objective data. Subjective evaluation often includes asking significant individuals to record their personal impressions of various aspects of the program, typically using a "Likert-type" scale. These scales provide a number of items to which respondents give their reaction by indicating some degree of agreement or disagreement. In constructing such a scale, the evaluation designers go through a series of relatively straightforward steps as follows (Adams & Schvaneveldt, 1985):

1. Develop a pool of items or questions relevant to the program being investigated. This pool of items should contain approximately equal numbers of favorable and unfavorable items in a random mix.

2. Provide a response category for each item. These are typically five-point response categories for each item, including (1) strongly agree, (2) agree, (3) undecided, (4) disagree, (5) strongly disagree.

3. State some items positively and others negatively. This minimizes the tendency of respondents to simply mark one column down the page.

4. Develop approximately 20 to 30 items. This provides a good sample without being too cumbersome.

5. Administer the instrument, and analyze the data. Usually this analysis is based on numerical values (1 to 5) being assigned to each of the five responses, typically with a score of 5 representing a most favorable response. These individual item scores then can be analyzed.

Some possible types of subjective data that might be gathered include both educator and student perceptions of aspects of cooperative teaching such as the quality and effectiveness of help that students who are struggling receive; the perceived clarity of lessons that are presented; and the overall level of personal and professional satisfaction of the educators engaged in cooperative teaching, as well as that of their students. For example, all educators participating in cooperative teaching might respond to an item that says, "I learned new instructional strategies from my partner." If the average score for this item among the respondents is 1.9 (disagree), then one might conclude that the potential for cooperative teaching to allow participants to learn from one another is not being fully recognized in the present system. In addition, one might also sum up all scores from each respondent to obtain an overall subjective interpretation of how effective the processes have been, and to gain a sense of how favorably any particular respondent feels overall about the processes inherent in cooperative teaching.

Neither purely objective nor purely subjective evaluative information alone provides a comprehensive and completely accurate picture of the effectiveness of the various processes involved in cooperative teaching. The combination of both kinds of information yields the most complete picture.

In order to be able to effectively interpret any data there must be some point of comparison. Thus at least two data sets are recommended: one prior to the implementation of cooperative teaching and a second at some point after implementation. Additional ongoing evaluations provide an even better picture of how the impact of the program is evolving over time.

In evaluating cooperative teaching, typically evaluators would collect information on whatever factors have been identified as significant prior to actual development and implementation. (A number of suggested factors are provided later in this chapter.) This initial pre-implementation set of data then serves as a baseline, or initial point of comparison, for a second set of data that is collected after the program has been in operation long enough to begin having some impact. Comparison of these two sets of data then allows evaluators to ascertain specific ways in which the program is having greatest effect.

Process Evaluation Versus Outcomes Evaluation

Most educators have had the experience of implementing some program that was described as "can't miss," going through the prescribed training and subsequent instructions and procedures exactly as specified, only to find the results disappointing, discouraging, or unsuccessful. Given the inexact nature of interactions with human beings in all their complexity, it simply is not possible to develop educational programs that possess the degree of specificity and predictability of results that one finds in sciences such as physics and chemistry.

Given this reality, it may be useful for evaluative purposes to distinguish between two distinct and different aspects of cooperative teaching. These two distinct aspects are the individual component processes that in total make up the program and the resulting outcomes of the implementation of cooperative teaching. Evaluation of both these dimensions may be necessary to gain the most knowledge.

Process evaluation. Any replicable program requires certain procedures and processes to be followed if it is to be successful. For example, effective implementation of cooperative teaching requires (among many other things) that the cooperative teaching partners meet regularly to discuss, plan, and analyze their work. In the absence of the process of planning, cooperative teaching is unlikely to be successful.

Thus one approach toward evaluating cooperative teaching is to identify and evaluate the various component processes involved. For example, the evaluators might base their analysis in part on an examination of processes such as the frequency of planning for cooperative teaching, the productivity of those sessions in generating practical plans, and so forth.

At its simplest level, process evaluation involves two steps. First, the evaluators (along with the educators engaged in cooperative teaching if these are not the same individuals) must identify and agree upon those component processes that the program requires. This identification procedure requires and is based on a logical analysis of the program's process requirements. (Chapter 3 provides a starting point for identifying the essential components or processes required in cooperative teaching.)

Second, those identified processes are then evaluated. This stage of the evaluation may involve the use of objective information, subjective perceptions, or both.

Outcomes evaluation. Presumably any innovative program is designed and implemented to respond to some perceived needs that presently are unmet, and to achieve some desirable results. Evaluation of any program then must include an assessment of the degree to which these needs were met and the degree to which the desired outcomes were achieved.

As is the case in process evaluation, the evaluation of outcomes can be primarily objective, subjective, or both. Typically the development and implementation of cooperative teaching is designed to achieve both objective and subjective outcomes.

For example, a cooperative teaching effort may be designed and implemented in part to provide students with more effective instruction in basic academic skills. Measures of the effectiveness with which that outcome is achieved might include data such as schoolwide scores on standardized achievement tests, informal reading inventories, curriculum-based assessment measures, and so forth.

However, a second desired outcome of the implementation of cooperative teaching might be to foster a sense of camaraderie among educators at that school, that is, a feeling that they all share the same goal, which is the effective education of all students in that school. Evaluating this personally subjective outcome might require the construction of a Likert-type scale that includes items such as, "After having participated in cooperative teaching, I now believe that I have greater professional responsibility for all students at this school." Individual participants' responses to this item can yield a data base from which to judge whether the desired outcome of shared responsibility among all educators is being achieved.

Thus, as was the case in process evaluation, two steps are required in outcomes evaluation. First, the desired outcomes that were anticipated from cooperative teaching must be identified. Second, those identified outcomes must be systematically evaluated to determine if indeed the desired outcomes were achieved.

It is possible (and even typical) for a program to be more successful in one of these types of evaluation than in others. The relative weight and importance of these four types of data should of course be predetermined on an individual basis relative to the needs and desires of any particular situation. More on each of these types of data follows.

Determining Sources of Information

As previously noted, the evaluation of cooperative teaching should be guided in large part by a review of those factors that led to the adoption of the approach in the first place. These factors should be among the first reviewed as educators organize evaluations of cooperative teaching.

One way to begin is to group all the possible sources of information into four general categories of outcomes data that might be examined. These four categories include information gathered from and about (a) students, (b) the educational system, (c) professional educators, and (d) parents and other outside parties.

Student Information

In considering the issue of the restructuring of schools, Blum and Corbett (1993) effectively argued that this restructuring must begin with defining student outcomes (what students should know and be able to do) and then working backwards from that information to identify the rules, roles, and relationships that will be necessary to support those outcomes. Their fundamental premise was that there should be only one reason to restructure schools: to more effectively educate students, better preparing them to become responsive and responsible citizens in the future.

The primacy of student outcomes as a foundation for evaluating the effectiveness of cooperative teaching is difficult to argue. However, it will come as no surprise to most educators that there are a myriad of ways in which the impact of cooperative teaching (or another educational innovation) on student outcomes might be measured.

Subjective student information. The evaluators might choose both subjective and objective sources of information about student outcomes in determining the effects of cooperative teaching. Subjective sources of information might include the development and administration of a Likert-type scale. This instrument could then be given to all students (both those with and without special needs) who are involved in cooperative teaching to provide a source of comparison. An instrument designed to evaluate student outcomes subjectively might include such items as:

- "Cooperative teaching is helping me learn how to study better."

- "When both teachers are in the room our class has to slow down more for students who are having trouble learning."

- "I think other teachers should come into our class to help students who need help, instead of the students leaving our class for help."

(This chapter's concluding activity provides additional suggestions for developing or selecting evaluation instruments and individual items.)

Objective student information. Objective data may in some cases be easier for evaluators to collect and may also have greater impact with initially skeptical audiences. These data are typically used in evaluating school efficacy. Objective sources of information can be obtained from students who are participating in cooperatively taught programs and compared to that obtained from similar students who are not participating in these programs. Sources of objective information include:

- standardized test scores

- curriculum-based measurement results

- grades on homework, tests, and other educator-based evaluations of student performance

- observations of rates of social interactions

- observations of rates of on-task and other academic behaviors

(list continues)

• mastery of IEP goals and objectives

System Information

In addition to better meeting student needs, many schools implement cooperative teaching to respond to perceived problems in the current way the system is structured. One such example is the present physical, social, and professional isolation of support services providers from their general education colleagues. Thus, a second source of information about the impact of cooperative teaching is its impact on the overall system.

Subjective system information. As is the case with student data, evaluators may want to collect both subjective and objective information. Subjective and personal opinions on the effects of cooperative teaching on the educational system may be solicited from a variety of professionals who have been involved. These respondents might include general education teachers, support services providers, or administrators. The Likert-type scale developed to gather this information might include items such as:

- "Fewer students fall through the cracks in classes where cooperative teaching is implemented."

- "Cooperative teaching is more effective than the present arrangements in preventing small problems from becoming large ones."

- "Cooperative teaching is a less efficient use of professionals' time than is the present system."

Objective system information. A variety of objective data also exists that can be examined to evaluate the impact of cooperative teaching on the overall system. Sources of this data include:

- frequency of suspension, expulsion, and similar behavior-management interventions

- rates of absenteeism and dropout

- rates of grade retention

- numbers of students identified as having disabilities

- numbers of students removed from the general classroom for segregated support services (e.g., Chapter 1, special education, speech and language, gifted and talented)

Educator Information

A third source of information about cooperative teaching is gathered by determining the impact of cooperative teaching on the professionals providing educational services in the schools. These individuals include (but are not limited to):

- general education teachers
- special education teachers
- school administrators
- Chapter 1 teachers
- gifted and talented teachers
- speech and language therapists
- occupational therapists
- physical therapists
- school psychologists
- school counselors
- paraprofessionals, teacher aides, and instructional assistants
- specialized area teachers (e.g., art, music, physical education)

Subjective educator information. A great deal of subjective information can be gathered from educators that will provide a more complete and accurate picture of the effects of cooperative teaching. A Likert-type scale for these respondents might include such items as:

- "I enjoy working in cooperative teaching arrangements more than I enjoyed working with the old system."
- "I believe I have lost some degree of professional independence since beginning cooperative teaching."
- "I now am spending more time in planning than I was before I began cooperative teaching."
- "Cooperative teaching allows me to make better use of my unique teaching and professional skills."
- "After working in cooperative teaching I now believe students with disabilities can succeed in general classrooms."
- "I feel more stress working under cooperative teaching than I did under the previous system."

Again, the selection of the specific questions to be used in the scale would be driven by those educator-based factors that led to the decision to implement cooperative teaching in the first place.

Objective educator information. Objective data also may be gathered on the impact of cooperative teaching on the professionals in the schools. A few of these sources of data include:

- educator burnout rates (educator retention data)

- rate of transfer requests

- number of educators interested in cooperative teaching (e.g., who sign up and attend training sessions or volunteer to participate)

- number of workshops, staff development seminars, and graduate courses educators pursue and complete

- number of referrals for special education made by educators

- number of students continuing to be removed from the general classroom for the provision of support services

Each school likely will have specific educator-based data that can provide especially sensitive indicators of the effects of cooperative teaching on its unique professional staff.

Parent and General Public Information

It is important for educators to remember that from the perspective of many in society ultimately it is the general public that is the "consumer" of the "product" of the educational system. This product is an educated and literate citizenry. Those members of the public who presently have children in the schools are especially significant consumers.

In this sense it is to the tax-paying public that educators are ultimately answerable. The significance of evaluating the impact of cooperative teaching upon these individuals should not be overlooked. These individuals include:

- parents of students without special needs

- parents of students with special needs

- members of parent–teacher organizations

- school board members

- politicians

- employers

- other citizens in the community

Subjective parent and general public information. Subjective data can be gathered through Likert-type scales completed by these individuals. For example, a survey of parents could include such items as:

- "Students with special needs are not likely to have their needs best met in the general classroom, even when a support services provider is there."

- "My child is best educated in a classroom characterized by great diversity."

- "Cooperative teaching may be effective for less able students but is not as good for the most able students."

- "I believe that cooperative teaching allows all children to receive a better education."

Objective parent and general public information. Objective data on the effects of cooperative teaching on these individuals might include information such as:

- attendance at parent–teacher meetings

- rates of responsiveness to school messages sent home

- attendance rates at IEP meetings
- voting patterns of school board members and politicians

Perhaps the single most critical aspect of evaluation data is its continuance on an ongoing and proactive basis, shaping and determining the future of cooperative teaching. In the absence of this function, evaluation has questionable utility.

The data collection process is incomplete until the data have been synthesized, analyzed, interpreted, and disseminated to appropriate audiences. Chapter 9 identifies a variety of forums and audiences appropriate for this dissemination process.

Conclusions

At this point the schoolhouse remodelers have collected and analyzed enough information to determine that the schoolhouse remodeled with the cooperative teaching blueprints is now ready to occupy. However, when home owners move into their remodeled homes, they often find that a certain period of adjustment is necessary before the new surroundings truly feel like home. Similarly, educators moving into classrooms with cooperative teaching often sense an initial period of uneasiness. The next chapter examines this phenomenon in greater depth and suggests ways in which the "moving in" process can be accomplished most smoothly and successfully.

Chapter 5 Activity
Cooperative Teaching Outcomes
Evaluation Guide

One of the more difficult aspects in initially developing an implementation plan for cooperative teaching is determining exactly what it is that should be evaluated. Again, the two dimensions of cooperative teaching that might be evaluated are the various individual processes involved in cooperative teaching, and the subsequent outcomes of cooperative teaching.

The following presents an "if . . . then" format for assisting in the evaluation of cooperative teaching. This guide has assisted a number of schools and districts that have implemented cooperative teaching as they developed their evaluation plans.

Cooperative Teaching Outcomes Evaluation Guide

I. If You Are Interested in Student Changes in . . .

a. *grades*, then review grades of students in cooperatively taught classrooms with those of similar students in one-teacher/traditionally taught classrooms.

b. *social interactions*, then compare levels of social interactions of students in cooperatively taught classrooms with those of students in traditionally taught classrooms.

c. *behaviors*, then compare levels of those behaviors of students in cooperatively taught classrooms with those of similar students in traditionally taught classrooms.

d. *self-concepts*, then administer tests of self-concept to students before they join cooperatively taught classrooms and again after learning in cooperatively taught classrooms for some period of time.

e. *attendance*, then compare attendance records of students in cooperatively taught classrooms with those of similar students in one-teacher/traditionally taught classrooms.

f. *attitudes*, then construct and administer to all students a "School Attitudes" instrument, comparing the results from students in cooperatively taught classrooms with those from similar students in one-teacher/traditionally taught classrooms.

g. *skills acquisition and academic achievement*, then administer either a curriculum-based or a commercially available academic skills test or academic achievement test to all students, comparing the skills of students in cooperatively taught classrooms with those of similar students in traditionally taught classrooms.

h. *attitudes toward diversity*, then construct and administer to all students a survey measuring attitudes toward diversity, comparing the results from students in cooperatively taught classrooms with those of similar students in one-teacher/ traditionally taught classrooms.

II. If You Are Interested in System Changes in . . .

a. *referral rates for special education and other support services programs*, then compare the numbers of referrals generated by educators who are participating in cooperative teaching with the number of referrals generated by educators who are not participating.

b. *placement rates in pull-out programs*, then compare the number of placements of students from classrooms participating in cooperative teaching with the number of placements of similar students from one-teacher/traditionally taught classrooms.

c. *amount of time students with disabilities are integrated with students without disabilities*, then review Individualized Education Plans and other data to determine the amount of time students with disabilities who are in cooperatively taught classrooms are participating in general education versus similar data from similar students who are in one-teacher/traditionally taught classrooms.

d. *suspension and expulsion rates*, then compare data from students in cooperatively taught classrooms with data from similar students in one-teacher/ traditionally taught classrooms.

III. If You Are Interested in Educator Changes in . . .

a. *attitudes toward student diversity*, then construct and administer to all school professionals an informal survey measuring attitudes toward student diversity, comparing results from educators participating in cooperative teaching to those from educators not participating.

b. *teaching behaviors*, then identify a list of specific characteristics sought (e.g., time spent in direct teaching, time spent in individualized instruction, number of explanations given), measure those behaviors in educators participating and educators not participating in cooperative teaching, and compare.

c. *collegiality*, then identify behaviors associated with collegiality (e.g., time spent in professional discussions, materials loaned and shared), measure those behaviors in educators participating and educators not participating in cooperative teaching, and compare.

d. *job satisfaction*, then construct and administer to all school professionals an informal survey measuring overall job satisfaction, comparing results from educators participating in cooperative teaching to those from educators not participating. Alternatively, compare resignation and transfer rates of educators participating in cooperative teaching to those of educators not participating.

e. ***stress***, then administer to all school professionals a stress survey, comparing results from educators participating in cooperative teaching to those from educators not participating.

IV. If You Are Interested in Parent Changes in . . .

a. ***attitudes toward the school***, then construct and administer to a sample of parents an "attitudes toward our school" survey, comparing results from parents of children in cooperatively taught classrooms to those from parents of children in traditionally taught classrooms.

b. ***responsiveness***, then compare the ratio of parent responses to educator communications in classrooms that are cooperatively taught to that in one-teacher/traditionally taught classrooms.

c. ***overall parental involvement***, then compare the frequency of behaviors such as attendance at parent–teacher meetings, participation in parent–teacher organizations, and classroom volunteering of parents of students in cooperatively taught classrooms to parents of students in one-teacher/traditionally taught classrooms.

Using the above format as a model, you should develop a similar "if–then" guide to use in evaluating the specific processes you employ in your cooperative teaching and the desired outcomes of those processes. To do this, you should first:

a. determine exactly what specific outcomes of cooperative teaching are most significant, important, or desirable in your program;

b. determine exactly what fundamental processes make up your individual cooperative teaching effort (e.g., identify cooperative teaching partner, develop schedules, decide on the frequency and duration of meetings, describe nature of interactions over time, and determine specific nature of cooperative teaching arrangement); and

c. determine the most desirable or useful nature of the evaluation of each of these individual processes and outcomes (i.e., objective data, subjective data, or both).

References

Adams, G. R., & Schvaneveldt, J. S. (1985). *Understanding research methods.* New York: Longman.

Blum, R., & Corbett, D. (1993). Thinking backwards to move forward. *Phi Delta Kappan, 74,* 690–694.

McLaughlin, J. A., & McLaughlin, V. L. (1993). Program evaluation. In B. Billingsley (Ed.), *Program leadership for serving students with disabilities* (pp. 343–370). Richmond: Virginia Department of Education.

6

Moving In
Resolving Issues
in Cooperative Teaching

"Trust is the result of risk successfully survived."
—Jack Gibb

After the finished remodeling project is inspected and approved, home owners eagerly move back into their remodeled residence, anticipating the great advantages the renovated structure will now provide. However, it usually takes some time before the home owners are completely comfortable with their new surroundings. The revised physical arrangements of the home are likely to disrupt previous routines and ways of doing things and may actually lead to unanticipated problems. In short, some period of adjustment is necessary before the new structure truly feels like home again.

Similarly, educators have lived in a schoolhouse that has remained fundamentally unchanged for much of this century. The basic architectural arrangement of the schoolhouse has been one educator in one classroom with near-total responsibility for one group of students, either for an entire day (at the elementary level) or for one class period (at the secondary level). At the same time, various groups of students with special needs were removed, with educational responsibility for these students parceled out to various specialists (e.g., ESL educators, special educators, remedial reading teachers). The places to which these students were sent (often literally the basement of the school, or portable classrooms outside the main schoolhouse) sent an additional message about the perceived significance of these students in the overall functioning of the school.

Remodeling the schoolhouse using the blueprints of cooperative teaching results in a substantially changed teaching environment, one fundamentally quite different from the one that educators have become so accustomed to over the decades. In developing and implementing cooperative teaching, school personnel are dramatically redefining themselves and their professional roles, especially in the area of interpersonal relationships.

Historically, teaching has been a profession characterized by great isolation from colleagues (and in fact from all other adults). It is not unusual for many educators to see colleagues only briefly before the start of school, again briefly during a (too-short!) lunch break, and again briefly after school. This is in stark contrast to almost all other occupations, which require coworkers to cooperate with colleagues actively and intensively as integrated teams to complete work projects.

As educators move into cooperative teaching, they will be moving into a work environment radically different from the one to which they have become accustomed. New social demands, and issues such as "turf" and trust, are emerging to become critical for educators embracing cooperative teaching. Perhaps the best way to understand these changes is to see them in terms of a paradigm shift.

Paradigms and Paradigm Shifts

Futurist and educator Joel Barker began talking about paradigms and paradigm shifts almost 20 years ago as a way to understand the

behavior of people as they encounter inevitable changes in their worlds (Barker, 1992). A paradigm is the way in which individuals perceive and understand their surroundings. It is the set of written and (especially) unwritten rules and regulations that establish the widely understood boundaries and behavioral expectations of one's world. The paradigm that is dominant at any certain time is so fundamental, so established, so taken for granted that it is like the air: unquestioned and usually unrecognized.

From time to time powerful changes develop in the fundamental beliefs that a society holds, and in the ways a society thinks and acts. Barker referred to these changes as paradigm shifts. It is critical that these paradigm shifts be recognized early in their development, as they represent changes in the rules and fundamental ways in which a society operates.

Any given paradigm is maintained because it is useful at solving some set of problems. In the initial stages of a paradigm its effectiveness often is limited, as many individuals continue to cling to comfortable (though increasingly inappropriate) old ways of thinking and responding. As the new paradigm becomes more well-established and more clearly understood, its problem-solving capabilities increase rapidly. While it does not (and likely cannot) resolve all problems, the new paradigm does so often enough, and with enough success, that the few problems it does not seem to address effectively can be put on the back burner for a while.

At this point the new paradigm becomes widely accepted and appears to be "correct." Even though new alternative paradigms may begin to emerge during this successful period, the very success of the paradigm presently in place keeps new ones from becoming well-accepted for some period of time. However, as time goes on seemingly intractable problems remain or emerge, problems that the old paradigm seems to find impossible to resolve effectively. It is at this point that the new paradigm (or the remodeling of the present structure) begins to emerge, become accepted, and ultimately evolve into the widely accepted paradigm for its time.

A paradigm shift in American society that occurred during the mid-20th century with enormous implications was that from racial segregation to integration, a shift that is still evolving. A similar shift toward inclusion of increasingly diverse groups of students in the mainstream is occurring in public education as well.

The present paradigm of public education, a paradigm that in most places has existed at least since the establishment of compulsory education in the early 1900s, has a number of well-established rules and boundaries. These include the following.

- One educator works with, and has responsibility for, only one specified group of students.

- Educators work alone, not together, as they teach.

- As educators work in isolation, they are responsible for (especially at the secondary level) and teach in primarily one discipline.

- An educator works with any group of students for only one year.

- There are at least two clearly discernible and distinct groups of students: typical students and students with special needs.

- These two distinct groups of students have entirely different needs in terms of curriculum and instructional techniques.

- Only educational specialists have the skills that students with special needs require; thus, general educators are not appropriate educators for these students.

- Educational specialists have little to offer typical students.

Initially when most countries instituted compulsory education in the early part of the 20th century, usually only average to above-average students were admitted to or stayed in school. At that time the schools' organizational structures were based largely on the then-new assembly-line approach to factory production. Thus, students who evidenced significant learning or behavior differences were excluded routinely from participation in public school programs, much as factories would discard raw production materials that fell below some preestablished standard.

In most places exclusion of these students (to varying degrees) was the paradigm that dominated educational thought and practice through the 1970s. However, the switch to a paradigm emphasizing inclusion is rapidly emerging, both in the society at large as well as in the public schools, which mirror that larger society.

For example, through the 1940s and 1950s there was great debate over the question of whether students with disabilities should even be in the public schools. Similar debate occurred in the early 1970s concerning students with severe disabilities. When both groups of students initially were admitted into the public schools, often it was only to separate segregated schools for students with special needs. With the advent of legislation in the mid-1970s mandating that students with disabilities be educated in the least restrictive environment, many public schools instituted separate classes in the schools for these students, maintaining functional segregation and exclusion.

Through the 1980s, students with special needs began to be placed into general education classes for much (though rarely all) of the school day. As this occurred, it became more and more obvious that the existing general education paradigm (which included such rules as "educators work by themselves" and "educators lecture to large groups of passive students") was *not* the most effective for the increasingly diverse student needs found in contemporary classrooms.

Students in general education classrooms were no longer all of average and above-average ability, as they had been for much of this century. Instead, student populations represented much greater linguistic, ethnic, cultural, learning, and behavioral diversity. The schools were becoming significantly more heterogeneous, as was the greater society. Educators increasingly were encountering problems that were unresponsive to solutions based in the old educational paradigm. A new paradigm that could respond to these new problems was required. The emergence and widespread acceptance of cooperative teaching is one particularly significant indicator of this new emerging paradigm.

Role Changes

As Sarason and his colleagues noted in 1966, teaching is a lonely profession. Rarely do educators have the opportunity to discuss problems or successes with colleagues (Sarason, Levine, Goldenberg, Cherlin, & Bennet, 1966). Similarly, Rudduck (1991) noted that education is among the last vocations where it is still acceptable to work alone. Based in the old educational paradigm, professional and social isolation historically has characterized the professional experience of most educators.

This old paradigm led automatically to a number of consequences. The professional isolation of educators made it difficult for them to share new ideas and better solutions, inhibited the recognition of success, and permitted incompetence to exist and persist to the detriment of both students and educators (Fullan & Hargreaves, 1991). It also allowed (if not produced) conservatism and resistance to innovation in teaching (Lortie, 1975).

An especially significant consequence of this isolation is the near total absence of feedback concerning one's performance. While most school personnel receive pro forma evaluations, these occur infrequently and typically contain little of substance that can actually be used to improve skills. In a recent study of schools, Rosenholtz (1989) concluded that the typical pattern of educator isolation and uncertainty results in educational settings in which learning potential is diminished. The combination of isolation, uncertainty, and individualism contributes to, and helps to sustain, educational conservatism, since educators have little access to new ideas and the opportunities associated with them. School personnel then naturally return to their familiar, safe practices, which do little to respond to rapidly changing student needs (Fullan & Hargreaves, 1991).

This professional seclusion is so engrained in the old educational paradigm that many educators are unable to imagine, and have never actually considered, any working arrangement other than teaching alone. The physical architecture of many schools contributes to this problem, with educator isolation further exacerbated when they work in portable classrooms or other separate locations. This often has been the case with programs targeting students with special needs (e.g., special education, bilingual education).

The emerging educational paradigm, one in which educators work not in isolation but together, has significant and fundamental implications for redefining the very nature of their work. As Barker (1992) noted, when a paradigm shifts, all concerned go back to zero. In other words, no matter how skilled an educator was at doing his or her job under the old paradigm, under the new paradigm all participants essentially are back at the starting line.

To understand this more clearly, one need only imagine manufacturers of horse-drawn wagons and coaches at the turn of the century, as the transportation paradigm was just beginning to shift. Two possible options for carriage manufacturers at that time were to (a) concentrate on making bigger, stronger, and more deluxe horse-drawn carriages; or (b) acquire the skills and machinery necessary to survive in the emerging "horseless carriage" paradigm. The futures inherent in each of these options are clear in hindsight. Regardless of their skill in producing the very finest horse-drawn carriages, those companies that failed to perceive and adapt to the new paradigm perished.

Similarly, in the schools it may well be that the old paradigm (in which educators worked in isolation) was effective for the educational tasks of the time. However, school personnel cannot ignore the reality that the old educational paradigm is increasingly ineffective at meeting the increasingly diverse needs of the present-day student population, as well as the needs society will have of these young citizens tomorrow. As the old educational paradigm falls, in the future educators will be asked to work in the way almost all workers do throughout society: cooperatively.

Under any new paradigm, one's past record of achievements becomes less important, much as one's skills in manufacturing horse-drawn carriages became essentially irrelevant in the 20th century. Instead, what is likely to be more important is how well one can adapt to, and professionally thrive under, the new educational paradigm of cooperative teaching. This has great implications for all school personnel.

Under the old paradigm, most educators participated only in one-way interactions, giving help to (typically) passive students. In

cooperative teaching the daily professional interactions of school personnel will be expanded from one-way interactions with students to include more symmetrical and balanced ongoing two-way interactions with other professionals. In the new educational paradigm based on educators working together in a collegial fashion, each will be help receivers as well as help givers. In addition to the traditional role of giving help to others, educators now will be actively receiving substantial amounts of assistance from their partners in cooperative teaching.

Interpersonal Skills

After a recent home remodeling project, one of the authors found that a previously frequently used path to a door was blocked and less convenient, and that a new route had to be learned. While seemingly inconsequential, it nevertheless was several months before this behavioral adjustment became second nature. For most educators, the single most significant change involved in remodeling the schoolhouse using cooperative teaching blueprints is the new professional relationships they must develop with their teaching partners. This change may well represent the single greatest challenge in implementing cooperative teaching and pose the greatest difficulty for educators accustomed to working in isolation. It takes work and skill to develop and maintain a harmonious and productive working relationship with another professional, given the complex nature of human interactions.

When in place, effective interpersonal skills allow people to initiate, develop, and maintain productive relationships. Johnson (1990) identified four basic interconnected and overlapping components of interpersonal skills. These are:

1. knowing and trusting each other;

2. communicating with each other accurately and unambiguously;

3. accepting and supporting each other; and

4. resolving conflicts and relationship problems constructively.

Coming to know and trust another person requires that each discloses how he or she feels and thinks. This in turn requires that each knows himself or herself and is aware of personal reactions, so that those reactions can be accurately shared with the other. This process of self-awareness followed by self-disclosure is fundamental for the development of trust over time.

Any social relationship requires at least two individuals. For a symmetrical and balanced relationship each must be open with, and be open to, the other. An individual who is open with another shares personal ideas and feelings, letting the other know who he or she is. One who is open to another must learn who that person is and accept him or her. These processes require self-disclosure.

Self-disclosure is the deliberate revealing of information about oneself that is significant and that normally would not be known by others (Adler & Towne, 1987). It does not (necessarily) mean revealing intimate details of one's past or present life but instead means sharing one's honest reactions to events both are experiencing in their cooperative teaching relationship. Only through mutual self-disclosure can individuals truly get to know one another, a mandatory requirement for effective cooperative teaching. Ongoing, mutual self-disclosures between two individuals help build a similar, shared, and consistent view of their world. While there is potential risk in self-disclosure, as one repeats the process and begins to trust the other, the risk diminishes. In addition, the act of self-disclosure makes it easier for the other also to self-disclose, again enhancing and building the level of mutual trust.

Information that is shared through self-disclosure has two dimensions: breadth and depth (Altman & Taylor, 1973). Breadth refers to the variety of subjects that are discussed. For example, two educators beginning in cooperative teaching are likely to start their relationship by sharing information on such topics as where each went to school, previous jobs, and so forth. As their relationship grows these topics are likely to expand into their lives away from work, hobbies, and similar areas.

While shallow, surface relationships may or may not have great breadth, strong relationships usually are characterized by great depth. Depth of self-disclosure refers to the degree to which the information that is shared is personal and revealing. As trust develops in a cooperative teaching relationship, each member becomes more and more secure and thus more comfortable in sharing information that is potentially sensitive. One way to consider depth of self-disclosure is in four levels: social clichés, factual self-disclosures, opinion-based self-disclosures, and personal feelings (Adler & Towne, 1987).

The first of these, social clichés, are those verbal exchanges people use routinely with each other. Interactions along the lines of "How are you?" "I'm fine; how are you?" and "Oh, I can't complain" illustrate this surface level of interaction. Nothing personal is revealed, and nothing is risked (nor is it possible for much to be gained).

At a somewhat deeper level are self-disclosures based on facts. A statement such as "Math has always been difficult for me. My grades in my college math courses were my lowest," while factually based, conveys a deeper level of self-disclosure.

The sharing of opinions operates at a still deeper and more intimate level than do fact-based self-disclosures. In sharing one's opinions one is more clearly revealing exactly who one is, while simultaneously exposing oneself to greater risk of a critical or hurtful response from the other. A statement such as "I've never participated in cooperative teaching before" is a factual one. However, saying "I'm not sure that cooperative teaching can work in our school" is a much more revealing level of self-disclosure.

The deepest types of self-disclosure are those describing one's personal feelings. One partner in a cooperative teaching relationship might say to another, "When you say you'll finish a task and you don't, I feel angry and taken advantage of." This level of self-disclosure is quite intimate, because revealing one's feelings to another opens one up to criticism at a most vulnerable level. However, when accomplished in a mutual atmosphere of trust, it also provides each participant with an additional sense of togetherness.

Obviously, no qualitative values should be assigned arbitrarily to these four levels. Each is appropriate in certain circumstances and inappropriate in others. What is important in a relationship such as cooperative teaching is that all participants are able to self-disclose and communicate at all four levels, since such a mutual ability facilitates the most complete, comprehensive, and situationally appropriate exchanges.

The process of self-disclosure is most effective when done at a deliberate and moderate pace, not advancing to deep levels inappropriately early in the relationship. Too rapid self-disclosure can scare another away. Strong relationships usually are built gradually. Conversely, too slow self-disclosure will hinder the necessary development of mutual trust. Essentially the pace of advancement along this continuum of depth of self-disclosure depends on the level of mutual comfort with each other that is being established.

Self-disclosure requires that one be self-aware. There are a number of ways to develop this self-awareness. Much as educators learn to watch students in order to determine who they are, they also can learn to watch themselves objectively, taking note of their own behaviors to learn more about themselves. Using other school professionals as benchmarks or comparison points in these observations, especially those who are similar in key ways, also helps to enhance self-awareness.

In self-disclosure one describes one's feelings and reactions. In doing so one typically finds that these thoughts and feelings become clearer and easier to understand. In addition, as one self-discloses, the reactions of others to those disclosures help one become more aware of the nature of one's beliefs and actions. This effect can be enhanced by soliciting feedback concerning one's self-disclosures.

Trust

In a 1989 study of team effectiveness, Larson and LaFasto found that teams are most productive when the surrounding atmosphere is one of trust. They identified several reasons that explain why trust is necessary for teams to function well together.

First, when team members trust each other, they can stay problem focused and goal oriented, rather than concentrating on guarding and protecting themselves. In the absence of trust, personal agendas come to the forefront, and considerable energies are expended in developing and protecting against personal attacks.

Second, an atmosphere of trust yields a more efficient use of time. Individuals can speak frankly and directly, without others trying to determine "what he's *really* saying."

Finally, when team members trust each other, each feels comfortable in proposing answers or solutions that may be risky. Each is willing to propose possibilities that have some chance of failure. Participants feel comfortable in self-disclosing and will contribute ideas and suggestions freely, without worrying about potentially hurtful personal criticism. In social interactions characterized by mistrust, people tend not to propose answers, or to propose only those that are conservative and safe. This self-censoring results in many potentially valuable contributions never emerging.

Self-disclosure in the absence of trust is risky. If one does not trust the person to whom self-disclosure is being made, one may anticipate rejection and ridicule. In general, self-disclosing to another can result in either harmful consequences or beneficial ones. Trust exists when one anticipates that the other will respond in a way that produces beneficial consequences.

Mutual trust builds as two individuals increasingly self-disclose to each other, receiving acceptance and support in return. Trust grows as each participant learns that (a) no criticism will follow any self-disclosure and (b) all concerned will guard the self-disclosures made in that context and not gossip or share those self-disclosures with others. Expressions of warmth, accurate understanding, and cooperative intentions all serve to increase trust in a relationship, even when the involved parties have unresolved conflicts.

More specifically, trust among two or more individuals builds as a result of involvement and autonomy (Larson & LaFasto, 1989). In cooperative teaching, both participants must feel involved from the very early planning stages. Together the educators plan a strategy for implementing their cooperative teaching, jointly determining their roles and responsibilities.

With an overall goal for the cooperative teaching established, the involved partners then must perceive autonomy in their venture. That is, they must feel that the program is theirs and that they are in charge. Such a sense of professional autonomy for decisions that traditionally have been made by school administrators will facilitate a sense of mutual trust between the cooperative teaching partners, yielding the most productive end results.

Trust can be lost or destroyed in several ways. If one's self-disclosures are met with rejection, ridicule, criticism, or nonacceptance, any trust that has been built up to that point will be damaged. In addition, to develop mutual trust, both participants must self-disclose. If the degree to which the two are willing to self-disclose is significantly unbalanced, the person who is more often self-disclosing may begin to feel overexposed and vulnerable.

To a large extent trust functions as a self-fulfilling prophecy. If one enters into a relationship expecting rejection, one's behaviors are

likely to be suspicious and guarded, the opposite of behaviors conducive to the development of mutual trust. In such a situation the other is indeed likely to be wary of or even reject the suspicious individual, thus confirming his or her initial negative expectations. However, if one enters into a relationship anticipating that the other will be warm and worthy of trust, and expresses support and acceptance of the other, it is likely that he or she will receive such support in return.

Turf

In many major urban centers, ongoing violence associated with youth gangs often revolves around the issue of "turf." Often a gang will identify a section of the city as its own, mark that section with identifying symbols, and defend that turf from other gangs, using violent retaliation against intruders and outsiders. While this is perhaps an extreme example, the tendency to identify physical or social space as one's own and to feel uncomfortable when others invade that personal space is a very human one.

This is no less true for school personnel than for anyone else. In moving into cooperative teaching, one of the more difficult adjustments educators must make is the inherent shift from professional autonomy to professional sharing. After having had sole responsibility for, control over, and personal and professional privacy within one classroom or with one group of students, educators now are being asked to move into a psychologically very different climate, one in which another adult is present. Having a colleague move onto one's turf is often unsettling, even for the best-intentioned educator.

There are a number of "turfs" where partners in cooperative teaching must learn to cohabit. The first of these is the actual physical environment that the two will now share. Most educators have come to see the actual classroom environs as their own and have taken pains to decorate and personalize their space. Many will actually confess to a bit of discomfort when another school professional is in that space for any length of time.

It has been speculated that the reason many educators resist other adults in their classrooms is that the only time most educators have had visitors for any length of time was when they were being evaluated, an intimidating (and even humiliating) experience for most (Fullan & Hargreaves, 1991). Going back even to student teaching, the presence of another professional in the room usually has meant that the educator was being scrutinized and evaluated. Given the

stress inherent in most evaluative situations, it is not surprising that most educators become uncomfortable when another school professional is in the room, especially for more than a few moments. This likely is part of the reason why many educational innovations that include some sort of teaming component find widespread acceptance difficult to achieve quickly.

In addition to the actual physical space, a second type of turf that must be shared is that of educational materials. Over the years the typical educator assembles a set of customized curricular materials, much of it often purchased not with school funds but with the educator's personal monies. This ownership (literally as well as figuratively) may have been appropriate under the old paradigm of the solitary and autonomous educator. However, in cooperative teaching these materials must be collectively held. Yielding sole control and ownership of some set of materials laboriously compiled and assembled over the years is difficult.

An especially significant challenge for many educators beginning cooperative teaching is moving from the traditional dichotomous identification of students as either "mine" or "yours." One of the authors recently conducted a follow-up training workshop for educators who had been involved in cooperative teaching for a complete academic year. The participants were enthusiastic about the results of their work and were eagerly awaiting the next year. One of a pair of cooperative teaching partners had been a general education fourth-grade teacher, while the other previously had been a special educator working with students who had mild disabilities. While the two educators spoke of "our" classroom, "our" curriculum, "our" materials, and "our" program, it was nonetheless discouraging to hear the former special educator go on to say, "But on the statewide academic competency testing, her kids did better than mine." This educator had adopted almost all aspects of the philosophy of shared ownership and responsibility inherent in cooperative teaching. However, it was obvious that, when it came to students with disabilities, she still clearly saw those students as hers, with educational responsibility for those students falling primarily on her and not jointly with her cooperative teaching partner.

Given the natural tendency to look for solutions that are easiest to implement, when two educators move into cooperative teaching they frequently decide to establish joint residency in the previous classroom (typically the larger one) of one or the other. While such a decision initially appears to be reasonable and logical, what follows naturally evolves from the fundamental fact that one educator is at home while the other is a visitor. Though this is covert and often not even recognized (much less stated), it nonetheless can have a significant and detrimental impact on the desired goal of shared educational ownership and responsibility.

To avoid this problem, if possible it is best for the two new cooperative teaching partners to move into a new room, one in which neither previously has worked. This new physical environment provides an atmosphere more suitable for the fresh beginning the educators seek in their professional work, while simultaneously avoiding even the subconscious suggestion that either is a visitor. The two partners move in together and jointly develop the sense that the new environment belongs to both.

If this is not possible, the next best solution is to dramatically rearrange the physical environment of the room. Both educators should substantially rearrange (or even exchange) furniture, work together on room decorations, and so forth. This way the room becomes less clearly identified as belonging to the previous tenant and instead comes to be seen as shared space. What is sought is a sense of shared ownership, of the room being not "yours" or "mine" but "ours."

In fact, a clear indicator of the success (or failure) of the partners in cooperative teaching in overcoming these obvious and not-so-obvious issues of turf is their use of language as they gain experience working in this venture. The increasingly frequent use of such shared language as "we" and "our," instead of such traditionally autonomous language as "I" and "mine," suggests that the cooperative teaching partners have internalized the shared ownership and responsibilities inherent in cooperative teaching.

Flexibility

As educators begin moving into cooperative teaching, a consistent theme that emerges as their relationship develops is the tremendous need for mutual flexibility. Professional and personal flexibility is absolutely essential as school personnel continue to evolve in ways consistent with the newly emerging educational paradigm of shared responsibilities. No matter how extensively, comprehensively, or thoroughly one plans ahead, it is simply not possible to anticipate and plan for the nearly infinite variety of problems that are encountered once new arrangements are implemented.

For example, any home remodeler can tell stories of plans going astray when pipes or wiring were not where they were expected to be, when walls could not be moved because of unexpected circumstances, when required materials became unavailable or prohibitively expensive, and so forth. Knowing that such unexpected developments are virtual certainties in any remodeling project makes their inevitable appearance less stressful and disturbing.

Many problems encountered by educators implementing cooperative teaching are not responsive to familiar or straightforward solutions. In the absence of professional flexibility of both cooperative teaching partners, these problems may continue to present eventually insurmountable obstacles.

As referred to here, flexibility includes substantial tolerance for ambiguity. Flexible school professionals are able to receive much conflicting information without forcing premature closure on the situation. Educators who are flexible are able to look at problems from

many different sides and are comfortable moving from one perspective to another. They can drop previous ways of thinking about things and adopt new ones easily.

In addition, school personnel who are flexible and adapt to changing situations typically experience less stress in their professional lives than others. The ability to respond easily and smoothly to changing situations without worrying endlessly over them helps any educator easily roll with the day-to-day surprises that inevitably emerge in school programs.

Conclusions

The home owners have now moved into their remodeled house and gradually are becoming comfortable with the changes resulting from the remodeling. However, it is not unusual to find that the previous arrangements of the furniture and other furnishings no longer work as well in the newly remodeled structure as they did in the old. Either the old furniture and furnishings must be rearranged in a new way to better fit the newly remodeled area, or new furnishings must be obtained. The next chapter explores how educators moving into cooperative teaching must similarly examine their social arrangements, shifting and rearranging them as necessary to maximize their professional effectiveness in their newly remodeled schoolhouse.

Chapter 6 Activity
Assessing Flexibility

As noted in this chapter, flexibility is key to successful implementation of cooperative teaching. A helpful starting point is to have some idea of how flexible one is before trying to blend with a partner in cooperative teaching.

Raudsepp (1990) developed a self-survey of one's overall flexibility that has been adapted here to allow an educator to determine his or her own level of educational flexibility. While the adapted survey has not been empirically validated, many educators nonetheless have found it a useful and enjoyable exercise in personal analysis. For maximum benefit, it is useful to first estimate one's own perceived level of flexibility, from very flexible to very rigid.

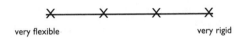

very flexible   very rigid

Following this initial self-estimate, completing the following exercise can yield enhanced insights into one's own personal flexibility.

Instructions

For each item record:

> A for *Almost Always*
> B for *Sometimes*
> C for *Rarely*
> D for *Never*

Perhaps needless to say, these answers should reflect one's own personal reality, not the way one wishes one were. The accuracy of one's self-awareness is an important first step in developing a productive and fulfilling relationship in cooperative teaching.

_____ 1. It is important for me to have a specific place for everything.
_____ 2. I make strong demands upon myself.
_____ 3. I feel very uncomfortable when I have to break an appointment.
_____ 4. When leaving home or work I find I have to check and recheck doors, lights, windows, the desk, and so on.
_____ 5. It bothers me when people do not put things back exactly as I left them.
_____ 6. I do not like to stray very much from my planned and scheduled activities.
_____ 7. I get upset if things do not go as planned.

_____ 8. After completing a task, I have doubts about whether I did it right.

_____ 9. I do certain things over and over again even though I know it is pointless to do them.

_____ 10. I don't dwell on my problems too long.

_____ 11. I worry about a lot of things.

_____ 12. I react quickly to unexpected situations.

_____ 13. I am meticulous with most of my possessions.

_____ 14. I strive for perfection in what I do.

_____ 15. I don't care if people laugh at my ideas.

_____ 16. I feel I miss out on a lot of opportunities because I don't act quickly enough.

_____ 17. I find time to relax and simply do nothing.

_____ 18. I move, walk, and eat rapidly because I don't like wasting time.

_____ 19. I go back and forth searching for the right decision.

_____ 20. I'm very punctual.

_____ 21. Stress makes me disorganized.

_____ 22. I like to make detailed lists of my daily tasks and activities.

For the remaining questions simply score A for *Agree* and B for *Disagree*.

_____ 23. I often feel anxious or apprehensive even though I don't know what has caused the worry.

_____ 24. I frequently get rattled or annoyed at others for not keeping on schedule with plans we've made.

_____ 25. I seldom act without critically thinking.

_____ 26. I sometimes get a kick out of breaking the rules and doing things I'm not supposed to do.

_____ 27. I tend to dwell on things I did but shouldn't have done.

_____ 28. I'm frequently tense or nervous.

_____ 29. There is frequently a discrepancy between the way I want to behave and the way I actually behave.

_____ 30. My work tends to pile up so much that I have difficulty completing it.

Scoring

After all answers are recorded, they should be scored according to the following key:

1.	A=5	B=3	C=2	D=1
2.	A=6	B=4	C=2	D=1
3.	A=4	B=3	C=2	D=1
4.	A=6	B=4	C=2	D=1

5.	A=6	B=4	C=2	D=1
6.	A=7	B=4	C=2	D=1
7.	A=7	B=4	C=2	D=1
8.	A=5	B=3	C=2	D=1
9.	A=5	B=3	C=2	D=1
10.	A=1	B=2	C=4	D=6
11.	A=7	B=5	C=2	D=1
12.	A=1	B=2	C=4	D=6
13.	A=6	B=3	C=2	D=1
14.	A=7	B=4	C=2	D=1
15.	A=1	B=2	C=4	D=7
16.	A=6	B=3	C=2	D=1
17.	A=1	B=2	C=4	D=7
18.	A=7	B=4	C=2	D=1
19.	A=7	B=4	C=2	D=1
20.	A=6	B=3	C=2	D=1
21.	A=7	B=4	C=2	D=1
22.	A=5	B=3	C=2	D=1
23.	A=6	B=1		
24.	A=5	B=1		
25.	A=6	B=1		
26.	A=1	B=6		
27.	A=7	B=1		
28.	A=6	B=1		
29.	A=6	B=1		
30.	A=6	B=1		

Total score _____

The total score should be recorded on the following continuum.

Actual score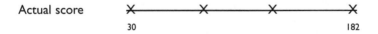

30   182

Now compare the previous pretest estimate of flexibility to the actual score obtained after completing the self-survey.

Interpretation

Scores from 30 to 52 suggest very high levels of flexibility, making adapting to new situations relatively easy. Scores from 53 to 84 indicate some inflexibility. Scores from 85 to 132 suggest a significant degree of inflexibility, which is likely to cause problems from time to time as new situations are faced. Too much attention to insignificant details may hamper success. Scores from 133 to 182 indicate very high degrees of inflexibility. This often is accompanied by feelings of nervousness that "things aren't right" because not every *i* is dotted and *t* crossed. Unless they take steps to become more flexible, school personnel with scores at this level are unlikely to be able to deal effectively with rapid and substantial change, such as cooperative teaching.

Implications

Many educators are surprised to find scores suggesting that they are less flexible than they may have anticipated. Such findings can serve to guide further thinking, planning, and mutual growth as partners in cooperative teaching begin working together.

Educators whose scores suggest a high degree of inflexibility can take deliberate steps to loosen up and become less rigid and more flexible. The primary vehicle for this is to take more risks.

Such activities as speaking out early on a controversial school issue, changing one's routines, and going out of one's way to interact with people normally not encountered all serve to "shake things up" and allow one to achieve a fresh perspective. By changing daily routines and moving into unfamiliar ground one can become more comfortable with change in general. In doing so, educators will become better prepared to benefit and grow from the inevitable innovation and change in the schools.

In addition, many cooperative teaching partners have found it useful to share their flexibility ratings with each other, specifically noting and commenting on areas of special flexibility as well as on areas of rigidity each may have identified in this exercise.

References

Adler, R. B., & Towne, N. (1987). *Looking out/looking in.* New York: CBS Publishing.

Altman, I., & Taylor, D. A. (1973). *Social penetration: The development of interpersonal relationships.* New York: Holt, Rinehart & Winston.

Barker, J. A. (1992). *Future edge: Discovering the new paradigms of success.* New York: William Morrow.

Fullan, M., & Hargreaves, A. (1991). *What's worth fighting for? Working together for your school.* Andover, MA: The Regional Laboratory of Educational Improvement of the Northeast and Islands.

Johnson, D. W. (1990). *Reaching out: Interpersonal effectiveness and self-actualization* (4th ed.). Englewood Cliffs, NJ: Prentice-Hall.

Larson, C. E., & LaFasto, F. M. (1989). *Team work: What must go right/what can go wrong.* Newberry Park, CA: Sage.

Lortie, D. (1975). *School teacher: A sociological study.* Chicago: University of Chicago Press.

Raudsepp, E. (1990). Are you flexible enough to succeed? *Working Woman, 15*(10), 106–107.

Rosenholtz, S. (1989). *Teachers' workplace: The social organization of schools.* New York: Longman.

Rudduck, J. (1991). *Innovation and change.* Bristol, PA: Open University Press.

Sarason, S., Levine, M., Goldenberg, I. I., Cherlin, D., & Bennet, E. (1966). *Psychology in community settings: Clinical, educational, vocational, and social aspects.* New York: Wiley.

....

7

Rearranging the Furniture
Adjusting to Cooperative Teaching

....

"Change is inevitable; pain is optional."
—Anonymous

The completion of almost every home remodeling project is followed by a period of change and adaptation. Various placements and combinations of the furniture, paintings, wall hangings, and plants must be tried out before the right fit is achieved. In addition, the home owners may become alarmed in noticing that there are gaps at the base of a wall that the molding does not completely hide, that one corner of a room has an unpainted spot, that a door does not swing freely, and so forth.

The appearance of these things typically causes great distress in the home owners. However, the reality is that, given the magnitude and complexity of any substantial remodeling or rebuilding project, such developments must be expected. Indeed, it would be rare not to find any problems after a large remodeling job is completed. However, to avoid the feeling that "Everything is wrong!," it is useful to anticipate the presence of these things beforehand. Then, when problems do make their inevitable appearances, the home owners are psychologically prepared to plan and take corrective actions.

Educators now are moving into schoolhouses that are fundamentally different, having been remodeled following a set of cooperative teaching blueprints. As they do so, the educators also will encounter inevitable discrepancies between the ideal situations people naturally anticipate when they plan a remodeling project and the real world, which will contain the educational equivalents of unpainted walls and gaps that the molding fails to cover.

After living in the newly remodeled schoolhouse for a period, school professionals must expect to spend some time doing the educational equivalent of moving furniture around in order to fine tune their new structure. The significance of the changes that will be necessary following a rebuilding project of this magnitude should not be underestimated. Educators must realize beforehand that a variety of adaptations will be required before the new arrangements in the schoolhouse feel natural. One way educators can better prepare for this adaptive process is to go into it with a basic understanding of the nature of change.

Change

In a substantial analysis of change in the public schools, Fullan (1993) identified a number of lessons that have been learned as school systems have encountered change in a variety of forms over the last 50 years. Several of these, along with other findings from studies of change, have direct implications for school professionals as they move into cooperative teaching. Two of these lessons are that problems are friends and that it is important to stay connected with the wider environment.

Problems are Friends

At first glance this statement seems illogical. Most people seek to avoid problems. However, the reality is that avoidance of problems is usually ultimately unsuccessful. Problems emerge and continue regardless of whether people acknowledge them or not. More often, when ignored, these problems stay (and even grow) until a solution or effective response finally is developed, implemented, and evaluated. Unfortunately, educators frequently will respond to problems resulting from change by pulling out of the new approach and retreating to the apparent security of the old ways.

In comparing successful and unsuccessful schools, Louis and Miles (1990) found a primary difference in how these two groups of schools responded to problems. The least successful schools simply continued on in the usual ways, ignoring the increasing significance of the problem.

Problems are friends in that it is only through them that solutions can be found. Problems inherently hold the key to their own solutions; they contain within themselves the seeds to the answers. To identify these answers one must first become absolutely familiar with a problem, including all its components, before developing effective and comprehensive solutions. It is only by becoming intimate with the problem that educators can find solutions. The key is for the educators to persevere through this uncomfortable learning phase.

As educators begin to work together through cooperative teaching, problems are inevitable. In fact, a total absence of problems would suggest that any change implemented is superficial and trivial. When a problem does emerge (as one will in any substantial change), solutions will be developed only by pulling the problem into discussion and teasing it apart until the educators are close to it and understand it.

Connection with the Wider Environment

A typical response of many home owners when they are dissatisfied with the immediate results of a remodeling project is to seek outside help. They may get ideas for fine-tuning their new arrangements by talking with friends, architects, or interior decorators. In addition, they may check out home design books from the library, pick up the latest copies of *Architectural Digest*, *Better Homes and Gardens*, or *Sunset*, and pore over their colorful pages seeking new ideas and possibilities.

When moving into cooperative teaching, educators will be looking with great intensity at themselves, their students, and their schools as they seek to develop those strategies that will work best for their unique situations. In working together on this, however, they must be aware of and resist the temptation to become so self-centered that they ignore outside sources of input and information.

Nias, Southworth, and Campbell (1992) reported that schools effectively implementing collaborative structures were aware of and responsive to innovations evolving elsewhere in curriculum and instruction. Specifically, these effective schools analyzed developments at schools elsewhere and incorporated those developments so that they became a part of their program. In customizing and assimilating external developments, the schools came to develop ownership of the entire package as an integrated whole.

As educators begin to implement cooperative teaching at their own schools, they must remember that ideas gleaned from other schools, consultants, books, professional workshops, and other sources of staff development can only enrich the good ideas they develop in-house. Effective and successful programs avoid isolationism and instead remain tapped into outside sources of ideas.

Building Working Relationships

As previously noted, perhaps the single most significant change educators will experience as they move from traditional service delivery systems into cooperative teaching is the switch from professional isolation to an evolving identity as a team member. At the risk of oversimplification, as many successful coaches stress to their players, there is no *I* in *TEAM*.

What this means is that many professionals in the school will be asked to develop professional interpersonal skills in working with colleagues, skills that heretofore have been only minimally required for many. While the ability to work with students has always been an obvious necessity for educators, the equivalent ability to work with other adults in the school, or *collegiality*, has not.

Collegiality

The professional frontier of collegiality is a new place for many educators. Some analysts have suggested that collegiality may be the least common type of relationship among educators (e.g., Barth, 1990). Collegiality is not the same as *congeniality*, which simply refers to friendly and cordial relationships. Collegiality has greater substance, depth, and complexity. It implies productive work completed through interpersonal interactions in which all participants contribute. When effectively developed and implemented, it possesses great power. Most people function best when teamed up with at least one other person.

In a way, cooperative teaching can be conceptualized as one concrete and systematic way in which collegiality can be developed effectively in a school. For example, while not referring specifically to cooperative teaching, Barth (1990) suggested that the optimal number of adults working together in a classroom is two. One person alone quickly becomes depleted and exhausted, while more than two spend too much time in meetings trying to achieve consensus. As identified by Little (1981), several characteristics of collegiality are applicable to partners in cooperative teaching.

First, collegial educators talk about their practice. They make a point to discuss what it is they are doing, analyzing both their teaching and their students' learning. These conversations are concrete, direct, and ongoing.

Second, collegial educators observe each other as they work. It is these observations that provide the material for their ongoing discussions about their work. To facilitate the development of collegiality these observations must occur in a noncritical and open manner. To be observed as one is teaching is one of the most threatening experiences in an educator's life, since in most places such episodes typically are followed by evaluation and criticism from a superior. In a collegial relationship, the educator must see that the other's observations are being conducted in an atmosphere of mutual trust and support and that the information that emerges in subsequent discussions will be used to strengthen, not hurt.

Third, collegial educators work together on curriculum and instruction matters. This includes planning, designing, and evaluating both what they present to their students and how they present it. The key here is that the work is the product of a team, not of two discrete and separate individuals.

Finally, collegial educators teach each other what they know. Almost every professional who works in the schools has some unique area of expertise, talent, or skill that other educators at that school (and elsewhere) would profit from learning. Collegial educators specifically set out to share their unique skills with others and to learn from their colleagues that body of knowledge and those skills that will improve their level of professional competence.

When collegiality is implemented correctly in a school, decisions are of better quality and are more completely and effectively implemented. Morale is higher, with adult learning more likely to be sustained. Some evidence even suggests that, in schools characterized by collegiality, student motivation and achievement rise (Barth, 1990).

Conflict

Home owners engage in the tedious and stressful task of home remodeling because they realize the remodeling can effectively address a need or resolve some problem. However, a nearly inevitable side effect is that some unforeseen difficulties will accompany this remodeling.

Any change combines new advantages and new drawbacks, new possibilities and new pitfalls. When educators remodel the schoolhouse with a set of cooperative teaching blueprints, they typically discover a wealth of advantages of working with another professional in the classroom. However, the presence of another educator in the room also brings to that environment a different set of values, beliefs, perceptions, and ideas. The simultaneous presence of two school professionals in the room can lay the groundwork for possible disagreements and conflict that did not and could not occur when there was only one educator in the room.

For example, if an educator's only criterion for implementing cooperative teaching is initial ease in moving into cooperative teaching, then it would be easy to look for another educator with an identical set of beliefs and professional practices. However, such a professionally sterile arrangement does not, and cannot, yield the wealth of professional growth potential that comes through developing working relationships with colleagues with differing practices and perceptions.

Most educators have learned over the decades how to work effectively with administrators or superiors in a top-down approach, following suggestions, directions, and guidelines from "on high." Similarly, most school professionals have learned how to work with aides, volunteers, and other educational assistants, outlining for these individuals work responsibilities and directions. However, in both cases the relationships are essentially hierarchically structured and thus inherently asymmetrical and unbalanced, with one person clearly the boss and the other a subordinate.

In traditional school arrangements each educator was assigned work responsibilities that required little collaboration with other school professionals. Since educators seldom interacted with colleagues, especially on matters of substance, the likelihood of professional conflicts was remote.

Learning to coexist and work on an intensive and extensive basis with a colleague, one who is neither subordinate nor superior but instead is a peer, requires an expanded set of professional skills. Chief among these is the ability to resolve differences so that neither is the loser, that is, the ability to identify, develop, and implement win–win solutions.

The ability to understand and resolve conflict is therefore a relatively new skill required of school professionals. Friend and Cook (1992) summarized definitions of conflict by concluding that conflict generally refers to a situation in which one person (or group) perceives that another person (or group) is interfering with his or her goal attainment. They further identified three types of conflict.

The first of these is conflict between individuals with different goals. For example, if one cooperative teaching partner wants students in the cooperatively taught classroom to work in small groups while the other believes fervently that students must learn to work alone, significant potential for conflict exists. Similarly, at the secondary level one educator may feel responsibility to cover all content in the textbook while his or her partner in cooperative teaching argues that it would be more useful and practical to identify and focus exclusively on a few select concepts. In either of these cases, if one of the participants entirely wins, the other loses.

A second type of conflict is between individuals who have the same goals, but goals that cannot be achieved by both partners. Scheduling problems often are of this sort. For example, two cooperative teaching partners at a high school both may want to take a professional day to attend the same districtwide workshop. However, the school principal has made it clear that only one will be allowed to go. Similarly, an elementary education teacher may want to reserve the time immediately before morning recess for content instruction, while the cooperative teaching partner may want to use that same period for learning strategies instruction.

A third type of conflict, and one that is a bit beyond the scope of this discussion, is internal conflict. It may be that a cooperative teaching partner has spent years pulling together a rich source of materials to use in teaching in the area of science applications. While in cooperative teaching it might be expected that those materials would be shared with one's partner, there may be reservations about simply "giving away" the materials one had worked long and hard to acquire. This internal conflict ultimately can result in external conflicts as one struggles to resolve the problem.

In essence, some degree of conflict is inevitable whenever two or more human beings interact. In the rush to minimize conflict, the potential benefits of conflict should not be overlooked. Conflicts force people to become active, to think. Many significant social developments, including labor unions, civil rights legislation, and even the United States of America, emerged out of conflicts. Thus the task is not necessarily to eliminate conflict, but instead to understand it, minimize its risks, and maximize its benefits (Bolton, 1979).

Obviously, the easiest way to address the problem of conflicts is to structure relationships so that conflicts simply do not emerge. This is probably not possible in realistic day-to-day educational settings which feature high levels of intense interactions among professionals. Thus conflict-resolution strategies are required competencies for partners in cooperative teaching.

Conflict-Resolution Strategies

A typical couple in their remodeled house might be happy with nearly everything, except the unexpected question of where their oversized sofa should now be placed. As they (as well as professionals in the schools) seek to resolve conflicts, there are diverse strategies that may be called into play. Unfortunately, several of these conflict-resolution approaches, although occasionally appropriate, usually will lead to unpleasant or less-than-successful consequences (Bolton, 1979).

Less Effective Approaches to Conflict Resolution

Denial. ("There's no problem with the sofa.") Every individual who has ever been in conflict has at some point sought to resolve the problem by telling himself or herself that there really is no problem, that things are okay. One in essence pretends that everything is all right and deliberately ignores or does not acknowledge the reality of the situation. On rare occasions this strategy may actually work, as sometimes conflicts either do not actually exist or exist for only a very short time and then disappear seemingly on their own. However, more often the denial strategy simply results in conflicts growing larger, more complex, and ultimately more difficult to resolve. When this phenomenon occurs in cooperative teaching, the typical result is that the educators retreat to their previous roles of educational isolation, concluding that cooperative teaching does not work.

Avoidance. ("I'll just watch TV in the other room.") In avoidance people acknowledge that a problem exists but simply do not enter into situations where the conflict is likely to emerge. If two cooperative educators have very different beliefs about appropriate behavior-management strategies for their students during school assemblies, one way to resolve this is for only one of them to be at an assembly at any time. This way the source of the conflict can be completely avoided.

In some cases avoidance may be temporarily appropriate. As Friend and Cook (1992) noted, when conflicts are extremely serious and emotionally laden, avoidance can buy time to allow things to cool down a bit. It also may be a useful strategy to employ when more time is necessary to think through complex issues or, conversely, when the matter is of little consequence.

In general, though, avoidance is ultimately unproductive. Avoidance can seem on the surface to allow many people to go on with their lives despite conflicts. However, what is actually happening is that the involved individuals also are withdrawing from each other, so that ultimately all that is left of their relationship is a hollow shell, with the involved parties both having retreated from further interactions. Avoidance also facilitates the development of denial.

Capitulation. ("Okay, put the darn thing wherever *you* want it.") Since conflicts are inherently unpleasant for most people, some will simply give in whenever there is a conflict. Regardless of how unreasonable or illogical the other's position is, some people will almost automatically go along with whatever it is the other person wants. Capitulation may be appropriate when the issues are of minimal consequence. However, the long-term use of this as a consistent strategy is unproductive.

Individuals who routinely practice capitulation as a conflict-resolution strategy typically avoid eye contact with others and allow themselves to be interrupted frequently in interactions with others who hold different positions. They withhold information or opinions they may have and frequently make apologies. Their indecisiveness and lack of contributions make them unproductive team members.

On the surface capitulation may appear to minimize conflict. However, this result is achieved at the expense of the integrity of the capitulator, who ultimately will come to see that he or she is being devalued in the process. Results consistently achieved through capitulation fail to take advantage of the potential of all involved parties.

Domination. ("I said, the sofa goes against the back wall!") In many ways the opposite of capitulation, domination involves one person simply imposing his or her will upon another. The domineering individual simply generates a solution designed to meet his or her needs and then pushes and pushes the other person, ignoring all protests, until she or he submits or gives in. While domination may allow one to gain a particular result, overall it destroys the relationship between the two individuals.

People who often use domination as a means to settle disputes tend to interrupt and socially subordinate their colleagues. They often have intense if not glaring levels of eye contact, and their physical posture and demeanor is one of invasion and arrogance. They tend to be poor listeners and frequently resort to sarcasm and accusation in order to achieve their ends. In essence their goal is to win at any cost.

There are times when it might be arguable that this domineering approach is defensible. In situations where there are significant ethical issues at stake, the ultimate acceptance of one's position might justify such an approach. When an individual is absolutely, beyond the shadow of a doubt, positively convinced that he or she is right, domination may be the only means to the correct end. Finally, when a decision must be made for which one person will have ultimate responsibility, then that individual may be justified in using this approach.

However, these would be most rare circumstances. A more likely outcome of domination is the development of a two-directional resentment. The person who is being dominated comes to dislike and distrust the dominating partner and usually will withdraw from further interactions, as any individual would seek to escape from a punishing situation. Conversely, the dominator comes to see the other as weak, not to be respected, and ultimately not a true peer. Thus, a relationship in which one party dominates the other sacrifices all advantages that can be gained through cooperative teaching.

Individuals who are being dominated may strike back through sabotage, passive resistance, and emotional distancing. In addition, any agreements reached through domination are unlikely to be actively implemented by the individual who was not allowed to participate fully in the preceding decision-making process.

Both capitulation and domination are win–lose propositions in that for one person to get needs met, the other must sacrifice his or hers. Given the actual outcomes of both, in practical terms both approaches ultimately end up being lose–lose.

Deference to expertise. ("We agreed that we'd do what the decorator said.") In cooperative teaching the two educators bring to their work different sets of skills and areas of expertise. Historically, support services providers have developed particular expertise in areas such as curricular and instructional adaptations and individual behavior-management and learning strategies. General educators have instead developed such skills as large group instruction and management techniques and curricular sequencing.

Thus one approach to resolving conflicts is to defer to the more knowledgeable or comfortable of the two, depending upon the nature of the question. For example, if the question is one of maintaining discipline of the entire class, then the support services provider might defer to the general educator's suggestions, since he or she likely has had greater background and experience in such matters. Conversely, if the management question centers around the behavior of one or two students, the general educator might then defer to a support services provider such as a psychologist or special educator, whose training and professional experience likely has emphasized the applied behavior-analysis procedures most applicable to the management of individual behaviors.

However, this deference model has some problems. Its basic premise may distort to some degree the essential philosophy of cooperative teaching: that the two individuals involved are peers. In addition, as the two learn from each other and gain knowledge from the expanded range of educational experiences both are now involved in, the question of who is the expert and most knowledgeable about any given situation may not be so easy to answer.

Compromise and negotiation. ("Okay, you can put the sofa there, but your guitars and amplifier have to go in the garage.") In negotiating and compromising, people reach agreements by each yielding to some degree on their initial wishes. It is a frequent result of conflict; in fact, most of the world's democratic societies depend heavily on compromises to make it possible for their governments to function. However, a compromise means that neither party actually obtains what it wants. What usually happens is that each party ends up only partially satisfied.

Compromise is usually better than avoidance, capitulation, or domination. It may be appropriate when two individuals who both tend to be competitive or dominating are involved. Often the solution generated through compromise is at least workable, if not the best or first choice of anyone concerned.

While compromise is often a simple solution, it is not terribly powerful, nor does it often result in the best solution. In this situation each party essentially ends up in a partial win–partial win arrangement. Since neither is completely satisfied, conflicts emerging from the same fundamental issues are likely to recur at a later time. What is needed is a truly win–win resolution strategy. One such strategy is collaborative problem solving (Bolton, 1979).

A More Effective Conflict-Resolution Strategy: Collaborative Problem Solving

All of the previously noted approaches to conflict resolution shared a common characteristic. That is, in each approach conflicts were perceived as "me versus you, one winner and one loser" scenarios. The two individuals saw themselves in competition with each other. As such, only one person could and would be satisfied.

The perception of conflicts held by most people is that of situations in which not all involved can have their needs met simultaneously. Thus, for someone to win, someone else must lose. However, this need not be the case. There truly are conflict-resolution strategies that can consistently generate win–win outcomes. When people are able to move away from the perception of conflicts as win–lose scenarios and toward one in which it is understood that all parties *can* have their needs met effectively and completely at the same time, great progress has been made.

Conflicts simply present another way, and another type, of sharing. As is the case with any other situation cooperative teaching partners encounter, by working together and pooling their talents and skills they can generate effective solutions.

The fundamental win–win principle underlying collaborative problem solving is quite different from the previously noted, less effective approaches toward conflict resolution. Collaborative problem solving is also philosophically consistent with cooperative teaching. In cooperative teaching the partners commit to a fundamental professional sharing: a sharing of responsibilities, students, and instruction. As part of this professional sharing, when the inevitable problems and conflicts emerge, they too are shared through a collaborative problem-solving process.

For many people faced with conflicts, the first reaction is simply to immediately try the first possible solution that comes to mind. The tendency to try almost anything in order to be doing at least *something* is a natural and understandable one. However, this tendency usually does not result in the most effective resolutions. This is especially true when engaged in collaborative ventures.

Bolton (1979) offered an especially effective collaborative problem-solving process, a system based on Dewey's (1916) rules of logic in problem solving. The six steps of this simple yet effective process are as follows.

Step 1: *Define the problem in terms of needs, not solutions.* Much of the conflict in conflicts comes about when two individuals propose different solutions to a problem. When these two solutions are incompatible, arguments and animosity develop. What is necessary instead is for each to describe the problem in terms of their primary needs, not in terms of the secondary solutions each developed based on his or her individual (and perhaps idiosyncratic) analysis of the problem.

For example, assume that a general education teacher has several students in need of speech and language therapy. The support services provider (the school's speech therapist) has proposed that she work with each of these students individually on a pull-out basis in the therapy room. However, the teacher is opposed to this proposal, arguing instead that the students should stay in the classroom.

At this point each educator is arguing from a solutions perspective. The teacher's thinking is as follows: "The students lose too much instructional time when they leave the room each day. While the therapy might be useful, it is even more important that they learn the curriculum being presented in my classroom. In addition, they lose the possibility of learning from each other when they are isolated in the therapy room. The solution is for them not to receive the proposed therapy."

The speech therapist's thinking is as follows: "These students each have speech and language problems that are significant and severe enough to warrant intensive therapy. The solution is for me to bring them to my therapy room so that I can provide the intense therapy that is required."

At this point conflict is emerging because each educator is presenting only the solutions each has generated independently. To establish initial perspective, it must be kept in mind that it is only these solutions that are in conflict, not the individuals themselves. Each of their proposed solutions is based on the needs that each perceives. Although each is sharing with the other the solutions generated, the basic needs each professional has that led to the development of those conflicting solutions in the first place have not been shared. The first (and most critical step) in collaborative problem solving is for each person to reflect on the overall situation, sharing with the other not the solutions each has individually generated but instead the needs that the proposed solutions were designed to address.

Thus the teacher might share with the speech therapist the following: "When students leave the room they miss out on important curricular content, group learning activities, and social interactions that are important. I need them to be in the classroom to experience these things."

Similarly, the speech therapist might share her need as follows: "These students all have speech and language problems that require intensive intervention. I need to be able to provide these services to these students."

One effective way to help discover the needs that another has (which led to the solution he or she proposed) is to find out why the other wants the particular solution he or she initially proposed. What is the reason this particular solution is proposed? What advantages does it hold for the individual?

In essence, what is necessary is for the cooperative teaching partners to be able to distinguish between means and ends, that is, between solutions and needs. Once the fundamental *why* underlying each of the proposed solutions is understood by the other, the collaborative problem-solving process can begin in earnest.

Perhaps needless to say, the identification of the underlying needs that led to the particular solutions that are in conflict is often easier said than done. The skill of being able to reach below the surface and analyze one's proposed solution to identify the underlying need is not one that comes naturally to many people. One way to help ensure that that is being done is through reflective communication.

In reflection, one individual explains his or her underlying needs while the other listens attentively. The listener then states back to the first speaker the needs as he or she heard and understood them. The other then either affirms that the needs were understood correctly or reexplains them until they are. A bonus of this reflective communication is that as each hears his or her position as perceived and stated by the other, he or she can gain additional perspectives and understandings. The use of reflecting statements will improve significantly the chances of creating a successful problem-solving venture (Knackendoffel, Robinson, Deshler, & Schumaker, 1992).

One can further enhance the effectiveness of the communication through the use of active listening strategies. By assuming a posture of involvement (e.g., leaning the upper torso slightly toward the other person, shoulders and face directly facing the other) one communicates one's receptiveness to the other. Ample time spent in eye contact also communicates an interest and desire to listen. A too-serious facial expression can inhibit communication, so it is helpful to relax and smile and laugh when appropriate. These nonverbal behaviors all serve to facilitate effective communication (Knackendoffel, Robinson, Deshler, & Schumaker, 1992).

This first step in collaborative problem solving, defining the problem in terms of the fundamental underlying needs rather than the solutions that have been generated to meet those needs, is the most important, and typically the most time-consuming, step in the entire process. However, its value in this process cannot be overstated. Bolton (1979) noted its importance by quoting the old saying, "A problem well-defined is half solved."

Step 2: Brainstorm possible solutions. In brainstorming, problem solvers seek to generate rapidly as many ideas and solutions as possible without initial consideration as to their individual merits and potential. The idea is to create quickly a large and diverse pool of possibilities, which will be more carefully considered and evaluated at a later time.

In the early stages of brainstorming it is important not to slow the rush of ideas by being critical in any way. All proposals and ideas are initially equally acceptable and as such are recorded for later review and discussion regardless of their early apparent feasibility or lack thereof. This approach assures the widest possible beginning pool of ideas that can be further considered and evaluated. Several guidelines will help this process be as productive as possible.

■ *Don't evaluate.* If each idea is criticized as soon as it is proposed, people soon will stop contributing. After all, why should they open themselves up for immediate and repeated criticism? When a group accepts all ideas regardless of how apparently outlandish or unworkable they are, people feel safe in making even the most off-the-wall contributions. Sometimes even the seemingly silliest ideas contain seeds that on further analysis contribute to the final solution. This perspective will help to generate the widest and most diverse pool of possible solutions, which is the purpose of this phase.

■ *Don't explain.* At this point contributors should not clarify or go into detail about their proposals. This slows down the rapid flow of possibilities. During this phase the participants are looking for possible ideas, not fully developed blueprints. Thus, participants should simply toss out a single-phrase or sentence contribution, then another pithy suggestion, and so on, all as rapidly as possible. There will be time for any needed explanations after this early phase is concluded.

Making suggestions without offering clarifying explanations is difficult for many professionals in the schools. Over the years most educators have developed sophisticated skills in explaining ideas to colleagues, parents, and students. This explanatory tendency is difficult to shake off easily. However, for the creative problem-solving process to be most effective, participants must be able to throw out an idea and immediately continue in further creative explorations without feeling compelled to explain or defend each idea the moment it is proposed.

■ *Remove limits.* Participants in brainstorming sessions should understand that there are no constraints whatsoever upon their contributions. As a result, they also should be willing to accept eagerly even the most foolish proposals at face value. This is done for two reasons. First, criticism of anything may well inhibit the subsequent contribution of other, more solid, proposals. Second, even the most apparently foolish proposal may either have a germ of an idea within it or spark someone to think in a different way to come up with a useful contribution.

■ *Prompt.* Someone (perhaps the recorder) should periodically cue the others by saying, "Okay, what else?" or words to that effect. This encouragement solicits still more suggestions while helping the group focus on the task at hand.

■ *Expand on the ideas of others.* Some of the most effective proposals are made by piggybacking on the ideas of others, using the ideas as springboards for other possible solutions.

■ *Record all contributions.* The person serving as recorder should list each person's contribution on a blackboard or large easel, using a few key words to capture the idea so the group can see and use the previously offered ideas for further inspiration. All participants must see that each contribution is group property; that the solution ultimately developed likely will be one created with input and changes suggested by everyone. Thus the ultimate solution will belong to the group, not to any one individual. This process can be helped by *not* listing each contributor's name by his or her contribution, a practice that is counterproductive to the collaborative spirit.

■ *Listen for natural break points.* A common mistake in brainstorming sessions is for someone to say something along the lines of "Okay, let's spend 5 minutes brainstorming this situation." The problem here is that often 5 minutes (or any other arbitrary figure) is too long. Often the ideas that ultimately are most useful are proposed early on. The remainder of any arbitrarily established time limit then results in individuals "burning out," getting off task, or becoming otherwise distracted along unproductive side avenues.

A better guideline is to avoid establishing a predetermined time limit on brainstorming. Instead, the individuals should listen for lulls. A typical pattern of idea production in these sessions is an initial flurry of suggestions for some short period of time, a pause, a second smaller flurry, pause, and so on. A useful guideline is to wrap up the brainstorming session after this second lull or pause.

In the aforementioned situation with the speech therapist and the teacher, after presenting their positions in terms of needs instead of solutions, they sat down in the school's conference room to brainstorm possible solutions to their problem. After a few minutes, they generated the following possible solutions.

1. providing therapy on a rotating basis after school

2. providing therapy by bringing the students into the therapy room during nonacademic times

3. providing therapy in the classroom

4. providing therapy on a less frequent basis than initially planned

5. embedding speech and language activities within the typical classroom tasks and activities

They were then ready to move on to the next step in collaborative problem solving.

Step 3: Select the solution (or solutions) that will best address the previously identified needs of all concerned. At this point any proposals that initially were not clear should be further explained. This process in itself may spark new possibilities as off-shoots of ideas are realized.

When no more contributions are forthcoming, it is time to begin identifying those solutions that hold the greatest promise. The best way to approach this step is for each person to select privately the solutions that appear to meet his or her needs. (It is critical throughout this entire process that the emphasis begin with and stay on the meeting of needs, and not on the initial conflicting solutions individuals had proposed.)

For this collaborative problem solving to achieve workable and acceptable solutions, all participants must sense that their needs truly will be met with the selected solution. If not, some sense of compromise will set in and participation will be only half-hearted, because the individuals will see themselves as having given in and not having their needs met. This can only result in an ineffective resolution.

After each person has privately identified one or more solutions that appear to meet his or her needs, these individually compiled lists are compared to find the choices selected in common. If the preliminary groundwork on defining the problem in terms of needs was done well, usually there will be one (or more) solutions identified by all participants as being good solutions.

Part of this selection process might include some forethought concerning possible outcomes of each possible solution. While not all outcomes can be predicted, some time given at this early point to consider possible outcomes can help avoid unpleasant results down the road.

In the example of the speech therapist and the teacher, as they reviewed their list of proposed solutions they found that they had two solutions in common: providing therapy in the classroom and embedding speech and language activities in the ongoing classroom activities. After some discussion they concluded that both should be chosen and incorporated into the educational program. Each believed that, when fully worked out and structured, this arrangement could satisfy their previously identified needs.

Step 4: Plan who will do what, where, and by when. At this point the actual transformation of a theoretical solution into a concrete and practical plan must occur. The proposed solution will have implicit and explicit expectations for each involved party concerning who will do what and where and when these duties will be carried out. These must be clear to all concerned. A written record of these determinations and agreements is helpful as a reminder in preventing future questions or problems, as specific details may be overlooked in the excitement of having reached a promising solution. This record also should include a plan for evaluation so that necessary data can be collected throughout the implementation. This evaluation plan should be complete enough to provide an effective foundation for evaluation without being so time-consuming that it interferes with the actual delivery of instruction.

In the example of the speech therapist and the teacher, their general agreement was that therapy services would be provided in the general classroom. In addition, ongoing classroom activities would contain special language-enriched content embedded within them. They then collaboratively developed the following plan.

Three days a week from 1:00 to 2:00 the speech therapist would come into the classroom. During this one-hour period the students would be divided into small skill groups, with these groupings based in part on similarity of speech and language needs of the students.

The teacher, a parent volunteer, and the speech therapist would each take one group for 20 minutes. Each group's lessons would include specific speech and language goals and objectives for each student, as well as language enrichment curricula common to all. During each group's 20 minutes with the therapist, each student with specific speech and language needs would receive intensive therapy in the small group and would benefit from similar therapy being provided to the other students in the group.

The second component of their new plan involved the embedding of language enrichment and stimulation activities that would help address the linguistic needs of the students in the class. In their previously arranged planning times the speech therapist worked with the teacher to help him identify adaptations of the typical classroom activities that would help accomplish speech and language goals.

For example, in the past the teacher had required his students to work on end-of-chapter questions independently. The speech therapist worked with him to help identify ways in which this activity could be adapted to be more linguistically enriched. One outcome of this was that these activities were now to be completed cooperatively, on a small group, oral basis. If each group had eight students and a chapter ended with nine questions, one question would be discussed and answered by all students. Each student would then choose (in a negotiated fashion) two additional questions to be answered orally in a round-robin format. One student would serve as the recorder, responsible for activating an audiocassette recorder for further speech and language analysis by either the teacher, therapist, or both cooperatively. Other student roles in each group would include a time watcher (to monitor that the tasks are completed in the allotted times), a noise watcher (to check with the teacher for cues concerning noise levels), and a "gopher" (to leave the group to go for help or materials).

This plan appeared to meet the basic needs identified by the teacher and speech therapist. First, the students would not be leaving the classroom and in the process losing valuable instructional time as well as the opportunity to learn from their peers. Thus the teacher saw his needs met with those students requiring more intensive speech and language services remaining with their classmates in their room.

In addition, the speech therapist saw that she would be able to provide intensive therapy to the students, which was the primary need she had identified. She also saw the possibility of additional learning occurring as she worked with other students in each group who had similar speech and language needs. Thus, her needs could be met and additional benefits gained. This win–win potential is characteristic of successful collaborative problem solving.

Step 5: Implement the plan. At this point it is time to translate the carefully developed plans into action. Assuming that the collaborative problem solvers have effectively and completely identified all the necessary steps that must be accomplished and have agreed on who will do what and when, the next step is to actually do these things.

It is at this stage that any lack of clarity in the developed plan, or any situations that the plan fails to account for, will come to light. The participants should recognize beforehand that even the most carefully and comprehensively developed plans will have gaps and oversights in them, simply because it is impossible to completely anticipate all potential scenarios.

This should not cause a fundamentally sound plan to be abandoned. Instead, the involved parties simply should return to the problem-solving system to resolve these issues as they occur. The process should be simpler and more efficient at this point, as the involved parties have come to see that their goals are harmonious and that the necessary foundation of trust is well-established.

For example, in the previously described situation, the speech therapist found that her supervisor had planned a number of Friday afternoon staff development programs that frequently would interfere with her ability to go into the classroom on that day. After meeting with the classroom teacher, she identified a number of possible solutions. These included having her come in on Thursdays instead of Fridays; having her develop a series of lessons on audiocassette or videocassette beforehand that her groups could go through independently; and having the volunteer take over the groups on the days when the speech therapist was out. The two educators reviewed and discussed these options and concluded that the solution that would best meet their needs was simply to shift the Friday sessions to Thursdays.

Step 6: Evaluate the plan. The final stage in the collaborative problem-solving process is evaluation. As noted in the previous chapter on evaluation, there are at least two dimensions that can be assessed. These are the processes, or individual components of the plan that is developed, and the outcomes, or the results of those processes.

To begin with, school professionals should look at the individual processes of the plan they developed. At this level of evaluation they might check to see if there are any missing components, if each component can be implemented practically, and so forth. (As part of this evaluative process the partners in cooperative teaching might carry out a similar analysis concerning the effectiveness of the overall collaborative problem-solving system.) If no deficits or problems in the individual processes involved in the plan are evident, educators then should move on to the evaluation of outcomes.

Simply put, the question the school professionals must answer at this point is this: Is the plan yielding the successful results that were anticipated? In the ongoing example, the speech therapist and the classroom teacher anticipated that their proposed plan would accomplish two outcomes (or respond to their two needs). First, the students who needed specific speech and language services would have their deficits remediated. In other words, the proposed program would be responsive to their specific special needs. In addition, it also was anticipated that these students would maintain adequate academic progress by staying in the classroom rather than being pulled out for specialized therapy services.

Both these sets of outcomes might and should be measured. First, the speech therapist might evaluate each special-needs student's speech and language progress by using whatever evaluative criteria seem most professionally appropriate. In addition, the teacher would maintain ongoing records of the students' academic progress. These records might include documentation of academic skills acquisition based on such sources as classroom tests, work samples, and standardized schoolwide academic achievement tests.

As noted earlier, in this evaluation phase the collaborative problem solvers might also evaluate their problem-solving strategies. For this purpose it is often useful to adopt a similar dual evaluative strategy. That is, they should assess both the processes and the outcomes of their problem-solving approach.

To this end the partners in cooperative teaching might conduct evaluations of all the involved processes periodically to make sure that all six steps in their collaborative problem-solving sessions are present. If steps are skimpy, incomplete, or altogether missing, are there problems arising that may be attributable to these missing steps?

Similarly, the involved parties also should evaluate the outcomes or results of their collaborative problem-solving activities. The primary criterion for this evaluation is obviously the effectiveness with which needs are met and conflicts avoided or resolved satisfactorily.

Given the inherently high degree of personal subjectivity and perception present in almost all human interactions, a possible third component to evaluate is how each feels about the problem-solving process, how satisfied each is with the overall system of collaborative conflict resolution. Each participant might take time to think independently about things such as what was best liked and least liked about the process, any regrets each might have about something said or done, and what each might do differently and better the next time around. After each has had a chance to contemplate these issues independently, they might then come together to discuss them. These additional analyses of the process can help ensure that it works as well as possible.

Figure 7.1 graphically illustrates the six steps of collaborative problem solving. The questions associated with each of these six steps can help to ensure productive and effective collaborative problem-solving sessions.

Troubleshooting

Needless to say, no process guiding interactions of people is consistently perfect, including collaborative problem solving. The following suggestions, some of which amplify previously introduced ideas, are offered as ways to resolve the most commonly encountered types of problems in this approach (Bolton, 1979).

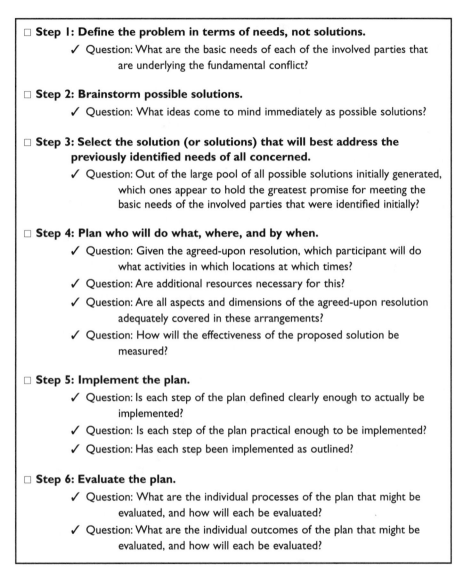

□ **Step 1: Define the problem in terms of needs, not solutions.**
  ✓ Question: What are the basic needs of each of the involved parties that are underlying the fundamental conflict?

□ **Step 2: Brainstorm possible solutions.**
  ✓ Question: What ideas come to mind immediately as possible solutions?

□ **Step 3: Select the solution (or solutions) that will best address the previously identified needs of all concerned.**
  ✓ Question: Out of the large pool of all possible solutions initially generated, which ones appear to hold the greatest promise for meeting the basic needs of the involved parties that were identified initially?

□ **Step 4: Plan who will do what, where, and by when.**
  ✓ Question: Given the agreed-upon resolution, which participant will do what activities in which locations at which times?
  ✓ Question: Are additional resources necessary for this?
  ✓ Question: Are all aspects and dimensions of the agreed-upon resolution adequately covered in these arrangements?
  ✓ Question: How will the effectiveness of the proposed solution be measured?

□ **Step 5: Implement the plan.**
  ✓ Question: Is each step of the plan defined clearly enough to actually be implemented?
  ✓ Question: Is each step of the plan practical enough to be implemented?
  ✓ Question: Has each step been implemented as outlined?

□ **Step 6: Evaluate the plan.**
  ✓ Question: What are the individual processes of the plan that might be evaluated, and how will each be evaluated?
  ✓ Question: What are the individual outcomes of the plan that might be evaluated, and how will each be evaluated?

Figure 7.1. Collaborative problem solving.

1. Handle emotions first. Strong emotions have such a significant impact on the interactions of people that they must be dealt with first. The primacy of emotions is such that, if they are present and ignored, little of practical substance will be achieved.

Sometimes these emotions are based on unstated but nevertheless substantial hidden agendas. When it appears that there are obstacles preventing productive problem solving, especially in the early stages of the process, it is useful to suggest that there may be some other unstated problem in the relationship and to ask in the most nonthreatening way possible if there are any concerns. Often subtle cues ultimately will reveal these hidden agendas. Once out in the open, they can be resolved through the six-step collaborative problem-solving process previously described.

2. Define the problem. For collaborative problem solving to be effective, each participant must be willing and able to share his or her specific primary needs, not the solutions each participant independently generated in response to his or her own perceived needs. This perspective and skill is so different from the initial impulse of most individuals that it is easy to overlook. However, if the conflict is not first defined in terms of needs, little further progress towards collaborative solutions can be made.

3. Don't interrupt brainstorming. The process of brainstorming, of putting one's ideas out for public scrutiny, is such a fragile one that even under the best conditions (when an atmosphere of optimism, support, and trust has been established) it is difficult for many people to participate actively. When someone in the group begins evaluating, criticizing, laughing or snickering, or even simply commenting on ideas as they initially are offered, many participants will quickly stop generating or submitting ideas. To be effective in generating the largest and most diverse pool of ideas, this initial brainstorming must be free of evaluations and interruptions. All participants involved must be receptive to all contributions, no matter how silly or far-fetched they may seem at first.

4. Work out the details. In the excitement and pleasure at having arrived at an apparent solution to a conflict, it is easy to skip over the nuts and bolts aspects of the actual mechanical implementation of the solution. While perhaps not as rewarding for many as the initial creative generation of the overall plan, the specifics of how the plan will actually be carried out must be given careful consideration or the chances of ultimate failure are greatly increased.

5. Follow through and follow up. The road to hell (and to nasty conflicts in the here and now) is paved with good intentions. Human nature being what it is, many well-meaning individuals will find that follow-through is more difficult than anticipated. Thus it is important that each participant commit to following through with whatever tasks or responsibilities are agreed upon. This can be helped by making sure that the specific duties and responsibilities of each are clearly identified and that any agreements entered into are done so freely.

It also may be helpful for each to follow up on the other. The involved parties might prepare a written summary at the end of each

meeting that outlines the specific tasks each will be taking on. While trying not to appear pushy, the educators might check with each other in a friendly way to determine how progress on each task is going. If unanticipated hurdles are emerging, it is important to identify these early on, before they become insurmountable.

6. Recycle the process. In working with personal computers, it is not unusual to enter a command or series of instructions only to have the machine fail to respond. Frequently all that is necessary for the machine to respond is simply repeating the instructional sequence. While it is possible to go into a detailed, complex, and systematic analysis of why the first attempt failed, it is almost always easier simply to forget it and proceed on (while blaming the glitch on the momentary displeasure of the microchip gods).

Similarly, often the best way to approach an apparently failed collaborative problem-solving process is to recycle through and repeat the six steps. It is not unusual to find that this second time around results in a productive and successful solution (or solutions). What is critical to the success of this second attempt is that the involved parties approach each step fresh and anew, rather than simply generating the identical (and ultimately unsatisfactory) responses they did the first time. A conscious effort to think about the situation differently, or from a different perspective, will help.

Conclusions

The educators have now settled into their newly remodeled and refurbished schoolhouse and have spent some time applying touch-up paint, moving pictures around, rearranging the furniture, lubricating window blinds, and so forth. In short, they have completed the initial necessary fine-tuning of their new facility. In the rush of actually completing the remodeling project they may have had little opportunity to step back a bit from the project and think about the meaning of change and how it came about. The next chapter explores the nature of change, using the analogy of educators in cooperative teaching as change agents, who are aided and abetted in their efforts by change facilitators.

Chapter 7 Activity
Interpersonal Style Survey:
The Johari Window

This chapter has focused on enhancing the quality and productivity of interpersonal relationships among school professionals. As you move into collaborative structures such as cooperative teaching, you will be asked to participate in more intense social interactions with colleagues than have been required in the past. These new demands for social skills will ask of you greater levels of personal insightfulness and self-understanding.

The Johari Window (named after its creators Joseph Luft and Harry Ingham) is a visual aide designed to allow individuals to better understand themselves (Adler & Towne, 1987). The greater level of self-understanding that can be gained from completing this exercise can enhance your ability to communicate your basic needs to your cooperative teaching partner. If your partner also completes this Johari Window exercise, he or she will be able to reciprocate these communications more effectively, maximizing the effectiveness of your interactions.

To begin, you might imagine a frame that contains everything about you—all your personal characteristics, likes and dislikes, and so on, as illustrated below.

**Everything
about
yourself**

Next, divide this frame with a vertical line, separating everything about you into one of two categories: things that are known to you and things that are not known to you, as shown on the next page.

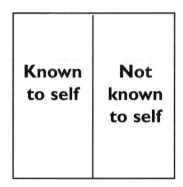

Now divide the first frame in two again. However, this time do this in a different way, with a horizontal line. These two top and bottom halves will represent those characteristics of you that are known to others and those characteristics that are not known to others, as follows.

Now the two divided frames can be superimposed upon one another to form quadrants, so that everything about you falls into one of four categories, as follows.

	Known to self	Not known to self
Known to others	**Area 1** **OPEN**	**Area 2** **BLIND**
Not known to others	**Area 3** **HIDDEN**	**Area 4** **UNKNOWN**

Area 1 represents information about yourself that both you and others are aware of (the OPEN area). Area 2 includes information about yourself that others know but that you do not know (the BLIND area). You acquire information in this area primarily through feedback from others.

Area 3 represents that set of information about yourself that you know but that others do not know (the HIDDEN area). This includes those unique sets of facts and information that people keep secret from others. Finally, Area 4 is that set of information about yourself that neither you nor others are aware of (the UNKNOWN area). This information must exist, since every person frequently learns new things about himself or herself.

The Johari Window can be refined by labeling and conceptualizing the two axes slightly differently. Rather than "Known to self/Not known to self," the horizontal axis might be labeled "Receptivity to feedback." Similarly, the vertical axis might be relabeled from "Known to others/Not known to others" to "Willingness to self-disclose," as illustrated in the following diagram.

Receptivity to feedback

Willingness to self-disclose

Each of these axes represents a continuum. Some persons will have very high levels of receptivity to feedback from other people and also will be very willing to self-disclose about themselves. Other individuals may be very disinterested in receiving feedback from others and also may be unwilling to share things about themselves. Still other people may have high degrees of one of these two characteristics but low degrees of the other.

Using the points along the continuum of each axis, every person can construct a Johari Window that gives a personalized set of the relative sizes of the four quadrants (OPEN, BLIND, HIDDEN, UNKNOWN). In this reconceptualized Johari Window, the larger Area 1 (the OPEN area) is, the more likely an individual is to both disclose information about herself or himself and solicit feedback and information about himself or herself from others. An example of such an individual's Johari Window follows.

Receptivity to feedback

**Willingness to
self-disclose**

This individual trusts others enough to disclose information about himself or herself, knowing that that confidence will not be abused. That trust in others extends such that this individual also solicits and is receptive to feedback from others. However, if Area 1 is extremely large it may cause some interaction difficulties, especially in the early stages of a relationship. This is because the level of social comfort and trust required for high self-disclosure and high receptivity to feedback from others usually requires some time to be established. Individuals who self-disclose too much too early and who too eagerly solicit and respond to feedback early on in a relationship make many uncomfortable.

Conversely, an individual may have a small Area 1, indicating little self-disclosure and little willingness to solicit or be receptive to feedback from others. Such a person's Johari Window is as follows.

Receptivity to feedback

**Willingness to
self-disclose**

This individual takes few risks and may appear aloof and uncommunicative. It is interesting to note that for this individual the largest quadrant is the UNKNOWN area.

Two other general patterns can emerge in Johari Windows. Some people are very receptive to feedback but engage in little self-disclosure. Their Johari Window pattern is similar to the following example.

Receptivity to feedback

Willingness to self-disclose

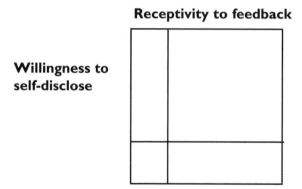

These individuals initially may seem highly supportive, because they frequently solicit ideas. Their unwillingness to self-disclose seems at first to be simply unselfishness. However, in the long term these individuals usually will be perceived as distrustful and fundamentally detached.

Finally, some people will discourage feedback from others but freely self-disclose.

Receptivity to feedback

Willingness to self-disclose

These individuals usually come across as self-centered. Perhaps the major problem for such people is the very large BLIND area. They remain unaware of how they appear to others.

The following questionnaire was developed to help you develop your own personal Johari Window, allowing you to understand your behavior in interpersonal relationships from a novel perspective (adapted from Johnson, 1981). As you go through the questionnaire, keep in mind that there are no right or wrong answers. The best answer is the one that comes closest to representing accurately your probable behaviors in each situation. In each statement, the first sentence or two outlines a situation and is followed by a possible reaction. Each of these scenarios is followed by a series of five numbers, whose meanings are as follows.

> 5 = You *always* would act this way.
> 4 = You *frequently* would act this way.
> 3 = You *sometimes* would act this way.
> 2 = You *seldom* would act this way.
> 1 = You *never* would act this way.

For each item, indicate the number that is closest to the way you would likely handle that specific situation. Try to relate each question to your own personal experience. Take as much time as you need to give a true and accurate answer for yourself on each item. There are no right or wrong answers. Trying to give the "correct" answer will make your answer meaningless to you. Be honest with yourself!

1. You have implemented a successful cooperative teaching relationship with a colleague, but some of her mannerisms and habits are getting on your nerves and irritating you. More and more you avoid interacting with her outside of the classroom.

1	2	3	4	5
never				always

2. In a moment of weakness, you give away a secret shared by a colleague. This person finds out and calls you to ask about it. You admit to it and talk with him about how to handle secrets better in the future.

1	2	3	4	5
never				always

3. Your cooperative teaching partner never seems to have time to meet to plan with you. You ask her about it, explaining how you feel.

1	2	3	4	5
never				always

4. A colleague feels you have inconvenienced him and tells you how he feels. You respond that he is too sensitive and is overreacting.

1	2	3	4	5
never				always

5. You had a disagreement with a colleague, and now she ignores you whenever you are around. You decide to ignore her back.

1	2	3	4	5
never				always

6. A colleague has pointed out that you never seem to have time to meet with him. You explain why you have been busy and try for a mutual understanding.

1	2	3	4	5
never				always

7. At great inconvenience you arrange to take your colleague to a meeting across town. When you arrive to pick up your colleague, you find she has decided not to go. You explain to your colleague how you feel and try to reach an understanding about future favors.

1	2	3	4	5
never				always

8. You have argued with a colleague and are angry with him, ignoring him when you meet. Your colleague tells you how he feels and asks about restoring the relationship. You ignore him and walk away.

1	2	3	4	5
never				always

9. You have a secret that you have told only to one other colleague. The next day another colleague asks you about the secret. You deny the secret and decide to break off the relationship with the person to whom you told the secret.

1	2	3	4	5
never				always

10. A colleague tells you about some of your mannerisms and habits that get on her nerves. You discuss these with her and look for some possible ways of dealing with the problem.

1	2	3	4	5
never				always

11. A colleague is involved in something illegal that you believe will lead to serious trouble. You decide to tell him how you disapprove of his involvement in the situation.

1	2	3	4	5
never				always

12. In a moment of weakness you give away a colleague's secret. She finds out and calls you to ask about it. You deny it firmly.

1	2	3	4	5
never				always

13. You have a partner in cooperative teaching who never seems to have time for you. You decide to forget him and to start looking for a new cooperative teaching partner.

1	2	3	4	5
never				always

14. You are involved in something illegal, and a colleague tells you of her disapproval and fear that you will get in serious trouble. You discuss it with her.

1	2	3	4	5
never				always

15. You work with a colleague and find that some of his mannerisms and habits are getting on your nerves and irritating you. You explain your feelings, looking for a mutual solution to the problem.

I	2	3	4	5
never				always

16. A colleague points out that you never seem to have time to meet with her. You walk away.

I	2	3	4	5
never				always

17. A colleague is involved in something illegal that you believe will lead to serious trouble. You decide to mind your own business.

I	2	3	4	5
never				always

18. A colleague is upset because you have inconvenienced him. He tells you how he feels. You try to understand and agree on a way to keep it from happening again.

I	2	3	4	5
never				always

19. You had a disagreement with a colleague, and now she ignores you whenever you are around. You explain how her actions make you feel and ask about restoring your collegial relationship.

I	2	3	4	5
never				always

20. A colleague tells you about some of your mannerisms and habits that get on his nerves. You listen and then walk away.

I	2	3	4	5
never				always

21. At great inconvenience, you arrange to take a colleague to a meeting. When you arrive to pick your colleague up, you find she has decided not to go. You say nothing but resolve never to do any favors for that person again.

I	2	3	4	5
never				always

22. You have argued with a colleague and are angry with him, ignoring him when you meet. He tells you how he feels and asks about restoring the collegial relationship. You discuss ways of maintaining it, even when you disagree.

I	2	3	4	5
never				always

23. You have a secret that you have told only to one other colleague. The next day, an acquaintance asks you about the secret. You call the colleague and ask her about it, trying to come to an understanding of how to handle secrets better in the future.

I	2	3	4	5
never				always

24. You are involved in something illegal, and a colleague tells you of his disapproval and fear that you will get in serious trouble. You tell him to mind his own business.

1	2	3	4	5
never				always

Survey Answer Key

In this survey there are 12 questions (the even-numbered questions) that deal with your willingness to self-disclose and 12 questions (the odd-numbered questions) that target your receptivity to feedback. Transfer your scores on each item to this answer key, reversing the score for all the questions listed that are followed by an asterisk on the answer key. (That is, for the questions followed by an asterisk, if you answered 5, record a score of 1; if you answered 4, record a score of 2; if you answered 3, record a score of 3; if you answered 2, record a score of 4; and if you answered 1, record a score of 5.) Then add the scores in each of the two columns.

Willingness to Self-Disclose	Receptivity to Feedback
1. _____ *	2. _____
3. _____	4. _____
5. _____ *	6. _____
7. _____	8. _____ *
9. _____ *	10. _____
11. _____	12. _____ *
13. _____ *	14. _____
15. _____	16. _____ *
17. _____ *	18. _____
19. _____	20. _____ *
21. _____ *	22. _____
23. _____	24. _____ *
TOTAL _____	TOTAL _____

After your scores in each of the two domains have been totaled, go to the following Johari Window figure and draw horizontal and vertical lines through your totaled scores on willingness to self-disclose and receptivity to feedback, respectively.

Generating your own personalized Johari Window can help to give you some perspective on your basic style of interaction with others. The more honest and accurate your responses to each item are, the more useful this activity will be. Use the results to help you determine how you might better be able to work with other school professionals in the intense professional relationships inherent in cooperative teaching.

Receptivity to feedback

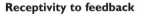

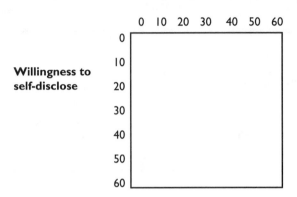

References

Adler, R. B., & Towne, N. (1987). *Looking out/looking in: Interpersonal communication.* New York: Holt, Rinehart & Winston.

Barth, R. S. (1990). *Improving schools from within: Teachers, parents, and principals can make the difference.* San Francisco: Jossey-Bass.

Bolton, R. (1979). *People skills: How to assert yourself, listen to others, and resolve conflicts.* Englewood Cliffs, NJ: Prentice-Hall.

Dewey, J. (1916). *Essays in experimental logic.* New York: Macmillan.

Friend, M., & Cook, L. (1992). *Interactions: Collaboration skills for school professionals.* New York: Longman.

Fullan, M. (1993). Innovation, reform, and restructuring strategies. In G. Cawelti (Ed.), *Challenges and achievements of American education: The 1993 ASCD yearbook* (pp. 116–133). Alexandria, VA: The Association for Supervision and Curriculum Development.

Johnson, D. (1981). *Reaching out: Interpersonal effectiveness and self-actualization.* Englewood Cliffs, NJ: Prentice-Hall.

Knackendoffel, E. A., Robinson, S. M., Deshler, D. D., & Schumaker, J. B. (1992). *Collaborative problem-solving.* Lawrence, KS: Edge Enterprises.

Little, J. W. (1981). *School success and staff development in urban desegregated schools: A summary of recently completed research.* Boulder, CO: Center for Action Research.

Louis, K., & Miles, M. (1990). *Improving the urban high school: What works and why.* New York: Teachers College Press.

Nias, J., Southworth, G., & Campbell, P. (1992). *Whole school curriculum development in the primary school.* Philadelphia: Falmer Press.

8 Reflecting on the Changes
Considering Administrative Implications of Cooperative Teaching

"Toto, I don't think we're in Kansas anymore."
—Dorothy in *The Wizard of Oz*

The decision to remodel a home is one that has significant and long-lasting implications for all who live there. It is rare for two home owners to be struck simultaneously with the idea to enter into a substantial remodeling project. More likely, one person came up with the original idea and then shared it with the other. That individual either quickly accepted the idea or did so reluctantly, only after encouragement and persuasion by the other. The home owner who first had the idea for the remodeling and then sought the other's support for that idea is in essence serving as a change agent. That person must be convinced of the necessity for change and be willing and able to convince another.

Similarly, as educators move into innovative practices such as cooperative teaching, they will in effect be serving as change agents in their schools. Change agents are key people with the expertise to administer the right changes in the proper dosages (Grossman, 1974). Clearly, school professionals implementing cooperative teaching match this definition.

Pioneers

As important as the role of educator as change agent is for today, it is especially critical for tomorrow (Fullan, 1993). Barker (1993) described those individuals who are at the forefront of change as pioneers. Such people possess three critical characteristics.

First, pioneers have the courage to take risks. For example, the pioneers of the American West blazed a trail to new territories, taking chances and encountering dangers on their journeys. These were risky ventures, fraught with a multitude of dangers.

The pioneers were followed by the settlers, who undertook the same journey after it first was made safe by the pioneers. These settlers were low risk takers compared to their pioneering predecessors. In the schools, educators developing and implementing cooperative teaching are pioneers, high risk takers. These educational pioneers see how things might be better and are willing to take actions to back up those beliefs and perceptions. They are taking chances, putting themselves on the line for possible failure instead of sticking with the (apparently) safe status quo.

It is difficult for most people to admit that there are problems with the status quo. One often can ignore problems for a while. This option is usually easier than the hard work involved in acknowledging that there are problems, identifying the specific nature of the problems, and then setting out to correct them. For example, when a business is not doing well its executives often refuse to acknowledge any problem and may even put forth impressive arguments to justify the poor showing. This truth dodging can go on for some time, forestalling any attempt to face the facts (Grossman, 1974). If one substitutes the words *school* for *business* and *educators* for *executives* in this analysis, this phenomenon can be seen as equally true of edu-

cation. It requires courage to point out problems and then to accept
the risks necessary to address the problems.

The second characteristic of pioneers is that they possess
insight and intuition. Whether in the American West in the mid-
1800s or in the schools today, by the very nature of their ventures
pioneers have little data to go on initially. They have no choice but to
make judgments based on their professional and personal intuition.
Their work is further complicated by the fact that no change that
depends on people (such as school restructuring) can ever be completely predictable, because people are never completely predictable
(Grossman, 1974). Thus to a large extent these pioneers must rely on
solid professional intuition.

This is not to negate the necessity for data collection, only to
acknowledge that in the early stages of any innovation there is a relative dearth of information on which one might rely. Early decisions
must be made using less-than-complete data sets. As more experience is gained with the innovation, more data become available to
facilitate more successful decisions throughout.

As home owners go through proposed blueprints trying to visu-
alize the completed remodeled structure, they often find it difficult to
sense how they will feel once the project is done. At some point they
must simply trust their intuition that led to the initially selected
plans. Similarly, educational pioneers moving into cooperative teaching must realize that they are moving into relatively uncharted terri-

tories. Given their pioneering status, when faced with the many questions for which no ready answers yet exist, they have little recourse other than to trust their professional judgments and instincts.

Finally, pioneers are characterized by endurance, the ability to persevere and continue on through difficult times and trying periods. They enter into their ventures with the clear understanding that any undertaking of substance takes some time to complete, with inevitable (and typically unforeseen) difficulties and setbacks along the way. Certainly not all pioneers are successful. In the American West, some gave up and returned, while others died in their efforts. Similarly, some educators will be tempted to quit and return to the safe and well-known territory of their traditional work in the schools. The ability to understand this basic reality of any pioneering effort, persevere through difficult periods, and then learn from these difficult times for the future is what makes successful pioneers successful.

As any home owner in the midst of an extensive home remodeling project will quickly and eagerly volunteer, there are many times when the question "Is this really worth it?" will arise. If the dust, noise, and general discomfort can be endured, the final results almost always are seen as worthwhile. Schoolwide reform will be difficult to accomplish, will be time and labor intensive, and will require rethinking and relearning on everyone's part (Muncey & McQuillan, 1993). Many educators moving into cooperative teaching will find the inevitable disruption and changes in their previously well-established professional routines to be distressing, confusing, and at times difficult. However, if they endure the initial unstable period, the stress levels almost certainly will diminish.

It is critical that pioneers in the schools emerge and professionals engaging in cooperative teaching and other educational innovations serve as agents of change because fundamental change must be based on a bottom-up approach. Instead of being mandated from those in authority, to be most effective change must come from practitioners.

. . . .

Change has considerable psychological impact on the human mind. To the fearful, it is threatening because it means that things may get worse. To the hopeful, it is encouraging because things may get better. To the confident, it is inspiring, because the challenge exists to make things better. Obviously, then, one's character and frame of mind determine how readily she or he brings about change, and how she or he reacts to change. (Whitney, cited in "Notable and Quotable," 1967)

. . . .

Significant Change Cannot Be Mandated

One of the consistent findings in business and education is that change is most successful when it is not based on directives from above but instead evolves from the individuals who are actually responsible for implementing the day-to-day functions associated with the change. Belasco (1990) noted that the CEOs of some of the world's largest corporations have concluded that change occurs only when all people involved see themselves as owners of that change, rather than simply passive recipients of management-dictated orders.

Top-down mandates can bring about only limited types of change in people (Fullan, 1993). Specifically, mandates can result in changes that do not require skill or thinking to implement and that can be monitored through close and constant surveillance. However, as educators move into cooperative teaching, they must make substantial changes in values and beliefs, behaviors, utilization of resources, commitments, motivations, and insights. Such fundamental internal and personal changes simply cannot be mandated. They instead evolve from significant changes in one's personal perception of how things should be, a paradigm shift.

Administrators cannot unilaterally force educators to think in substantially different ways. While an occasional nudge from above can help facilitate professional growth, to be truly effective cooperative teaching (or any innovation) must originate from those who ultimately will be responsible for implementing the change. As Ferguson noted (1987), "A belated discovery, one that causes considerable anguish, is that no one can persuade another to change. Each of us guards a gate of change that can only be unlocked from the inside. We cannot open the gate of another, either by argument or by emotional appeal" (p. 112).

In developing and implementing cooperative teaching, school professionals experience great changes in the way they go about their daily work. To overcome the inevitable fears and stresses associated with change, the educators involved must feel that they are responsible for the change and that its success or failure lies directly with them. Administrative mandates alone cannot do this.

Perhaps needless to say, most change begins with only a few individuals. These pioneers, or change agents, are the people who are cutting the new paths, who are among the earliest at perceiving and understanding the implications of a paradigm shift and developing appropriate responses. As Margaret Meade observed, "Don't think that a small group can't change the world. Indeed, that's the only way it can happen." If the change is to continue and become institutionalized, a "critical mass" of change agents must be established. This is the power that brings about change.

As educators move into cooperative teaching, at first there may be only a single pair of educators working together at any given school. What must then happen for the change to be embraced on a widespread basis is that others must see the value of that innovation and incorporate it into their own work. Other educators then must see these individuals implementing change, see its value, change themselves, and so on. As more and more people follow suit, the critical mass necessary for the fundamental change is rapidly achieved.

What essentially is happening at this point is a nonlinear domino effect, impacting people, curriculum, and instruction. Ultimately this results in a shift in the basic educational paradigm of how professionals in the schools work together.

Thus change agents must actively work for change to be incorporated on a widespread basis. However, widespread implementation of innovation may depend equally on another group of school professionals, the change facilitators.

Change Facilitators

While change cannot be mandated from above, in the absence of administrative support it is unlikely to develop and thrive. If educators moving into cooperative teaching are considered change agents, it may be appropriate to view supportive administrators as change facilitators. Change facilitators are those individuals who are in a position to provide assistance to those who are implementing change. In the public schools, change facilitators are usually school principals or other local, regional, or state-level school administrators.

In a multiyear study of change facilitators, Hord and his colleagues identified six functions that collectively describe what effective change facilitators do in helping schools develop and implement innovative school restructuring plans such as cooperative teaching (Hord, Rutherford, Huling-Austin, & Hall, 1987). They are as follows.

1. Develop supportive organizational arrangements. This function of change facilitators includes things such as assisting in scheduling and planning, and providing the personnel, equipment, and other resources required before implementation of the change can begin. This also includes the ongoing provision of those resources after the change has been implemented. Since requests and demands

for resources usually outweigh supply by a heavy margin, change facilitators often must become creative in the area of resources acquisitions. An evolving role of administrators as change facilitators is that of resource brokers, networking with their counterparts to maximize the use of local education agency resources.

2. Provide for staff development. School professionals must receive diverse training, initially on a knowledge/awareness level before the innovation is begun. This training must continue on an ongoing basis if the implemented change is to continue successfully. The change facilitator must assure that this training is tailored to fit the unique needs of the specific individuals and situations involved and must target all involved personnel.

3. Consult and reinforce. This type of support is less structured, less formal, and more individualized than training. Typically by offering support through a follow-up to training, change facilitators must make provisions to address the present and evolving needs of particular individuals in particular situations so that the implemented changes can be sustained.

4. Monitor. Effective change facilitators help develop and support functional and authentic evaluative procedures in their efforts to advance the changes. The act of gathering information, though critical to success, often is neglected. For example, some administrators stay away from their teachers out of the belief that their staff is intimidated by their visits (though often the reality is that these competent staff members may feel ignored or abandoned in the absence of such visits). Open-ended questions and face-to-face informal conversations are effective procedures to gather useful data and also serve to reinforce staff members about the significance and importance of the changes they are helping to bring about.

5. Communicate with others. A significant role of change facilitators is to elicit support from individuals and agencies external to the school. This includes such activities as public relations campaigns, networking with counterparts elsewhere, presentations to parent–teacher organizations, and so forth.

6. Disseminate. In order to help other schools adopt an innovation, administrators supporting and facilitating the change must be able to provide information that will assist those just beginning these efforts. Strategies include mailing descriptive brochures, offering implementation materials or videotapes, and even providing training through program representatives to help others design and implement their versions of the innovation.

These six functions are common to administrators effectively serving as change facilitators. However, several styles exist through which change facilitation can be carried out. Extensive research on schools actively involved in restructuring efforts has concluded that there are essentially three styles of change facilitators. These are *initiators, managers,* and *responders* (Hall & Hord, 1984).

Initiators are those administrators who hold decisive, long-range goals for their schools. They have a clear sense of what their schools should look like and take active steps toward changing their schools to match that vision. They solicit input from their professional staffs and then make decisions based on that input. They push themselves, their staffs, and their students to assure that they all continue to move in the same direction toward the same goals. They energetically seek and successfully obtain the resources necessary for the furtherance of the schools' goals and are creative at this task.

Managers are more moderate and are as much reactive as proactive. They are efficient and support the change agents in their schools without much fanfare. They protect their staffs from what they see as excessive demands and are sensitive to educator needs. They question changes at the beginning. When they see that change is being encouraged from sources such as the district's central office, they will support their staff in bringing those changes about. However, they may not go much past the minimum effort that is required for the change. They also find it difficult to delegate responsibilities and may try to do all the required tasks themselves.

Responders are most concerned with how others will perceive their decisions and the overall direction of their schools. They delegate decisions while soliciting as much feedback from all concerned as possible, making sure everyone has a voice. They are concerned with making school professionals and students content. They may make decisions based more on immediate circumstances than on long-range goals, perhaps based on a pervasive and strong desire to please others. Once a decision is made, responders tend to stay with that decision.

While it is likely that only a few change facilitators will fit exactly in one of these categories, the three types can be seen as points along two continua. Toward one end of the first continuum (which might be labeled "Receptiveness to Externally Imposed Change") is the responder, who is most receptive to change imposed from outside or above. Conversely, as illustrated in Figure 8.1, the initiator resists externally imposed change, instead being most sensitive to changes proposed or emerging internally.

On a second continuum (which might be labeled "Level of Personal Involvement in Change"), the responder takes a low profile in helping the change occur. Conversely, the initiator takes a most active role in outlining the directions of the change. The manager adopts a moderate position on both continua. Figure 8.2 displays the continuum of personal involvement.

To put it simply, responders let change happen; managers help change happen; initiators make change happen.

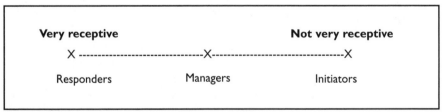

Figure 8.1. Receptiveness to externally imposed change.

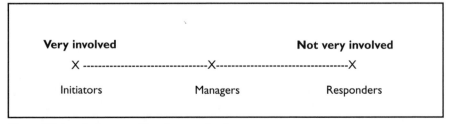

Figure 8.2. Level of personal involvement in change.

Emerging research correlates the style of the facilitator with the likelihood of the success of any innovations that are implemented in the schools. Hord, Rutherford, Huling-Austin, and Hall (1987) found a statistically very strong correlation (.76) between the style of the change facilitator and innovation success. Specifically, the change facilitator style most often associated with success was the initiator style, followed by the manager style. Responder-led schools were least successful in implementing change. The specific skills of the initiator-style principals that appeared to contribute most to the success of innovations included their strong vision, push, consistent decision-making, and priority setting. Perhaps needless to say, these qualities would be most desirable in an administrator of a school implementing cooperative teaching.

Conclusions

It is now time to show off a bit, to share the excitement of cooperative teaching with others. When home owners move into a new home or a substantially remodeled one, they typically share their excitement with their friends and neighbors by having a housewarming party, in which guests are invited to come see and enjoy the new structure, sharing the excitement.

In cooperative teaching, educators usually are eager to display their new schoolhouse with their colleagues, as the newly remodeled schoolhouse fits their needs so much better than did the previous arrangements. With school professionals actively involved as significant change agents in remodeling the schoolhouse through cooperative teaching, supported by change facilitators in administrative positions, the next step is to help others achieve similar results. This information sharing is critical if the improvements are to become widespread. The next chapter explains a variety of procedures educators have found to be effective in spreading the word about cooperative teaching, disseminating applications and results throughout their professional communities.

. . . .

Chapter 8 Activity
Checklist of Possible Actions of
Change Facilitators

. . . .

As noted earlier, Hord, Rutherford, Huling-Austin, and Hall (1987) identified a number of ways in which change facilitators can support change in their schools. In this adaptation of that work, a number of possible actions a change facilitator might take to support innovations in a school are listed, along with "YES" and "NO" columns. As you read each, simply check off whether or not the individual serving as change facilitator at your school is taking such actions. (Items that are not applicable should be left blank.)

This exercise has at least two purposes. First, some change facilitators may want to support an innovation such as cooperative teaching but are unaware of how to express that support. The following list of concrete suggestions may help to yield specific and concrete types of assistance that can be requested by the educators serving as change agents at that school.

Second, the overall pattern that emerges from the completed checklist may suggest how enthusiastically the change facilitator actually supports the change. A change facilitator who purports to be supporting the change but who in actuality is providing little of the following types of support likely is only nominally a change facilitator.

Effective change facilitators do the following . . .

1. Develop supportive organizational arrangements

Is the change facilitator assisting in . . .	YES	NO
a. developing innovation-related policies?	___	___
b. establishing global rules?	___	___
c. making decisions?	___	___
d. planning?	___	___
e. preparing?	___	___
f. scheduling?	___	___
g. staffing?	___	___
h. restructuring roles?	___	___
i. seeking or providing materials?	___	___
j. providing space?	___	___

	YES	NO
k. seeking or acquiring funds?	___	___
l. providing equipment?	___	___

2. Provide for staff development

Is the change facilitator . . .

a. developing positive attitudes?	___	___
b. increasing knowledge?	___	___
c. teaching innovation-related skills?	___	___
d. reviewing information?	___	___
e. holding workshops?	___	___
f. observing use of the innovation?	___	___
g. modeling use of the innovation?	___	___
h. providing feedback?	___	___
i. clarifying misconceptions?	___	___

3. Consult and reinforce

Is the change facilitator . . .

a. encouraging people one-on-one?	___	___
b. promoting innovation use one-on-one?	___	___
c. assisting in problem solving?	___	___
d. coaching small groups?	___	___
e. sharing tips informally?	___	___
f. providing personalized assistance?	___	___
g. holding ongoing conversations?	___	___
h. applauding progress?	___	___
i. providing small "comforting" sessions?	___	___
j. reinforcing individuals moving into change?	___	___
k. celebrating success?	___	___

4. Monitor

Is the change facilitator . . .

a. gathering information?	___	___
b. collecting data?	___	___
c. assessing progress informally?	___	___

	YES	NO
d. assessing progress formally?	___	___
e. analyzing data?	___	___
f. interpreting data and other information?	___	___
g. reporting and sharing outcomes data?	___	___
h. providing feedback on collected data?	___	___
i. collecting data from all significant parties?	___	___

5. Communicate with others

Is the change facilitator . . .

a. providing accurate descriptions to others?	___	___
b. reporting to appropriate other parties?	___	___
c. making presentations at conferences?	___	___
d. developing a public relations campaign?	___	___
e. gaining the support of important groups?	___	___

6. Disseminate

Is the change facilitator . . .

a. encouraging others to adopt the program?	___	___
b. mailing descriptive brochures?	___	___
c. providing start-up materials to others?	___	___
d. training visitors to the program?	___	___
e. facilitating staff development elsewhere?	___	___

References

Barker, J. (1993). *Paradigm pioneers* [Videotape]. Burnsville, MN: Charthouse International Learning Corporation.

Belasco, J. A. (1990). *Teaching the elephant to dance: The manager's guide to empowering change.* New York: Penguin Books, USA.

Ferguson, M. (1987). *The Aquarian conspiracy.* Los Angeles: J. P. Tarcher.

Fullan, M. G. (1993). Why teachers must become change agents. *Educational Leadership, 51,* 12–17.

Grossman, L. (1974). *The change agent.* New York: Amacom.

Hall, G. E., & Hord, S. M. (1984). *Change in the schools: Facilitating the process.* Albany, NY: State University of New York Press.

Hord, S. M., Rutherford, W. L., Huling-Austin, L., & Hall, G. E. (1987). *Taking charge of change*. Alexandria, VA: Association for Supervision and Curriculum Development.

Muncey, D. E., & McQuillan, P. J. (1993). Preliminary findings from a five-year study of the coalition of essential schools. *Phi Delta Kappan, 74*, 486–489.

Notable and quotable. (1967, June 7). *The Wall Street Journal*, p. 16.

9

Having the
Open House
Sharing Cooperative Teaching

"And now it's time for you and me to start a revolution . . ."
—Jefferson Airplane, circa 1969

When a home remodeling project is finally complete and the various minor bugs worked out, home owners typically look forward to showing off the results to friends and neighbors. After completing a substantial remodeling project, a housewarming party allows everyone to see how well the project turned out and how much better the remodeled structure is than the one it replaced.

At the party the home owners often will find their friends and neighbors admiring the new arrangements. Guests contemplating similar changes (and perhaps even those who were not until they saw the new structures) frequently will ask a variety of questions—recommendations from the home owners about things such as the best type of windows to buy, why this type of carpeting was selected over that, which of the consultants at the decorating center seems most knowledgeable, and so on.

As a small initial cohort of educators begins to restructure the schoolhouse using the architectural blueprints for cooperative teaching, the last step in the process is to share their ideas with colleagues so that they might benefit as well. This professional sharing is the best way that the educators benefiting from cooperative teaching can return the favor to those individuals who first shared knowledge and skills with them.

Dissemination

All professionals in the schools owe a tremendous debt to previous generations of educators who came before them. These predecessors spent years and careers identifying those procedures and practices that were most effective in furthering the fundamental purposes of education. They then passed those practices on through a variety of channels to their successors in the schools today. This tradition of sharing of knowledge and skills, common to all professions, allows others to step into roles with established baseline levels of competence, which simply would not be possible without this sharing. Almost all of what professionals in the schools do is based to some degree on information provided by their predecessors.

It has been said that each time an educator dies, a professional library burns. If the books (so to speak) are not taken from the library and read beforehand, that information is lost forever.

It is not possible to directly repay these individuals for their work. The only way this debt can be repaid is by present-day educators acquiring and passing on additional information to others in the same unselfish tradition. As school professionals move into innovative and effective programs such as cooperative teaching, dissemination efforts are a critical component of their work.

Dissemination refers to the promotion of thoughtful and appropriate use of effective innovative practices (Allen & Kliot, 1982). This goal is achieved by promoting awareness of the innovation among potential users, providing information to these individuals to facili-

tate their ability to make intelligent decisions about the use of the innovation in their work and giving assistance to help implement an innovation in a given situation. Dissemination activities include developing a dissemination plan, packaging the innovation for dissemination, training others in the use of the innovation, and establishing awareness activities and communication networks such as newsletters and brochures.

Essential Elements in Effective Dissemination

As home owners consider how they might let others know about their newly completed remodeling project, they can choose from a number of options. For example, they might send out letters or cards (with or without pictures) explaining the new addition; they may shoot and make copies of a videotape illustrating the new structure; or they might hold a housewarming party where friends and neighbors can come in and see it for themselves. In making a decision concerning the best way to achieve their goal of letting others know about the changes, the home owners would consider a number of factors, including who is to be notified and how best to do this.

Similarly, in planning dissemination activities for cooperative teaching, educators first must address several issues in order to make those activities most effective. These include (a) identifying the essential elements of cooperative teaching that make it unique; (b) making determinations concerning the fundamental purpose underlying the dissemination; (c) determining the target audience to receive that information or training; and (d) deciding how the dissemination might best be structured to achieve those purposes and reach that target audience.

Allen and Kliot (1982) developed a series of questions that can help the potential disseminator become more effective in making decisions concerning dissemination efforts. This information is adapted and provided in Figure 9.1.

Intended Purpose of the Dissemination

There exists a continuum of program dissemination functions, from simply informing others about the results of some program to providing intensive and extensive training to others so that they might then develop and implement similar programs on their own. For example, if a state or federal grant was used to assist in the development and implementation of cooperative teaching, a typical requirement attached to such grants is that a written report on the program be submitted. This sort of report usually is factual in nature, simply giving information on such things as personnel involved, time lines along which program development activities took place, and specific outcomes of the program. Numerical data often play a major role in these reports, including information such as number of educators involved and number of students impacted, as well as outcomes data such as achievement test scores and special education referral and participation rates. While these sorts of informational dissemination efforts may serve to persuade others to develop similar programs, this is not their major purpose.

Conversely, if the intention of dissemination is to bring about similar programs at other schools, then that effort must be much more intensive, or at least quite different. For example, if a school district becomes convinced that a pioneering cooperative teaching effort at a school was and continues to be successful in meeting preestablished district goals, then the district may want similar programs to be established at other schools in the district. In this case, a simple factual summary of the program is unlikely to be effective in bringing about these changes. Other forms of dissemination will be required.

1. Have the essential elements of cooperative teaching been specified adequately (e.g., cooperative planning, cooperative presenting, cooperative processing, cooperative problem solving?

Sources of information to determine this:

- review of program documents (e.g., the original proposal, progress reports)
- expert review (e.g., outside consultants) of cooperative teaching in operation
- observations of cooperative teaching
- interviews with others who are implementing cooperative teaching

2. Do the educators follow the essential elements of cooperative teaching as specified?

Sources of information to determine this:

- observation of educators in operation
- educator and student interviews
- expert review (e.g., outside consultants) of cooperative teaching in operation

3. Do the students served through cooperative teaching respond as predicted (that is, how well are all students succeeding in the cooperatively taught general education classrooms)?

Sources of information to determine this:

- observations of students
- interviews with students
- interviews or ratings by parents or school professionals
- examinations of student work and educator records
- standardized tests of knowledge and skills
- curriculum-based or other tests of knowledge and skills
- scales of attitudes, beliefs, and other similar dimensions
- behavioral observations and data recording

4. Do other parts of cooperative teaching (e.g., collegiality; job turnover and stability; changes in beliefs, knowledge, and skills) operate as specified?

Sources of information to determine this:

- observation of educators
- interviews with educators

5. What additional costs are involved in the development and implementation of cooperative teaching (e.g., initial and ongoing staff development costs, travel for visits to exemplary programs, release time, hiring of paraprofessionals)?

Sources of information to determine this:

- budgets
- expert cost analyses

Figure 9.1. Initial questions in planning dissemination efforts.

Target Audience

Chapter 5 identifies a number of individuals who might be targeted as recipients of information about cooperative teaching. These individuals include:

- parents
- educators at that school involved in cooperative teaching
- educators at that school not involved in cooperative teaching
- educators at other schools involved in cooperative teaching
- educators at other schools who are not presently involved in cooperative teaching but are considering whether to become involved
- professors in teacher preparation programs at universities
- staff development professionals and educational consultants in school districts or educational support centers
- school building administrators
- state department of education staff and administrators
- school district administrators
- local school board members
- educational researchers

The specific audience identified as a target for the dissemination efforts clearly influences the form, structure, and content of those efforts. For example, professors in teacher education programs might be especially interested in the theoretical foundations of cooperative teaching (accompanied by extensive lists of references), as well as statistically based data analyses of the program's effectiveness. Parents may be more interested in the direct practical implications of the introduction of cooperative teaching on their children's day-to-day school experiences, while administrators might be most interested in overall costs. Yet another possible audience, educators at other schools, might instead need to receive basic awareness activities initially, followed by some theoretical background as well as practical step-by-step implementation strategies. No one dissemination effort can effectively address the diverse needs of all potential consumers of this information. Any dissemination program clearly must keep the target audience in mind from the initial stages of planning.

Structures and Types of Dissemination Activities

Once those individuals responsible for dissemination have determined both the basic purpose of the dissemination efforts and the target audience, the next step is to identify possible ways in which that dissemination might take place and determine which ways best fit the specific purpose and audience. A number of options exist here, including conducting staff development activities, presenting at professional conferences, or writing for professional publication.

Conducting staff development activities for colleagues. It has been suggested that the rate at which the professional skills of educators becomes obsolete is ever quickening. During the 1940s, without ongoing staff development activities, educators' skills could be expected to be obsolete in 12 years. By the 1980s, that span was reduced to 5 years. It is anticipated by some that this quickening pace of obsolescence of professional skills in educators will continue into the next century (Idol, 1993). Thus ongoing staff development programs are more critical than ever.

In many ways workshops may be the most powerful and efficacious way to disseminate a practice, especially on the local level. It is primarily through on-site staff development activities that many educators update their professional credentials and skills, and it is on this face-to-face, intensive basis that educational innovators often can have greatest impact. Evolving video technologies (telecourses, teleconferences, and so on) are erasing many previous practical barriers such as travel and time.

Effective staff development workshops have several components (Browder, 1983). These include identification of goals and objectives for the workshop, the selection of presenters, determination of incentives for attendance, decisions about content delivery, and evaluation. Several of these are particularly relevant for the development of workshops on cooperative teaching.

The goals and objectives one has in mind for a particular workshop obviously determine the subsequent development of the workshop. A workshop designed to provide attendees with an introductory awareness of cooperative teaching will be structured very differently than a skill-based training program designed to result in attendees returning to their schools ready to implement cooperative teaching. The former realistically might be done in a single 1- to 3-hour session; the latter likely would require 2 to 3 full days of intensive training, with additional follow-up training sessions scheduled on an ongoing basis. It is a mistake to propose or agree to objectives that are simply not achievable in very short workshops.

The best presenters are those who combine skills in adult instruction with a wealth of practically derived information about cooperative teaching in the schools. Having two or three presenters simultaneously can be especially useful, as they can then demonstrate cooperative teaching strategies as they present the workshop.

Incentives for attendance are usually not under the control of workshop presenters. However, most educators recognize today the changing needs of their student populations and the increasing inadequacy of the old ways of doing business in the schools. If the preworkshop publicity emphasizes the advantages for educators in learning about and implementing cooperative teaching, and the potential for ongoing support is noted, most school professionals will be interested in attending. Often administrative support for cooperative teaching is contingent upon participants attending and completing training, a potentially powerful incentive.

The initial decisions made about the delivery of the content of the workshop on cooperative teaching will have great impact on its ultimate effectiveness. In reviewing the literature on effective staff development programs, Idol (1993) concluded that staff development programs are most effective when:

- the programs are based in the schools instead of universities;
- educators participate as helpers and planners of the programs instead of mere passive recipients;
- the program requires school professionals to construct and generate ideas, material, and behaviors, rather than having the attendees passively receive this information from the presenters;
- educators share ideas and provide material assistance to each other;
- the program is part of a long-term professional development plan;
- the program is specific, practical, and provides for hands-on experience; and
- observation of exemplary programs is possible.

These findings have direct and practical implications for workshop presenters who will be sharing information on cooperative teaching with their colleagues. To be most effective these programs should include frequent activities in which participants at the program become purposefully involved in small group or partner work, generating and then sharing with others possible solutions to scenarios posed by the presenters.

In providing staff development for busy and pressed colleagues, it is sometimes tempting simply to provide a practical how-to laundry list of tips for implementing cooperative teaching. However, without a basic theoretical background as a foundation on which those specific implementation strategies can be built, the subsequent success rate is significantly impaired. It is not enough for educators to know how to implement cooperative teaching; to be most effective they also must know the *why* underlying the procedures so that they can evolve their own procedures based on that solid theoretical foundation.

Keeping the necessity for a solid theoretical background in mind, the staff development program will be best received if it emphasizes practical strategies that are immediately translatable to classroom application. The use of real-life examples, of problems encountered and solutions generated, of mistakes made and corrected, all serve to give the session impact and clarity. Similarly, in activities where attendees are expected to work together to generate some sort of solutions or products based on cooperative teaching (for example, cooperatively designed lesson plans), using practical real-life examples as starting points for these activities will elicit higher levels of interactions and better end results.

At a minimum, then, effective staff development in cooperative teaching should include some basic theoretical information underlying the concept, some practical suggestions that can help practitioners implement cooperative teaching in their schools, and activities that allow the participants to become directly involved in problem solving and the generation of options and solutions. The plans should include variety in activities—from verbal presentations to the inclusion of overhead transparencies to the use of videotapes; from one-way talking to attendees to eliciting questions and responding; from activities in which attendees are relatively passive recipients to those in which they must become active. Activities also should vary in the amount of time allotted to each.

In the rush to try to cover a large amount of information in a short amount of time, presenters may overlook the reality that the attention of even the most dedicated professionals in the schools is finite. Few can listen to a near-nonstop, 6-hour lecture productively. The inclusion of a few short "brain breaks" and the simple courtesy of arranging for beverages and other light refreshments can significantly enhance the receptiveness of the audience.

Finally, staff development sessions on cooperative teaching are most effective when participants attend as cooperative teaching teams. The commonality of knowledge and skills they receive is invaluable when they return to their schools to begin the planning process.

To help plan staff development activities in cooperative teaching, Figure 9.2 presents a planning checklist (adapted from Browder, 1983).

An example of a possible outline for a 3-hour awareness workshop on cooperative teaching is provided in Figure 9.3.

(check boxes when completed)

I. Selection of workshop objectives

☐ Have participants been pretested to determine baseline levels of knowledge and skills?

☐ Has this information been used to determine workshop objectives?

II. Selection of presenters

☐ Are the presenters experienced in adult education and professional presentations?

☐ Have presenters been selected to represent diverse backgrounds and perspectives? (check all that apply)

___ teachers
___ support services providers
___ principals
___ other administrators
___ state department of education personnel
___ university teacher educators
___ private consultants
___ other _____

III. Determination of incentives

☐ Have incentives for attendees been determined? (check all that apply)

___ released time
___ payment
___ academic credit
___ salary step credit
___ certification renewal
___ personal recognition
___ ongoing support
___ other _____

IV. Delivery of content

☐ Has the structure of the workshop been thought out to include the following as appropriate? (check all that apply)

___ active participation
___ self-directed learning
___ fundamental theoretical background
___ practical application
___ live demonstrations
___ overhead transparencies and handouts of graphics
___ videotapes of cooperative teaching
___ opportunities for practice

V. Workshop evaluation

☐ Have plans been made to evaluate the effectiveness of the workshop? (check all that apply)

___ evaluation elements determined
    ___ overall content of workshop
    ___ the overall process
    ___ effectiveness of presenter
    ___ degree to which workshop objectives were met
___ workshop evaluation form developed

Figure 9.2. Planning checklist for cooperative teaching workshop.

I. Introduction
  • KWL (Know/Want/Learned)
  Find out from participants what they know about cooperative teaching at present, what they want to learn about cooperative teaching, and what they have learned about cooperative teaching (by the end of the workshop).

II. What is cooperative teaching?
    A. Definition (oral presentation and overhead transparencies)
    B. Component parts or elements (oral presentation and overhead transparencies)
        1. cooperative planning
        2. cooperative presenting
        3. cooperative processing
        4. cooperative problem solving

III. Why is cooperative teaching especially necessary now? (partner activity)
    A. The ongoing restructuring movement in the schools, which is altering the traditional rules, roles, and relationships
    B. Increased movement toward teams and collaboration throughout society

IV. What are the benefits of and barriers to cooperative teaching?
(small group assignment)
    A. Benefits
    B. Barriers
    C. Solutions

V. What is necessary to begin cooperative teaching?
(oral presentation and overhead transparencies)
    A. Identifying the first cooperative teachers
    B. Identifying and soliciting administrative support
    C. Developing training

Figure 9.3. Sample outline for a 3-hour awareness workshop on cooperative teaching.

In preparing for a staff development session on cooperative teaching, the presenters should organize all materials and content beforehand so that any last-minute scurrying about is minimized. The materials and notes to be used at the workshop should be assembled in their correct order and reviewed the day before the workshop. Presenting in and of itself is stressful enough; scrambling at the last minute to find a missing overhead transparency or needed piece of equipment makes the anxiety level unnecessarily higher and suggests a lack of preparation. Dress and appearance should be comfortable yet professional.

If possible, it can be enormously helpful to have a co-presenter (or at least an assistant who is familiar with the presentation) to aid with activities such as distributing handouts, operating video equipment, and turning room lights on and off. This allows the presenter to concentrate on keeping the flow of the workshop steady. Many presenters have found it effective to have this assistant distribute materials that match overheads shown on a projector. This helps those in the audience who wish to maintain a permanent record of any overhead displays. A marking pen helps the presenter in explaining overheads as they are displayed.

As is the case with any other skill, developing and presenting to adults is a skill that develops with practice. One component that is critical to this development is feedback. A typical way to receive feedback is to ask attendees to complete anonymous workshop evaluations. While numerical data often are necessary for administrative agency purposes, typically the most useful bits of feedback are the responses of the attendees to a set of open-ended questions.

A common mistake is the premature dissemination of evaluation forms in the preliminary packet all participants receive in preparation for the actual program. This early distribution of evaluation forms often results in the evaluations being completed well before the end of the presentation, thus generating inaccurate or incomplete data. To prevent this problem, the presenters should distribute any evaluation form only after the formal presentation has been completed. A sample evaluation form is presented in Figure 9.4.

Presenting at professional meetings. Professional conferences range from small informal district meetings to the international gatherings of the major professional organizations in education. These professional meetings and conferences can provide excellent forums for dissemination of information about cooperative teaching. The possibilities range from districtwide professional educator meetings to state, regional, national, and international conferences of such groups as the International Reading Association, the National Council of Social Studies, the National Science Teachers Association, the International Council for Exceptional Children, the International Association for Cooperation in Education, the Association for Supervision and Curriculum Development, and so forth. Especially at the state or regional levels, these meetings can be effective outlets to present reports concerning innovative programs such as cooperative teaching.

Typically professional organizations will announce a "Call for Papers" several months to a year before the actual meeting. At the national and state level these announcements often are carried in the back of professional journals, while state and regional conferences may send announcement fliers to universities and school districts, and even to all members in that state or region. A "Call for Papers"

Cooperative Teaching Workshop Evaluation Form

For each of the following items, please circle the number that best represents your evaluation of that item.

5=superior   4=very good   3=good   2=improvement is needed   1=very weak

I. How well did the presenter(s) describe the following components of cooperative teaching?

A. Definition	1 2 3 4 5
B. Rationale	1 2 3 4 5
C. Benefits and barriers	1 2 3 4 5
D. Critical elements	1 2 3 4 5
E. Process steps	1 2 3 4 5
F. Other content _____	1 2 3 4 5

II. How well did the presenter(s):

A. Pace the instruction	1 2 3 4 5
B. Use a variety of methods and media	1 2 3 4 5
C. Answer questions	1 2 3 4 5
D. Involve you actively in the workshop	1 2 3 4 5

III. What did you like best about this workshop on cooperative teaching?

IV. What suggestions could you make to improve this workshop on cooperative teaching?

V. What do you intend to do as a result of attending this workshop?

VI. What content should subsequent workshops on cooperative teaching include?

Figure 9.4. Sample workshop evaluation form.

212 · *Cooperative Teaching: Rebuilding the Schoolhouse*

usually explains clearly what information is required for the presentation proposal to be considered. Since there is sometimes a paucity of quality proposals (especially at professional meetings at the state level), this can be an especially attractive option for those educators just moving into the professional dissemination phase of their programs. These presentations often attract a prime audience of colleagues in similar situations and thus can be especially useful in helping others implement innovative programs.

In submitting a proposal, educators should remember the primary guideline proposal reviewers use: How appealing is this presentation likely to be for the typical attendee at that meeting? For the most part, proposals that have catchy titles, emphasize practical applications, and are supported by data to indicate their effectiveness are best received.

For a presentation to be most effective at these meetings, the presenter can prepare for the audience a single-page skeletal outline of the presentation. This outline also should contain the presenters' names, addresses, and phone numbers, so that later they can be contacted for additional information and assistance. This handout enables audience members to follow along generally with the presentation without being overwhelmed by a multipage handout. What often happens with detailed multipage handouts is that audience members simply read the paper without listening to the presentation itself or simply take the extensive handout and leave. Graphic additions, even those as simple as colored overhead transparencies, can add tremendously to the effectiveness of the presentation.

An especially valuable resource in presenting at conferences on cooperative teaching is the use of videotapes to show how the procedures actually look in practice. A procedure that has been found to work well for presentations on cooperative teaching is to first give a concise overview of the theory underlying cooperative teaching, explain some basic procedures involved in implementing cooperative teaching, and then go to the videotape to show those procedures in operation. It is usually these videotapes that illustrate the concepts and make the ideas come alive for audience members, and it is often the images from the videotapes that will stay with attendees as they return to their schools.

For maximum effectiveness a 27" video display with front-firing speakers should be provided for every 18 to 20 participants. Alternatively a large projection display could be used. If the video takes longer than 10 to 12 minutes, breaks or pauses should be taken periodically with the presenter helping the participants process what has been seen up to that point.

Finally, attendees can see the procedures most clearly if two presenters actually conduct the session using the procedures of cooperative teaching. For example, one presenter might maintain primary responsibility for the major content delivery, while the second presenter organizes activities to support the learning of the content. Seeing the presenters practice what they preach makes it much more likely that the attendees will understand the principles in action.

Writing for professional publication. In terms of the number of individuals that can be reached, professional writing is perhaps the most efficient outlet for professional dissemination of cooperative teaching. Many educators have never given serious consideration to writing for publication in the professional journals in their fields. In colleges of education such professional activities are seen as part of the job of professors and serve as a partial basis for determinations such as tenure, promotion, and salary increases. However, practicing professionals in the schools traditionally have received minimal support or encouragement for professional writing. This situation is unfortunate, as these professionals possess a wealth of invaluable knowledge and information that goes untapped because of this problem.

A number of professional journals in the field of education are increasingly aware of this situation and are actively seeking professional writings from practitioners. As an example, the journal *TEACHING Exceptional Children* (TEC) published by the Council for Exceptional Children (Reston, VA) deliberately features articles focusing on practical methods and materials for classroom use. TEC specifically has identified manuscripts submitted from educators in the field as its highest priority and upon request helps link up practitioners in the field with university teacher educators who can help with the preparation of a manuscript. Similarly, the journal *Intervention in School and Clinic* published by PRO-ED of Austin, Texas, has been very receptive to papers written by practitioners.

Unfortunately, even programs such as those described above have had only limited success at eliciting professional writing from practitioners. The majority of articles in professional education journals continue to be prepared by university professors in teacher education programs. However, the people who know best how schools function are those educators intimately involved in school operations on a full-time daily basis. Teachers, counselors, principals, and other school professionals all have access to classrooms and other school settings, as well as an abundance of ideas and methods that could be shared productively with colleagues elsewhere. The school affiliation of an author of a journal article might even elicit an immediately receptive audience among other practitioners reading the journal. Nevertheless, such dissemination efforts remain limited.

When asked why they do not write about their successful innovative programs for professional dissemination, educators offer a variety of obstacles they either anticipate or have actually encountered. Some of the more common of these include time constraints, the complexity of the subject, and fear of writing (Barth, 1990).

In the discussion in Chapter 4 on time management, many of the problems associated with the busy schedules of educators were identified. Good professional writing is time-consuming. Many who do write discover that the time this activity requires is difficult to find. However, the earlier discussion on time management also offered a number of practical suggestions on how blocks of usable time might be identified.

Another obstacle is the increasing complexity of schools and the innovative practices that are evolving there. The nature of the interactions of professionals with each other and with students in effective innovative schools is complex and multileveled. These interactions do not lend themselves easily to the logical analysis professional writing requires. The gap between the daily "illogical" reality of human interactions in the schools and the cold logic of the professional writing found in most journals is difficult for even the best writers to overcome.

A third reason many school practitioners hesitate to write for professional dissemination is that for many, writing is perceived as an onerous and demanding task, one likely to result in criticism and rejection. This perception often is realistically based on years of education in the schools during which most attempts at writing were returned covered in red ink. Such histories of criticism inevitably lead to people avoiding writing whenever possible and approaching it only with the greatest trepidation and reluctance.

Even given these realities, some educators are committed to professional writing. There are a number of reasons underlying and supporting such a commitment. The idea of the professional debt all contemporary educators owe their predecessors has been noted already. Sharing one's knowledge with others is the only way in which that debt can be repaid.

Most educators are in the schools because they want to help students learn and grow. An innovative and creative educator might significantly impact a few dozen students directly over the course of a school year. However, if that same educator prepares a manuscript describing an innovative program and it is published in a national journal, several thousand colleagues across the country may see it, many of whom then might use those strategies to better serve their students. Thus the effective educator's professional contributions can be magnified a thousandfold through dissemination via professional journals. Such contributions are natural outgrowths of the role of educator.

A second reason educators should write for professional publication is that it helps to clarify their practice (Barth, 1990). In order to prepare a strong manuscript for possible publication, one must logically and comprehensively think through the entire program being described. In writing a paper describing cooperative teaching efforts, the author must think clearly about it from beginning to end, from the initial establishment of agreed-upon philosophies of education to the final evaluation methodologies. Writing about one's educational efforts enhances the development of the educator as reflective practitioner. In one sense, whether or not the paper is ever published is almost irrelevant. The primary value of writing often comes in helping authors think more clearly about their work.

Whether overtly acknowledged or not, publishing a paper describing one's program yields a level of personal and professional recognition that is valued by almost everyone. Most educators find it rewarding to have a paper that describes their program appear in a professional journal under their names. One of the things that often happens as a result is that readers will call or write to ask questions, give comments, and so forth. It is not unusual for educators who have published a paper explaining some innovative program to find themselves perceived as experts and asked to present a staff development session on the topic. The idea of leaving one's mark on the professional landscape is an appealing one.

An early decision in writing for professional publication is determining an outlet. There are so many professional journals available that the choices can seem overwhelming. Perhaps the best way to begin is to start deliberately small. Smaller local journals usually accept proportionately many more of their submitted manuscripts for publication than do the national journals, so one starts off with a better chance of acceptance.

There are a number of excellent starting points of this sort for dissemination activities about cooperative teaching (Criscuolo, 1987). For example, many school districts or state departments of education have a monthly bulletin that contains routine district announcements and so forth. Often the editors of these bulletins are receptive to a proposal for a column along the lines of an "Educator Exchange," wherein a guest author describes an exciting program such as cooperative teaching that is being implemented. Educators are usually interested in what their colleagues have to say, especially if the piece helps address practical problems they are facing daily. Local newspapers also often are interested in the idea of a school-related column in the education section of the paper, written by local educators with a parent audience in mind. Such an outlet is a perfect vehicle to let parents (as well as colleagues) throughout the region learn about cooperative teaching. This service also serves as an excellent public relations tool for the schools.

Similarly, educators might submit a paper describing their cooperative teaching to the state journal or newsletter in their disciplines. Many of these publications are eager to receive and publish papers that will be useful for their readerships. If the paper is not accepted, most editors will explain their concerns about the manuscript and even offer a second review upon revision with those comments in mind.

After some writing success has been gained in these ways, it may be time to raise one's professional sights a bit and submit a paper to a larger journal, perhaps one published by a professional organization on the regional or national level. Although these journals (especially at the national level) typically accept only a minority of submitted manuscripts, they can provide a very high profile for dissemination. Outlets such as *Learning* magazine, published by Springhouse Corp. (Springhouse, PA), *Instructor* magazine by Scholastic Inc. (New York, NY), the journals *Preventing School Failure* by Heldref Publications (Washington, D.C.), *Intervention in School and Clinic* by PRO-ED (Austin, TX), *Cooperative Learning* by International Association for Cooperation in Education (Santa Cruz, CA), and *TEACHING Exceptional Children*, published by the Council of Exceptional Children (Reston, VA), are especially interested in publishing how-to manuscripts submitted by practitioners. It is often useful for the author to link up at that point with a university professor in teacher education, because many of these professors have experience in preparing manuscripts for national journals. (One might then consider what is evolving as "cooperative publishing"!)

Both authors of this book have published extensively in a variety of professional journals and currently are serving as journal editors or reviewers. As such they have identified a number of ways practitioners can increase the likelihood of a paper describing a cooperative teaching effort being accepted by a journal. Size is a significant consideration; papers approximately 10 double-spaced pages in length offer a good compromise for many journals between being concise and being comprehensive. Bigger usually is *not* better here. Some journals offer special theme issues, and themes targeting collaboration or collegiality are excellent opportunities to disseminate information about cooperative teaching. For some journals, including photographs helps increase the chances for acceptance. (A phone call to the journal editor asking about this and other questions before sending the manuscript is usually a good idea.)

It is also useful to read several recent issues of the journal being considered to learn about typical content and styles of papers published there. The paper should be directed toward the readers, not the editors. The use of jargon should be minimized, as should the excessive use of whatever buzzword is currently fashionable.

In addition, it is helpful to have an outside reader go through the paper before submitting it. This reader should be one who will be very critical; in fact, the reader who concludes the paper is "perfect as is" likely has not read it critically. One should deliberately seek out an honest and objective appraisal from someone who will read it skeptically (though such people can be hard to find and should be treasured). The prospective author should ask the person to be especially critical of overall clarity and the logic or organization and presentation of the paper. It is easier to receive criticism from that person than from the journal editors.

A useful strategy is to keep a manuscript folder close at hand. Whenever the authors observe something potentially interesting, they can jot it down and drop it in the folder. At some point a significant amount of information will have accumulated there. Then the cooperative educators (cooperative writers?) can pull out the folder, shuffle the various papers into related groups or topics, arrange the topics in a logical order appropriate for the paper, and start writing, with much of the hard preliminary organizational work already accomplished.

For most writers the most difficult part is getting started. What works best for most successful writers is simply getting something down on paper (or disk) and coming back to it later, using it as a starting point from which to continue and repeatedly reviewing and revising it. The first draft cannot be perceived as anything near the final version. Writing is a process, not a one-time event. When the writer accepts this reality, the writing becomes easier.

Finally, the prospective author should keep one inarguable point in mind. A paper that is never submitted will never be published. Simply by submitting a paper, one is automatically far ahead of most colleagues, who will never reach that stage. Every professional in education who has been successful in publishing has had many papers rejected. This is especially true in one's first few attempts, when the author is still learning basic professional writing skills. Some of the most productive writers in education have a rule about no manuscript staying at their desk for more than 48 hours. When one manuscript is rejected, it is revised in accordance with the editorial comments and resubmitted within 1 to 2 days of its receipt from the first journal. Persistence and endurance here truly does pay off, as success breeds success. After one has had a first paper accepted, the second usually is easier, the third easier still, and so on.

Resistance to Change

Any educator engaged in dissemination activities as part of the role as change agent routinely will encounter individuals who are resistant to change. Most school professionals have some degree of investment in the status quo (as would any other equivalent group). When first approached about cooperative teaching, many will flatly deny any potential value, express reservations, or demonstrate more passive resistance in other ways.

Such responses are very understandable. At least at first, any change will result in additional work and effort required of educators. Functions that have long been on autopilot now will have to be dealt with on a more active, conscious, and time- and energy-consuming basis. What individuals may be resisting is not the change per se but the inevitable uncertainty that accompanies change (Richardson & Margulis, 1981). Thus some resistance to change in the schools, especially to change that is as fundamental as cooperative teaching, is probable.

Resistance to change can be interpreted optimistically as a sign that those individuals are actively involved in and committed to the school and its programs. A passive educator who is willing to do anything and everything suggested to him or her, with no evidence of question or concern, likely is uncommitted to or cares little about anything, including the quality of educational services he or she delivers to students. In all probability such individuals are simply going through the motions to collect a paycheck. Educators evidencing resistance to cooperative teaching are at least involved in and thinking about how schools should function and are anticipating the possible impact of proposed innovations.

Some predictors exist that can help to identify professionals in the schools most likely to resist cooperative teaching. These include the following:

- educators who see no problems in the status quo;
- educators who see individuals from outside his or her school as "know nothing outsiders" who "don't know our situation here";
- educators who have been exposed to trendy innovation after trendy innovation over the past few years, none of which seemed to last;
- educators who see the imposition of cooperative teaching as a top-down mandate;
- educators who do not see themselves as active participants in the planning and development process; and
- educators who perceive no payoffs for changing.

As educators move into cooperative teaching, they often become eager to help their colleagues develop along similar lines. Sometimes in the process these change agents will feel hurt, confused, irritated, or rejected by the unexpected depth of the resistance to change they encounter from their colleagues. They then may respond in a number of unproductive ways, including becoming impatient and angry, proceeding only in a half-hearted way, getting into power struggles with their colleagues, or finally simply giving up.

Responding to Resistance

Obviously, none of the responses mentioned above are productive in the dissemination efforts. However, professionals in the area of counseling (Egan, 1982; Richardson & Margulis, 1981) as well as in business management (Grossman, 1974) have identified a number of ways to respond effectively to reluctance to change. Several of these may be especially useful as professionals in the schools who are successfully engaging in cooperative teaching seek to disseminate this information to skeptical colleagues through presentations and workshops. These effective strategies for responding to resistance include the following.

Recognize that some resistance is normal. It is important that resistors not be made to feel defensive about their concerns or objections about a radical innovation in the schools such as cooperative teaching. To this end it is often useful to begin a workshop or presentation by explaining that it is likely that many have concerns or reservations about the proposal and then soliciting comments that will allow these concerns to emerge early on. Alternatively, the workshop presenter may ask participants early on to identify possible barriers their colleagues are likely to offer to the implementation of cooperative teaching. Such a strategy allows participants to list the barriers and concerns they themselves feel without personally exposing themselves to risk and criticism. After listing these barriers on a large pad or overhead, the attendees then might participate in a generalized, brainstorming problem-solving session in which responses to each barrier can be generated.

Personal anecdotes describing how the presenter felt similar objections at first can help to establish a sense of unity, a feeling that "We all feel this way at first."

> **Workshop presenter:** "When I first heard of cooperative teaching, my first thought was how impractical and unworkable it was. Two educators present at the same time in the same classroom? How could that ever work? I also questioned . . . (go on to list one or two other typical initial concerns)."

Look for and find an area of agreement to start with. It is not unusual in the course of conducting a staff development session on cooperative teaching to find that at some point someone will speak up, offering a strongly worded argument against the adoption of cooperative teaching. A useful perspective to keep in mind at this point is that people want to be right and will do almost anything to sustain this. One of the most effective ways of dealing with resistance is to find a point on which to agree with the other. After validating the individual on that point, one can then use that as a launching point for further discussion. Consider the following scenario (adapted from Richardson & Margulis, 1981).

> **Workshop presenter:** "It is important to plan for cooperative teaching beforehand so that each educator knows his or her role, at least in general. This will also allow . . ."

Workshop attendee (interrupting): "Excuse me, but my day is already packed and hectic from the moment I get to school until I leave late in the afternoon. There just is no time available for this planning you're talking about, at least not at my school."

At this point the presenter has several options. She can say that the issue of finding time will be covered later. However, this may sound as if she is dodging the issue. The objector as well as other attendees are then likely to tune out everything until the time issue is finally addressed. The presenter also could say something along the lines of "Everyone has time, you just have to look for it." However, this response denigrates and devalues both the objector and his point, as well as everyone else in the audience who heard the objector's comment and thought, "Yeah, me too."

The presenter knows from the experience of thousands of educators who are involved daily in cooperative teaching that time *can* be found to do the necessary planning. However, at this moment the objector cherishes his belief to the contrary. To respond effectively the presenter must find a way to agree with him.

Presenter: "You're right, many educators feel exactly the same way. The workday for educators always seems to go from one task to another without a break. No good teacher I know seems to have much free time. So any changes we make cannot take away from the important work all of us are already doing."

Here the presenter is ensuring that the objector sees the two of them as being on the same side, agreeing on a very basic issue. She clearly is in agreement with the objector and his point, putting the two of them psychologically on the same side. This is further emphasized by the deliberate use of the word *we.*

Often when objections emerge they are based in problems from the past. This can form the basis for the next avenue the presenter might explore with the objector.

Presenter (continuing): "I understand your school tried using collaborative consultation last year. Some of you may have felt you were in meetings all the time."

Objector: "That's exactly right! Meetings every day after school, it seemed like! Plus I ended up with the same problems and really no more help than before."

By establishing early agreement, the workshop presenter made it safe for the objector to open up a bit and explain why he felt as he did. She can now begin to understand some of the reasons underlying his objections and can avoid stepping on any psychological land mines. While it may not fit her previously established workshop schedule, this might be a good time for the presenter to note the differences between cooperative teaching and other approaches. The presenter might use the objector's analysis of the previous approach to make the point even more directly, while simultaneously drawing him in almost as a temporary co-presenter. (As an aside, when individuals say that they do not have the time to do something they acknowledge would be beneficial for them, it is usually because they have some difficulty in managing time. The presenter then should go on to suggest a couple of the easier ways planning time for cooperative teaching can be arranged and might even offer specifically to sit down and help that individual conduct an analysis of time usage [as outlined in Chapter 4]. A direct offer of help is difficult to turn down when in essence it already has been requested.)

In initially establishing a solid area of agreement, the presenter made it easier for the objector to open up to her, which then gave her a better idea of the underlying issues. Had she instead immediately suggested that there was plenty of time for planning if he just looked for it or managed his time better, she would have established an adversarial relationship, implying that he was lying, professionally incompetent, or both. Instead, the two of them were established psychologically as working side by side. It is absolutely critical for presenters to keep in mind that dissemination programs cannot become a contest with winners or losers, with some who are right and others who are wrong. Although it is the natural reaction of very few people, the best way to deal with resistance is by first getting in agreement with it, rather than fighting it (Richardson & Margulis, 1981).

Accentuate the positives, and highlight any possible drawbacks in the most constructive way. People are attracted to things that seem beneficial. In disseminating information about cooperative teaching, presenters should highlight those aspects that are most appealing. For example, the characteristics of cooperative teaching that most educators find most desirable are the potential for working with another adult in the classroom and the sort of professional collaboration and assistance this provides. Thus dissemination efforts should highlight the inherent advantages of having a colleague simultaneously present to "bounce ideas off of."

Conversely, some educators fear that they will be asked to assume professional responsibilities in the context of cooperative teaching that they find difficult or impossible. Consider the following example.

> **Presenter:** "Cooperative teaching takes place at the high school level in much the same way. One common arrangement is to

have the high school content-area teacher, for example a biology teacher, paired with a special educator."

Attendee: "I have to confess that I don't see how that could work, at least for me. By training I am a special educator and know very little about advanced biological concepts."

At this point the workshop presenter might be tempted to say something like, "Oh, you could learn that material." However, that does little to allay these concerns. At a recent workshop conducted by the senior author, just such a concern was raised. The presenter responded to the point as follows.

Presenter: "Let's remember the basic idea behind cooperative teaching. The idea is to have two educators who bring complementary sets of skills to the room. The biology teacher's skills are in the mastery of the content being taught. What sort of skills might a special educator bring to that or any other classroom?" (This last question was directed toward the workshop attendees at large.)

First respondent: "The ability to alter materials?"

Second respondent: "Knowledge of academic survival or study skills?"

Third respondent: "Small group instructional strategies?"

Presenter (recording these responses on an easel or overhead): "Sure, all of these and many more. The idea is not for both educators to have all the same skills, because this is virtually impossible. Cooperative teaching does not involve identical twin educators, since having the same set of skills twice does little good. Instead we're looking for a package of two different but complementary sets of skills. So the special educator would not be expected to come in with the same knowledge of biology that the biology teacher possesses, though she may well learn much of that over time. Instead, she must bring to that situation the specific unique instructional skills she possesses that can help all students succeed in that biology class."

This discussion was then immediately followed by a videotape of a similar arrangement at a high school, where the educators involved repeated the basic point that the strength of the cooperative teaching program is that it combines the knowledge the science teacher has with the knowledge of curricular alterations and instructional strategies that the special educator brings to the class. Rather than requiring twice the skills of either of the involved educators, cooperative teaching effectively combines and synthesizes the two discrete sets of teaching strengths into one comprehensive and powerful instructional package. In this way, what the special educator perceived as a shortcoming of cooperative teaching was recast as an advantage.

Express curiosity or interest. By expressing interest in a point raised in an objection, the presenter can learn more about the objection. Sometimes in verbalizing his or her objection, the individual will begin to withdraw parts of it, making a response easier to develop and structure. In any case, when the presenter shows interest in hearing more about the objection the potential for the development of some sort of adversarial relationship is minimized. In addition, the more information the presenter has about the objection, the more effectively she can then respond to it.

> **Attendee:** "I don't see how cooperative teaching could work at our school. Most of the teachers I've talked with don't seem to like the idea of another teacher in the classroom."
>
> **Presenter:** "That's interesting. Tell me more about the kinds of things they said."
>
> **Attendee:** "Well, one teacher said she . . ."

Paraphrase the objection. As is the case in expressing curiosity or interest, when the presenter paraphrases the objection the objector usually will go on to elaborate or modify the objection. This gives the presenter additional information from which to respond and assures that the presenter clearly understands the concerns. The objector then also has the opportunity to either confirm that the objections were heard and understood correctly or, if not, to make the appropriate corrections or clarifications.

> **Attendee:** "I think the parents of our students with special needs would object if they heard that we were no longer going to remove those kids to come to the resource room."
>
> **Presenter:** "So it's your sense that these parents would conclude that their children would no longer be receiving intensive intervention if the support services provider instead came to the students' general education classroom."
>
> **Attendee:** "Yes, that's exactly what they would say. They want the intensive services."

At this point the workshop presenter clearly understands the concern and can respond appropriately.

Ask what it would take to convince the objector. It is sometimes useful to ask this question early in the workshop in order to get an initial idea of the directions in which the presentation might be fine-tuned. This also is a useful question to ask when some sort of impasse apparently has been reached. Often the objector will explain exactly what is required to convince him or her. This gives the presenter the additional information to continue problem solving. Asking the question also takes the pressure off the presenter and puts some burden on the objector while keeping the discussion moving.

> **Attendee:** "I'm sorry, but I just can't see cooperative teaching being accepted at our school."

> **Presenter:** "I understand that you have some reservations about this. What would it take to convince you that it might work?"

> **Attendee:** "Well, at a minimum I would have to see some written assurance that there would be administrative support. Also, . . ."

Suggest the opposite. In presenting information in cooperative teaching, it is sometimes useful to argue for the opposite position. It can be an eye opener for attendees at a workshop to hear a presenter on cooperative teaching come out strongly advocating the status quo (albeit subtly exaggerating the problems thereof). Such an approach almost automatically has the audience members quietly disagreeing with the idea that the status quo is good and instead coming to see that change is necessary. This receptive psychological status then becomes fertile ground for quickly switching gears and advocating for cooperative teaching.

> **Presenter (at the beginning of the workshop):** "I think it's clear to all of us that our present system of teachers working alone in their classrooms is the ideal educational system. It allows us to best meet the needs of every single student in our schools and uses the unique skills each of us has for the best advantage of all students."

Conclusions

As Fullan (1993) noted, most educators choose their profession from a sense of moral purpose. A recent survey of student teachers asked them why they had chosen careers in education. The most frequently reported reason given by these respondents was to make a difference in the lives of their students (Stiegelbauer, 1992). However, what happens too often is that the initial sense of moral purpose these educators bring to their work becomes lost in the day-to-day, mind-numbing repetition of most educational programs. The result of this is professional cynicism and ultimately resignation, either literal or psychological.

A promising solution to this sense of professional inconsequentiality (Farber, 1991) is a change in the role of school professionals, from maintainers of the educational status quo to that of change agents (Fullan, 1993). This evolution in roles is inherent in the development and implementation of cooperative teaching. As educators come to see themselves as agents of change, they simultaneously will address two issues that are critical for many school professionals: the ability to have significant and substantive impact upon student lives and the opportunity to overcome the sense of powerlessness that often develops in the present system.

The ability to have greater impact upon student lives directly appeals to the moral purpose of making a difference for students. For increasing numbers of students in contemporary schools, the status quo is ineffective in helping them acquire the skills that are needed in a rapidly changing world. Educators who seek to change their educational programs through cooperative teaching typically report that by doing so they are able to respond more effectively to the diverse needs of students. With cooperative teaching school professionals are able to bring to the classroom a combined educational package more potent than either possesses alone, yielding the potential to have more dramatic and substantial impact upon the lives of their students.

The second need cooperative teaching responds to is that of overcoming the sense of powerlessness school professionals often experience. Going through essentially the same experiences year after year after year, many educators come to see themselves as isolated components in a nonresponsive system. Through cooperative teaching they have the opportunity to renew themselves and their instructional programs, using individualized feedback from another professional in the classroom to guide and facilitate their own professional growth.

There are few occasions as exciting as moving into a substantially remodeled home. As the home owners look around their new structure, take in the new environment, and compare it to their previous dingy and inadequate structure, their excitement grows as they anticipate the substantial improvements they will enjoy in their daily lives.

Cooperative teaching offers every educator the chance to reignite the initial spark of excitement felt when first beginning a career in education. That excitement will be contagious, spreading to students and colleagues alike. To paraphrase Barker (1993), the world in general and the schools that must reflect that world are changing rapidly and dramatically. The educator frightened of and resistant to the inevitability of change will perceive only threats. The educator who is flexible, who welcomes change for the growth possibilities it presents, and who is eager to share with others instead will perceive opportunity.

. . . .

"When you give away some of the light from a candle by lighting another person's flame, there isn't any less light because you've given some away. There's more. When everybody grows, there isn't less of anybody. There's more of, and for, everybody."

—Kaleel Jamison

. . . .

Chapter 9 Activity

Together educators can ignite the spark that enlightens the environment for all. **Now go do it!**

References

Allen, C., & Kliot, L. A. (1982). Some guidance for the evaluation of dissemination activities. In G. Harrison & D. Z. Mirkes (Eds.), *Process to product* (pp. 131–158). Monmouth, OR: Western States Technical Assistance Resource.

Barker, J. (1993). *Paradigm pioneers* [Videotape]. Burnsville, MN: Charthouse International Learning Corporation.

Barth, R. S. (1990). *Improving schools from within: Teachers, parents, and principals can make the difference.* San Francisco: Jossey-Bass.

Browder, D. (1983). Guidelines for inservice planning. *Exceptional Children, 49*, 300–307.

Criscuolo, N. P. (1987). Encouraging teachers to write for publication. *Teacher Education Quarterly, 14*, 102–107.

Egan, G. (1982). *The skilled helper.* Belmont, CA: Wadsworth.

Farber, B. (1991). *Crisis in education.* San Francisco: Jossey-Bass.

Fullan, M. G. (1993). Why teachers must become change agents. *Educational Leadership, 51*, 12–17.

Grossman, L. (1974). *The change agent.* New York: Amacom.

Idol, L. (1993). *Special educator's consultation handbook* (2nd ed.). Austin, TX: PRO-ED.

Richardson, J., & Margulis, J. (1981). *The magic of rapport: How you can gain personal power in any situation.* San Francisco: Harbor Putnam.

Stiegelbauer, S. (1992, March). *Why we want to be teachers.* Paper presented at the Annual Meeting of the American Educational Research Association, San Francisco.

Appendix

Sample Time Log

In constructing a time log to meet the unique needs of any educator, the first step is the identification of all the activities one engages in throughout the professional day. These obviously will vary from individual to individual. The following possibilities, though far from exhaustive, can serve as a starting point for the generation of one's own individualized list of typical daily activities in the school.

- individual professional planning

- directly teaching or working with students

- miscellaneous school duties (e.g., lunchroom duty, playground duty, bus duty)

- athletic coaching or club/activity advisement

- meetings with other school professionals

- meetings with parents

- student advisement and counseling

- miscellaneous paperwork (e.g., filling out report cards, attendance forms)

- monitoring students as they work independently (e.g., in cooperative learning activities, at independent seatwork assignments)

- evaluation of students (e.g., grading tests, calculating report card grades)

- changing the classroom's physical environment (e.g., changing bulletin boards, rearranging student desks or tables and chairs)

This list should be added to as appropriate to reflect the specific activities one typically engages in at the school. Each activity should be recorded in one of the activity columns.

The next step is to informally estimate how much time one spends in each activity. This might be done on an approximate percentage basis or in terms of hours or minutes per day.

After this initial estimate is completed, the next step is to record one's typical daily usage of time. For a period of 3 to 5 days, one should record every 15 minutes the activity one was engaged in during the immediately preceding 15-minute period. At the end of each day the total time spent in each activity should be calculated and perhaps converted to a percentage of the entire time available during the school day.

After 3 to 5 days of data collection, the educators should compare that data with the initial estimates. Typically there are significant discrepancies between how one perceives one's time is being spent at the school and the reality. In such cases, is the situation a satisfactory one? Are changes indicated?

The reality for many educators is that additional time for cooperative teaching may not be able to be gained through lightened professional duties elsewhere. In such cases, the time necessary to plan and implement effective cooperative teaching must be secured from presently inefficiently used blocks of time.

Time Log

	Activity									Notes
8–8:15										
8:15–8:30										
8:30–8:45										
8:45–9:00										
9–9:15										
9:15–9:30										
9:30–9:45										
9:45–10:00										
10–10:15										
10:15–10:30										
10:30–10:45										
10:45–11:00										
11–11:15										
11:15–11:30										
11:30–11:45										
11:45–12:00										
12–12:15										
12:15–12:30										
12:30–12:45										
12:45–1:00										
1–1:15										
1:15–1:30										
1:30–1:45										
1:45–2:00										
2–2:15										
2:15–2:30										
2:30–2:45										
2:45–3:00										
3–3:15										
3:15–3:30										
3:30–3:45										
3:45–4:00										
4–4:15										
4:15–4:30										
4:30–4:45										
4:45–5:00										
Total										

Subject Index

administrative support
  developing and obtaining for
    cooperative teaching, 97–99
  expressions of, 99–101
  necessity for success of innovation,
    95–97
administrators as change facilitators,
  190–194
avoidance, as conflict-resolution
  strategy, 157–158

barriers to collaboration, 4–6, 11–16
brainstorming, as part of collaborative
  problem–solving, 164–166, 171, 172

capitulation, as conflict-resolution
  strategy, 158
change
  "bottom up" vs. "top down," 189–190
  identifying concerns about, 69–74
  impossibility of mandating, 189–190
  overcoming resistance to, 219–225
  resistance to, 218–219
  the nature of, 150–152
change agents, 186–188, 226
change facilitators, 190–194
  checklist of possible actions of,
    195–197
  definition, 190
  effectiveness of various styles, 194
  functions of, 190–192
  styles of, 192–193
classrooms, sharing physical space in,
  139–141
collaboration
  barriers to, 4–6, 11–16
  basic features of, 7–11
  collaborative consultation, 31–33
  cooperative teaching, 36–37
  definition, 6–7
  definition of direct and indirect, 29–32
  direct approach to, 36–39
  indirect approaches to, 31–36
  peer collaboration, 33–34
  questions to ask before implementing,
    41

readiness for, 18–24
teacher assistance teams, 34–36
types of, 30
collaborative consultation, 31–33
collaborative problem solving, as conflict
  resolution strategy, 160–173
collegiality
  as opposed to congeniality, 153
  characteristics of, 153–154
  explanation of, 153
complementary instruction
  as an approach to cooperative
    teaching, 53, 55–59
  combining with other arrangements,
    63–67
  explanation of, 55–56
  strategies within, 55, 57–59
  teaching acting skills through, 55
  teaching learning skills through, 55
  teaching thinking skills through, 55
compromise, as conflict-resolution
  strategy, 160
Concerns–Based Adoption Model
  (CBAM), 69–74
conflict
  definition of, 155
  inherent in collaborative relationships,
    154–155
  potential benefits of, 156
  strategies for resolving, 157–173
  types of, 155–156
connection with outside environment,
  importance of, 151–152
cooperative learning, 47
cooperative teaching
  approaches to implementing, 53–67
  as a direct approach to collaboration,
    30–31, 36–39
  benefits of, 37–38, 51–53, 67–68
  budgetary questions, 97
  considerations in evaluating, 108–109
  determining dimensions to evaluate,
    123–125
  determining sources of information for
    evaluation, 116–122
  developing evaluation procedures for,
    111–116

About the Authors

Jeanne Bauwens is a professor in the College of Education at Boise State University and conducts school staff development programs in cooperative learning and cooperative teaching. In addition to her university work, she works with thousands of educators each year throughout the United States, Canada, and Australia, helping schools integrate collaboration in teaching and learning. When not professionally engaged she combs the beaches near her home on the Oregon coast.

Jack J. Hourcade is a professor in the College of Education at Boise State University. He has published extensively regarding students with special needs and is an associate editor of the journal *TEACHING Exceptional Children*. In his free time he plays guitar and bass in Boise's premier classic rock band FLASHBACK.

Notes

Notes

Notes